THE LIBRARY OF HOLOCAUST TESTIMONIES

Recollections and Reflections

The Library of Holocaust Testimonies

My Own Vineyard by Miriam Akavia
From Thessaloniki to Auschwitz and Back by Erika Myriam Kounio Amariglio
Scorched by Irit Amiel
A Village Named Dowgalishok by Avraham Aviel
In Hiding by Benno Benninga
Journey through Darkness by Willy Berler
A Child Alone by Martha Blend
A Little House on Mount Carmel by Alexandre Blumstein
Like Leaves in the Wind by Rita Blattberg Blumstein
My Heart in a Suitcase by Anne L. Fox
Have You Seen My Little Sister? by Janina Fischler-Martinho
Good Beyond Evil by Eva Gossman
My Private War by Jacob Gerstenfeld-Maltiel
No Place to Run by David Gilbert
An Englishman in Auschwitz by Leon Greenman
Who Are You, Mr Grymek? by Natan Gross
Nešarim by Thelma Gruenbaum
A Life Sentence of Memories by Issy Hahn
Life Strictly Forbidden by Antoni Marianowicz
The Children Accuse by Maria Hochberg-Mariańska and Noe Grüss
With a Yellow Star and a Red Cross by Arnold Mostowicz
For Love of Life by Leah Iglinsky-Goodman
From the Edge of the World by Anne Joseph
Hasag-Leipzig Slave Labour Camp for Women by Felicja Karay
Out of the Ghetto by Jack Klajman with Ed Klajman
A Hidden Jewish Child from Belgium by Francine Lazarus
A Cat Called Adolf by Trude Levi
Wartime Experiences in Lithuania by Rivka Lozansky Bogomolnaya
Fire without Smoke by Florian Mayevski (with Spencer Bright)
Hiding in the Open by Zenon Neumark
The Jews of Poznań by Zbigniew Pakula
My Child is Back by Ursula Pawel
From Berlin to England and Back by Peter Prager
My Lost World by Sara Rosen
From Lwów to Parma by Klara Rosenfeld
Warning and Hope by William Samelson
Fortuna's Children by Paul and Imre Schonberger
Surviving the Nazis, Exile and Siberia by Edith Sekules
By a Twist of History by Mietek Sieradzki
Through Blood and Tears by Henry Skorr
Memoirs from Occupied Warsaw by Helena Szereszewska
I Was No. 20832 at Auschwitz by Eva Tichauer
I Light a Candle by Gena Turgel with Veronica Groocock
Lessons in Fear by Henryk Vogler
Trust and Deceit by Gerta Vrbová
The Girl in the Check Coat by Christine Winecki
Holocaust in the Ukraine by Boris Zabarko
A Warsaw Diary by Michael Zylberberg

Recollections and Reflections

How I Turned Despair into an Appreciation of Life

JACK BRAUNS

VALLENTINE MITCHELL
LONDON • CHICAGO, IL

First published in 2007 by VALLENTINE MITCHELL

Catalyst House,
720 Centennial Court, Centennial Park
Elstree, WD6 3SY, UK

814 N. Franklin Street,
Chicago, Illinois 60610, USA

www.vmbooks.com

British Library Cataloguing in Publication Data

A catalogue record has been applied for

ISBN 978 0 85303 749 1
ISSN 1363 3759

Library of Congress Cataloging-in-Publication Data

A catalogue record has been applied for

Contents

List of Maps

List of Illustrations

This book is dedicated to my family

'Scrivere un libro e meno che niente se il libro fatto non rifa la gente.'

'To write a book means nothing if the book does not influence people.'

Acknowledgements

Sir Martin Gilbert enthusiastically encouraged and guided me in every way. He graciously agreed to edit my book and provided me with historical data and maps that greatly enhanced my writings. I am forever grateful

Joyce, my lifetime companion, painstakingly researched facts, transcribed corrections, encouraged, guided and helped me to complete my autobiography.

My children, Suzette, Janine and Alicia were always available to give me their guidance and support. Janine for all the extra hours she spent meticulously organizing the pictures and illustrations for the book.

I am grateful and appreciate all the help, guidance and encouragement I have received from the following friends from my past as well as present, each one contributing important information in different areas. Without their input this book could not have been written.

Sally Wiger, with patience and understanding, transcribed my dictations.

Zev Birger, Si Frumkin, Irena Veisaite and Cesare Reyneri read parts of my manuscript, researched historical facts and with their wisdom gave me valuable suggestions.

Lady Esther Gilbert, Robert Lenzner, Jeff Goldshen, Arnold Einhorn MD, George Bierman, Tina Lunson, Patricia De La Rosa and Margaret Kimura, each in their field of expertise gave me help to make my book a reality.

Thanks to Susanna Zevi of Agenzia Letteraria Susanna Zevi for representing me.

I am very grateful to Mark Anstee of Vallentine Mitchell for constantly communicating with me and guiding me through all the steps of publishing. Thanks to all the staff at Vallentine Mitchell who worked on my book.

Special thanks to the publisher of Vallentine Mitchell, Frank Cass, for publishing my book, having the faith that my memoirs were important to share with people, young and old, to understand the value of education and recording historical facts.

Foreword by Sir Martin Gilbert

This memoir has been long awaited. Jack Brauns is a man of many qualities, one of which is a deep understanding of the human condition. This understanding did not come from books or theoretical discussion, but from the hard and at times almost unbearable school of life. Jack Brauns is a survivor of the Holocaust. His memoir takes us to the edge of the pit. It is also a story of childhood in happy times, of family and friends, school and vacations, before the storm, and of the long struggle for rehabilitation, renewal and a return to productive life, again with the focus of family.

Jack Brauns writes as he talks, with a vivid sense of communicating the past as if it were only yesterday. He brings us in these pages many fascinating vignettes about pre-war childhood in the Lithuanian city of Kaunas: a child's-eye-view of the lost world of East European Jewry. It also tells the tormented story of the Kovno ghetto as seen by a youngster whose father, Dr Moses Brauns, was a leading and respected figure in the medical life of the ghetto. With pain in his voice, the author then recounts the tormented route – through Stutthof and Dachau – to liberation. The death of his younger brother, Harry, is a shadow that never passes from him. It is a loss that can never be compensated.

Unusual for many memoirs, Jack Brauns has a remarkably full and entirely absorbing focus on the post-war years. The reader is at his side, urging him on as he makes a new life, organizing a medical education for himself in Italy, then struggling to establish himself in the land of endless challenge, the United States. A climax of this memoir is the way in which he obtained the release of his parents from the Soviet Union at the height of the Cold War.

Jack Brauns has written a most personal and engaging tale; not only is it a powerful factual narrative, also an uplifting one, in which the reader, like the writer, emerges above the cruelties and savageries of the Holocaust, to a landscape full of hope; even amid the grim years of the Holocaust there are powerful accounts of non-Jews who tried to help, and who held out a hand of kindness.

This memoir deserves to be widely read, not least by young people, for whom it is a clarion call to emulate the best instincts of humanity.

Martin Gilbert, Honorary Fellow
Merton College, Oxford
14 August 2006

The Library of Holocaust Testimonies

Ten years have passed since Frank Cass launched his Library of Holocaust Testimonies. It was greatly to his credit that this was done, and even more remarkable that it has continued and flourished. The memoirs of each survivor throw new light and cast new perspectives on the fate of the Jews of Europe during the Holocaust. No voice is too small or humble to be heard, no story so familiar that it fails to tell the reader something new, something hitherto unnoticed, something previously unknown.

Each new memoir adds to our knowledge not only of the Holocaust, but also of many aspects of the human condition that are universal and timeless: the power of evil and the courage of the oppressed; the cruelty of the bystanders and the heroism of those who sought to help, despite the risks; the part played by family and community; the question of who knew what and when; the responsibility of the wider world for the destructive behaviour of tyrants and their henchmen.

Fifty memoirs are already in print in the Library of Holocaust Testimonies, and several more are being published each year. In this way anyone interested in the Holocaust will be able to draw upon a rich seam of eyewitness accounts. They can also use another Vallentine Mitchell publication, the multi-volume *Holocaust Memoir Digest*, edited by Esther Goldberg, to explore the contents of survivor memoirs in a way that makes them particularly accessible to teachers and students alike.

Sir Martin Gilbert
London, April 2006

1. Europe, showing places mentioned in the memoir.

2. East Prussia and the Baltic States.

3. Central Europe.

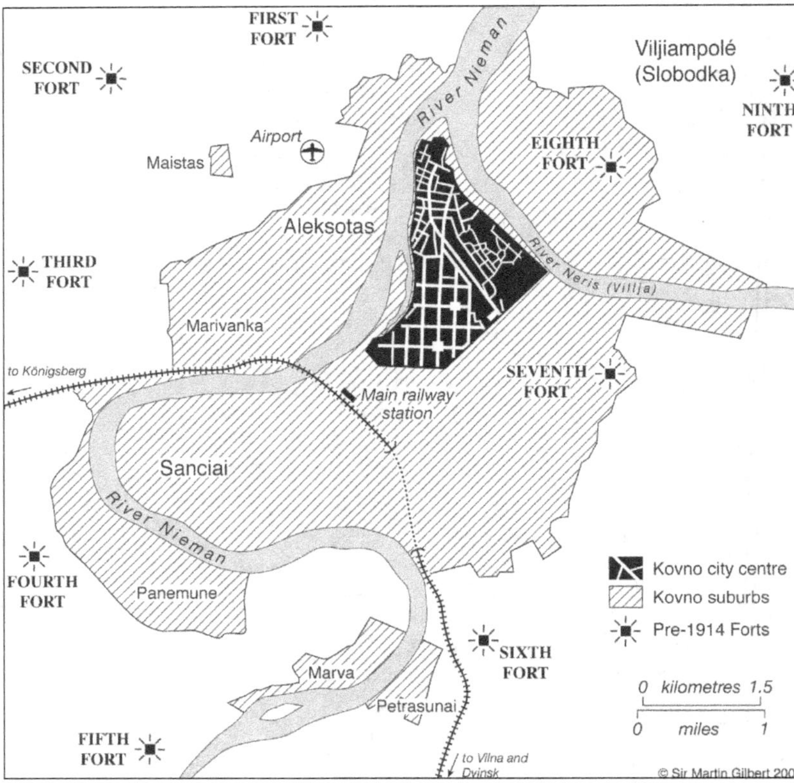

4. Kaunas (Kovno), showing the nine forts.

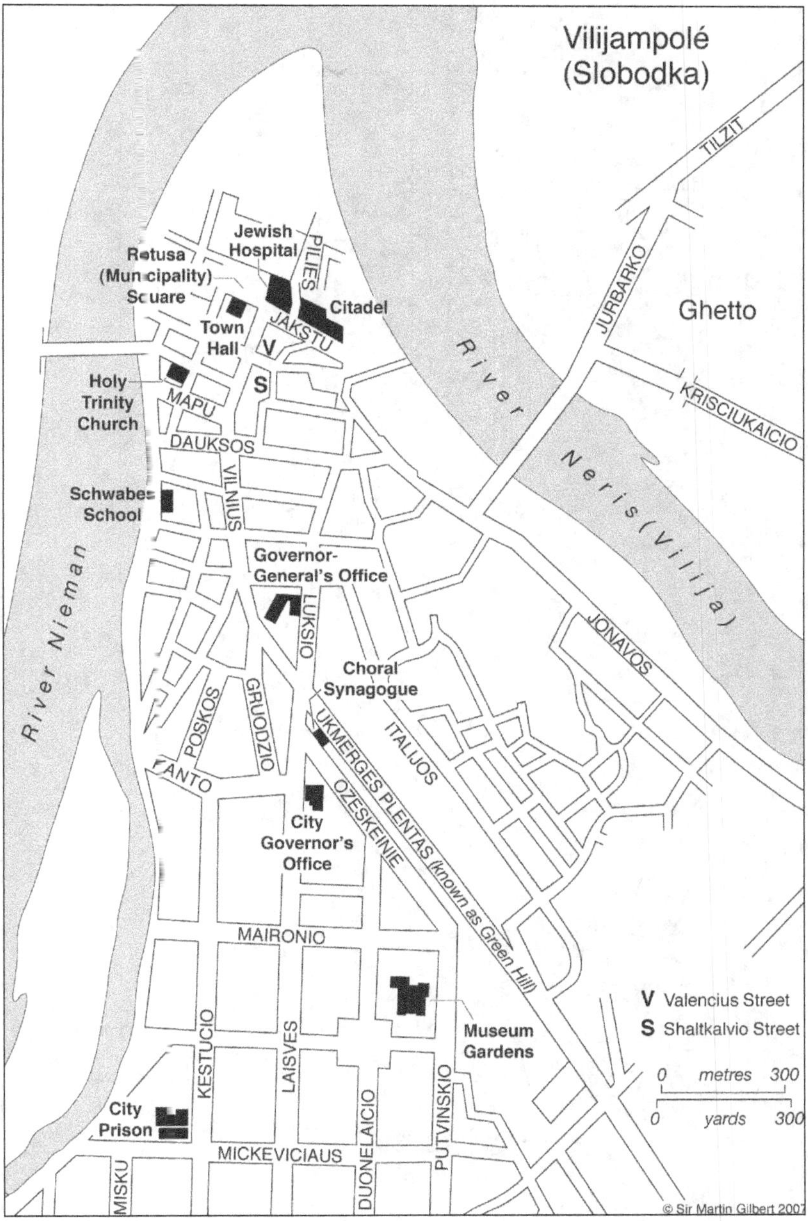

5. Kaunas (Kovno), city centre.

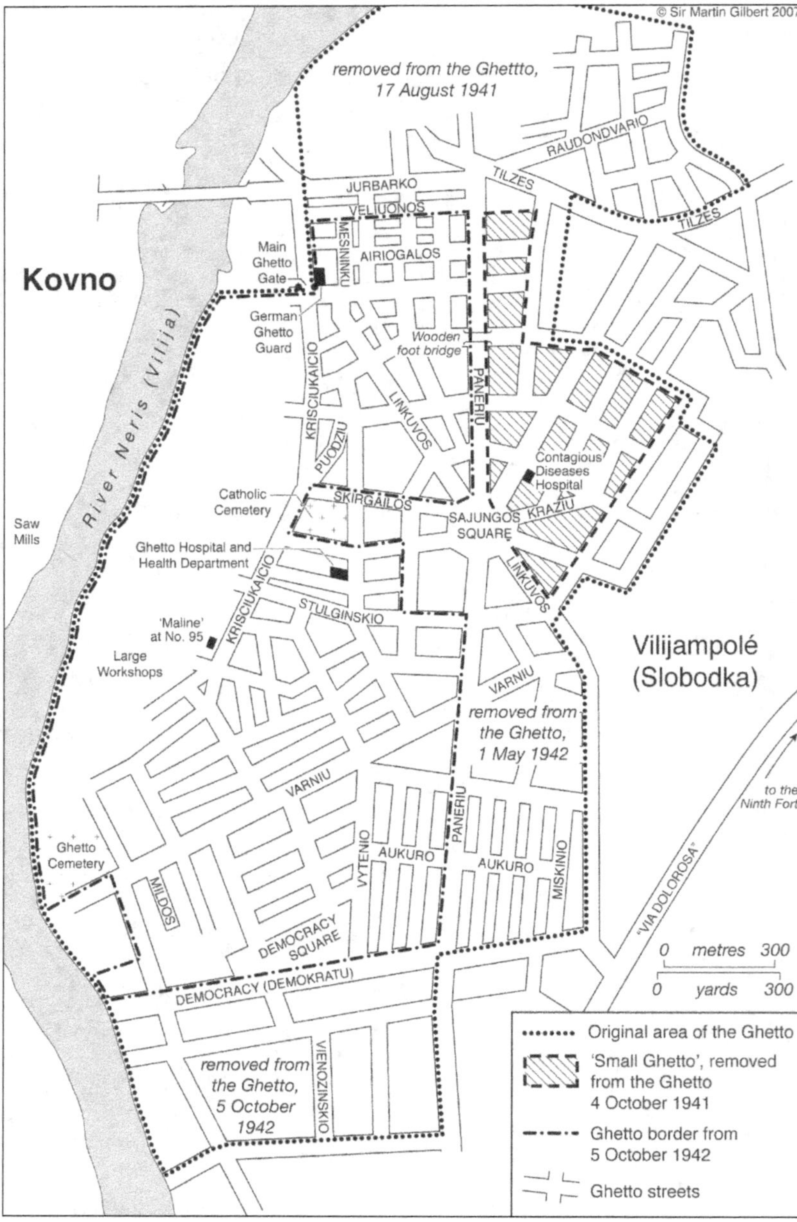

6. Kaunas (Kovno), the ghetto.

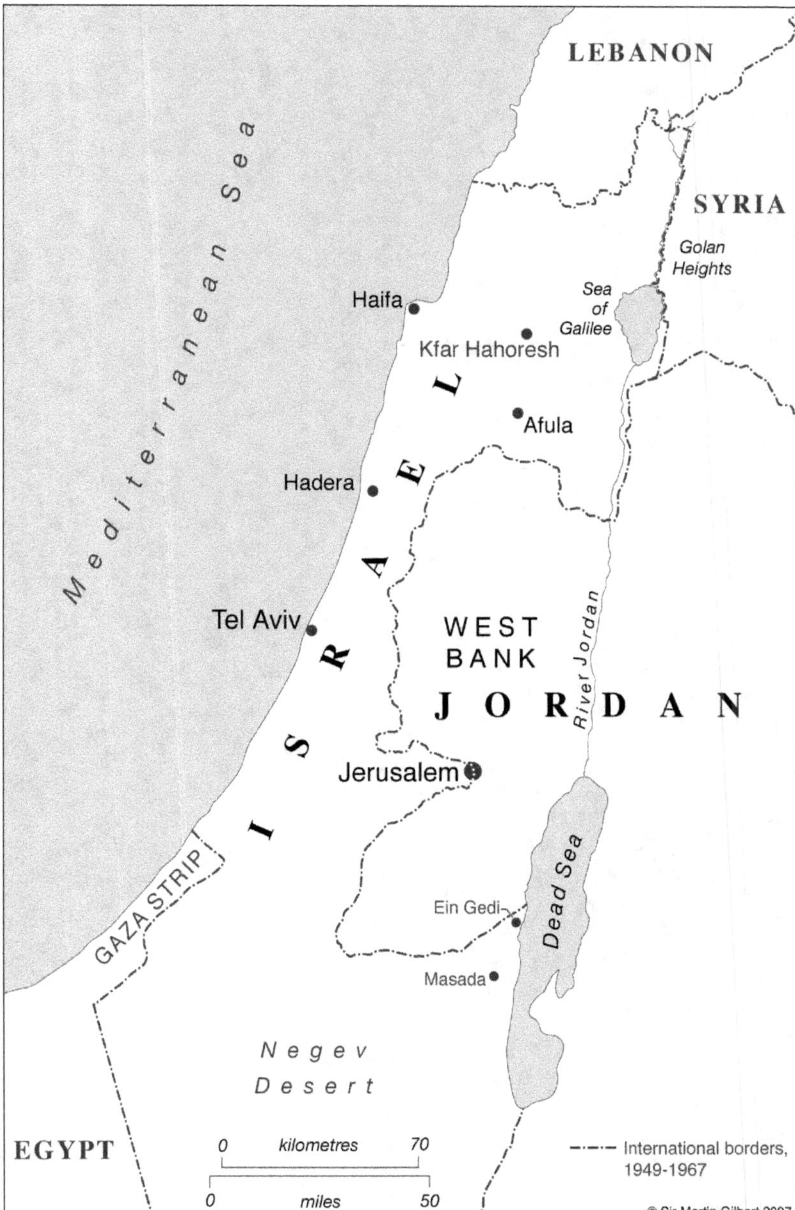

7. Israel, showing places mentioned in the memoir.

PART I

Revisiting Lithuania and My Past

1 Family Roots

On 29 April 1945, my life changed.

From having been an inmate of the Dachau Concentration Camp in Germany, I became a 'free' man. The challenge of surviving the Holocaust changed to the challenge of rebuilding my life and finding a place in the new world.

29 April is the day I celebrate my second 'birthday'. I had a life before that day.

I was born in Riga, Latvia and lived in Kaunas (known to the Jews by its pre-1914 Russian name, Kovno) in Lithuania. My family consisted of my father, mother, brother and myself. I benefited from my parents' love, education and guidance and how they taught me to appreciate life.

I went to the Hebrew high school (Schwabes) where all the subjects were taught in Hebrew, and where I obtained my education and learned the values and beauty of the Jewish religion and its philosophy.

On 22 June 1941, this way of life stopped and I was tossed into the whirlpool of the Holocaust. All the decisions I had to make were on my own, but each played a role in my survival – to be or not to be.

My friends and acquaintances came in and out of my life. Like the winds, some caressed me and some bruised me, but all of them helped to shape my character and my life.

My mother used to say the picture of life is like a mosaic made of small hexagons. If we had a good experience, that hexagon would be brightly colored. If we had a bad experience, that hexagon would be black. Together they would make up the mosaic of life.

After my liberation, education became my priority. I started my medical education at the University of Turin (Torino), Italy.

1. Father Dr Moses Brauns, Jack, mother Basia (Betty), brother Harry and grandmother Anna, Kaunas.

2. Jack as a boy scout, Kaunas.

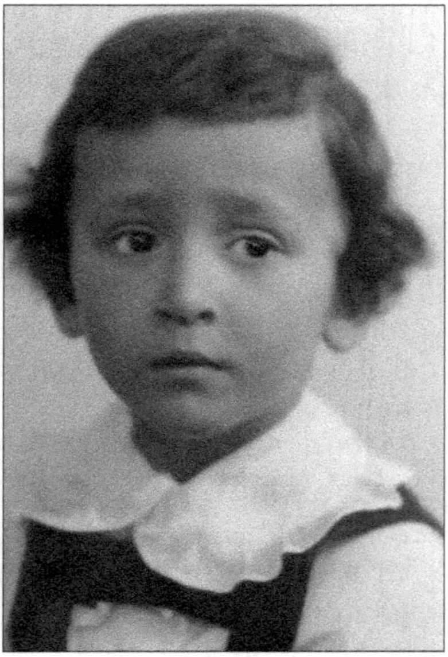

3. Brother Harry, before the Second World War. Killed in Stutthof – his crime? Being born Jewish.

Following emigration to the United States, I took my surgical residency in New York and a postgraduate course at the University of Pennsylvania.

In 1956, Joyce and I were married. I have to admit that my normal life started that day on 24 June 1956. It was Joyce who was responsible for rebuilding and bringing me to a normal life, and who influenced me in my daily thinking as well as decision making. She helped me to build a bridge from my past to the present.

We moved to California, where I started my surgical medical practice.

In 1960, with the help of Vice-President Nixon and Mrs Khrushchev, our family was finally reunited; my father and mother received a permit to leave the Soviet Republic of Lithuania. The only person missing in the reunion was my brother, who had perished during the Holocaust in Stutthof Concentration Camp at the age of 13.

In 1985, I had the privilege of meeting Sir Martin Gilbert. In the following years, our relationship developed into a close friendship. It was his friendship and perseverance that encouraged me to write my memoirs.

Then at the age of 72 I started writing my memoirs – not about me, but about my life and the people who played an important role in shaping my life's course. By writing and recollecting my life, I learned about my family, friends and mainly about myself.

It is very interesting – my mother was right: by continuously creating the pictures of the mosaic of my life and looking back, I can see the bright colors of the good experiences are shining even more; the black colors are not black any more – they have become gray as the years pass by. That is what life is about.

To understand the life of a person, you have to understand the mosaic to which the person was exposed. The mosaic changes several times in a lifetime, and the person has to adapt to each new mosaic to which he is exposed.

There are two important factors that determine a person's

life and behavior. First, the genetic factor: father and mother, grandparents, ancestors. Second, people and events that touch a person's life and leave a lifetime impression.

My father was born in Zagarai in 1895; Lithuania at that time was part of Tsarist Russia. His grandparents lived in Zagarai, which was in the Jewish Pale of Settlement. The Pale had a loose resemblance to a medieval ghetto. The difference between the ghetto and the towns in the Pale of Settlement was that people living in the Pale had no fences. They could leave during the day, but at night they had to return. They could, however, live or settle in other places designated within the Pale in Tsarist Russia.

The Jewish people living in the Pale adjusted to their life and worked hard to earn a living. They were deprived of higher education, however, because most of the towns within the Pale had no high schools or universities. There were exceptions granted to some Jews to live outside the Pale. These exceptions were that they had to be university educated; they had to be merchants of the first guild; they had to be guildmasters with diplomas; or they had to be former soldiers of the Tsar, Nicholas I, who served in the army for twenty-five years. There were other exceptions as well.

My father's grandparents owned a stable. They had forty horses, with equipment and wagons for carrying mail, and passenger coaches for transportation to the surrounding towns and cities. Escape from the Pale was through the door of education.

My father's father, Jacob, became a tailor. He had a diploma as a handicrafts man. Therefore, his family had the right to settle outside the Pale. His parents settled in Viljandi, Estonia, which also was part of Tsarist Russia. There, he opened a ready-made clothing store.

My father's mother returned to Zagarai to her parents' home to give birth to her first child (my father). He was born there on 29 October 1895. When my father was 1 year old my grandmother returned to Viljandi with him.

Viljandi was a small, clean town. There were about twenty-

4. Graduation of Dr Moses Brauns, Cologne Medical School, 1922.

5. Wedding photo of Moses and Basia Brauns, Riga, 15 May 1922.

five Jewish families and a small synagogue. My grandfather was the president of the Jewish community. They hired a teacher to teach the children Hebrew from prayer books and stories in the Bible. The teacher came from within the Pale, and it was illegal for him to live in Viljandi.

My father started his education in a German-language secondary school. Then he applied to a Russian governmental classic school or gymnasium (high school). As there was no gymnasium in Viljandi, my father had to apply to the gymnasium in Parnu, which admitted only 3 to 5 per cent of Jewish students. Luckily, he was admitted. But there was a legal problem: the fact that he had no right to live and go to school in Parnu. The principal of the school, who was a Russian ex-army officer – a general – was understanding of my father's problem and advised him to become an apprentice to a Jewish

6. Dr Moses Brauns and his staff, Contagious Diseases Department, Bikur Cholim Hospital, Kaunas, 1940.

guildmaster, a tinsmith, in order to obtain the right to live in Parnu. In the meantime, he would permit my father to attend the gymnasium. My father eventually graduated from the gymnasium there.

After his graduation my father decided to apply to medical school. In Tsarist Russia, there were nine medical schools and, once again, only 3 to 5 per cent of Jewish students were admitted. There were special exceptions for Jewish students. These included students who had lost a father or a brother in the Russian army, and students who had a wounded father or brother in the army, and students who had a father, brother or a close relative in the army, on whom the student was dependent.

My father's father had to obtain a medical certificate showing that he was mentally unable to care for his son, and gave this responsibility to his cousin, who was the head physician of the Cossack guard regiment stationed in Riga. I can imagine the humiliation that he had to overcome, as the leader of the small Jewish community. After the appropriate certificates were obtained, my father was admitted to Tartu Medical School located in what later became Estonia.

At the end of the First World War, my father transferred to Cologne Medical School, in Germany, to complete his medical studies. In February 1922, he graduated with a diploma in medicine.

My father's cousins, Jenny and Emma, and Emma's husband Abe Schecht, emigrated to the United States. Emma and Abe had two children; Ellie married Julius Kase and Howard married Laura. They lived in New York City. My father's brother, Heinz, emigrated to South Africa and became a textile industrialist. He married Sonia and they were blessed with a son, Aubrey, who also became a textile industrialist. Aubrey married Ella and had two sons. They lived in Johannesburg. Over the years my parents maintained a regular correspondence and shared many photographs. In later years all these relatives played an important part in my life.

My mother, Basia (Betty) Patursky, was born in Riga in 1896. Her maternal grandparents, whose name was Jacobson, came from the Swedish capital, Stockholm. They settled in Riga, where they started a canning factory that produced, among other things, the round cans, used to can sprats, that are still on the market today. She graduated from a French school in Riga, specializing in languages, and was fluent in French, German, Russian, Lithuanian, Latvian, English and Yiddish. She published several teaching books and was especially known for her first English teaching book in the newly independent Lithuania. The book was published in collaboration with Juozas Talmantas, who at that time was Minister of Education in Lithuania. Her sister Leny, and her husband Eugene Tal, both obtained medical degrees and emigrated to Argentina to practice medicine.

When my mother came from Riga to Viljandi to visit her uncle, she met my father and a romance developed. They were married in May 1922.

Lithuania was then independent. My parents settled in Kaunas, the temporary capital, in July 1922. My father started working there in the Jewish Hospital – Bikur Cholim. It was a 300-bed hospital and it contained a Department of Contagious Diseases with sixty beds. He became chief of the Department of Contagious Diseases, the only such department in Kaunas. There was another contagious diseases department in the Lithuanian Army hospital. In 1940 the University of Kaunas also opened a contagious diseases department.

I grew up in Kaunas. Our family consisted of my father Moses, my mother Basia (Betty), my brother Harry, and myself. My brother Harry was five years younger than me. Until I reached the age of 5, we spoke only Russian at home. After my brother was born, we gradually switched to German.

My mother's brother, Max Patursky, introduced me to photography and skiing. He bought me my first camera and my first pair of skis when he returned from France, where he graduated in chemistry from the University of Paris.

Jewish life in Lithuania was very rich and rewarding. We had several Jewish newspapers, several Jewish Hebrew schools, for boys and girls or co-ed, as well as rabbinical schools (yeshivas) where people came to study from all over Europe. There were also Jewish institutions, like orphanages, old-age homes and synagogues. The Jewish hospital treated 3,000 to 4,000 patients a year.

We had kosher food in our house and observed the Jewish holidays without having to check the calendar. We were members of the Choral Synagogue in Kaunas. For my bar mitzvah, we went to Viljandi in Estonia. Relatives from Riga as well as from Tallin arrived to participate in the celebration at the synagogue. Unfortunately, my grandfather Jacob had died a year or two before I was born. I was named after him. I met some of the community in Viljandi, including the people who were my father's and my grandfather's friends.

Summer vacations were very important. We usually had six to eight weeks of vacation between June and September. The months of July and August were the months of our family vacation and they were important to us because my father used to take off a whole month to spend with the family.

We alternated our summer vacations. Every other summer we would visit my mother's family. We usually stayed at the beach resort at Dzinghari, where my grandparents had a summer home. It was a beautiful place on the Baltic Sea. We traveled there by train from Riga. Aunt Raya, my father's sister, often joined us. She taught me to play tennis and to ride horses. I also had the opportunity to get to know my mother's parents and uncles.

The second place we used to visit was Viljandi, where my grandmother – my father's mother – had a home. Starting in my early childhood, I appreciated and enjoyed nature. I still recall my visits to my grandmother in Estonia. It was a picturesque, beautiful town in the mountains, with a large lake. Her house was within a short walking distance from the forest. Every morning I went out to the forest and I learned how to pick blueberries as well as mushrooms. I learned from her to distinguish between the poisonous and the edible mushrooms, from the ones I collected.

My father's family, his brother Wille and sister Raya, as well as my father's close friends, used to come to visit us in Viljandi. One of the people that I met there was Minister Jaan Lattik who was my father's closest friend. At the time my father went into medicine, Jaan Lattik became a Lutheran minister. I liked him very much. When he came to visit us he was already a very well-known person in Estonia. In spite of that, he always paid a lot of attention to me, and always spent time with me talking about my future and my plans, ambitions and goals.

Another place my family visited every other summer was Palanga, a sea side resort in Lithuania. We usually stayed at Gutman's Pension and always enjoyed it. Palanga was one of the most beautiful beaches I can recall in my life, in spite of my not having been there for more than fifty years. Many of my schoolmates used to come to Palanga. I had a great opportunity to spend a lot of time with my classmates and friends.

A close friend of my father, Dr Benjamin Zacharin, also stayed in Palanga. Often in the afternoon, my father and Dr

Zacharin used to take a walk in the forest and I would join them. Dr Zacharin was a well-known surgeon. I feel that during the time I spent with him he brought out the beauty of surgery and its application to medicine. Indirectly or directly, he played a very important part in my eventual decision to become a surgeon. At that time, Dr Zacharin was the chief surgeon at the Jewish Hospital in Kaunas.

One summer on vacation in Palanga, our family met the Balkin family – father, mother and two daughters – who had come from Germany for a vacation. They could not stop talking about the horrors they experienced as Jews living in Germany. They had to continue to live in Germany while waiting for an American affidavit to emigrate to the United States of America.

Some summers we went to Tallin, the capital of Estonia, and we spent some time with my uncles and aunts from my father's family. In the summer of 1937, we crossed the Gulf of Finland by ferry and visited Helsinki. It was an exciting trip, which left a big impression on me. The Estonian and Finnish languages are related, and it was not difficult for my father to communicate in Finland. That trip brought me closer to the Finnish culture. It was not until 1998 that I revisited Helsinki. To my amazement, I felt as if I had been asleep all those years and suddenly woken up in Helsinki. Little had changed. I was able to find my way easily through Helsinki. The names of the streets had not changed.

In 1939, the war started with the German invasion of Poland. Many of the Jewish Polish refugees fled to Vilnius to escape the German occupation. In 1940, the Soviet Union returned Vilnius to Lithuania, including all the Polish Jews who had found refuge there.

Politically, life was uneventful until Lithuania was occupied by Soviet forces. Things changed then. The Hebrew Schwabes High School was closed and Shalom Aleichem Yiddish school replaced it. We continued our studies in Yiddish. In our school there were basically two groups of students – the students who spoke only Yiddish and the students, including me, who were from the previous Schwabes (who in spite of being prohibited to speak the Hebrew language, spoke Hebrew among themselves; that was resented by the students who spoke only Yiddish). In spite of the merger of the schools, many of the teachers, especially the teacher I was so attached to and appreciated, continued to teach us.

Members of the Jewish Lithuanian community had opened their homes to the Jewish refugees from Poland. Each family adopted one or two refugees or a whole family. Money and clothes were collected and arrangements were made to help them to continue their journey to different destinations such as the United States or other escape options. Unfortunately, we were blinded and did not see the danger of anti-Semitism in Lithuania. That might be one of the reasons why most of the Lithuanian community perished during the Second World War.

In 1988 *The Kovno Ghetto Diary* was published in Hebrew in Israel, by the Bialik Publishing House. I had discussed with Avraham Tory – who had been the secretary of the Jewish Council (*Aeltestenrat*) in the Kovno Ghetto – the possibility of publishing this book in English. In 1990, with the title, *Surviving the Holocaust*: *The Kovno Ghetto Diary,* with introduction, historical notes and maps drawn by Sir Martin Gilbert, it was published by the Harvard University Press, Cambridge, Massachusetts.

It is the only surviving diary written at the time, and in such detail, of the events during the existence of the Kovno Ghetto.

For more than seven years, I tried to make a documentary or feature film about the Kovno Ghetto that would reach an audience for whom films would be more accessible than books. My daughter Alicia worked tirelessly to write the movie script with David Elton. They called it *The Last Leaves of Winter.* She accompanied me to Israel and interviewed many survivors to authenticate her narrative.

We decided to make the story into a documentary instead of a feature film. It was commissioned by the History Channel and made into a documentary by the film-maker, Herb Krosney, who felt that for authenticity, the filming should be done in Lithuania.

It would be my first trip to Lithuania since I was deported in 1944, fifty-three years earlier, to Stutthof, and was subsequently sent to Dachau. In order to make this trip I had to overcome my apprehension of visiting Lithuania again.

I arranged that my adopted sister, Irena Veisaite, who was living in Vilnius, would join us for the filming. I felt more comfortable that Joyce, my friend Martin Gilbert and Irena would be with me during this emotional trip.

It was early in the morning in Los Angeles when I walked to the American Airlines Gate 31. The walk was much more relaxed than my later walk to Gate 51 in Frankfurt. I fly frequently with American Airlines and am familiar with the Los Angeles Airport terminal, but in Frankfurt it was different. At Gate 51, I had to board a Lufthansa plane for a direct flight to Vilnius.

The first part of the trip was uneventful. After arriving in Frankfurt, I found my way to the lounge of Gate 51, where I sat down and waited for the flight to board. It was only then that I realized that I was really going back to Lithuania. Surveying the people waiting for the same plane, it looked to me as if there were some younger people on business, some elderly people possibly returning to Lithuania and a few Germans, probably on business, also going to Lithuania. I was proud of myself for my efforts – with the help of language tapes – to regain the ability to speak and understand the Lithuanian language, which I had not used for the past fifty-three years.

As I sat on the plane, I had no choice but to relive some of my past. It was a few days short of fifty-three years since I had entered the cattle cars and was deported from Kaunas to Stutthof.

I thought about my father and mother, and my brother. I thought about my life for three years in the ghetto, and the unbelievably harsh treatment by my so-called compatriots – even before the German Army occupied Lithuania. I saw the faces of my schoolmates who are still alive, and the ones who perished. My mind was working overtime. I relived my entire life in Lithuania before the plane landed.

The crew on the plane was efficient and friendly. Even if I could have tried to convey my thoughts to them, I am sure they would not have been able to understand. They were from another generation. It was fifty-three years later and I was on my way to Lithuania. By this time, I was prepared. With me, I had my lifetime companion and friend, my wife, Joyce. I had not shared my thoughts with her during the flight, but I am sure she had detected my apprehensiveness and concerns.

The announcement came on the intercom that the plane was in its landing pattern and that we would be arriving within seven to ten minutes in Vilnius. As I walked out of the plane, I saw two familiar people. One was my adopted sister, Irena Veisaite, whom I had seen just a few months before in London. Standing with her was my long-time friend and schoolmate, Dodik Judelevitz, whom I had not seen for fifty-seven years.

I knew then that I had really landed in Vilnius.

How wonderful it was, fifty-three years later, to be sitting around the table with such dear friends from my past. Irena had prepared an exquisite dinner. We discussed Irena's survival, with the generosity and help of a Lithuanian family who hid her during the war. Dodik described his family's evacuation to the Soviet Union in 1941 and his survival during the war years, as well as his return to Lithuania in 1945.

There were stories of joy and of sorrow, of pain and celebration. We learned the details of the daily survival of each of us. They were very interested in my survival in the ghetto and at Dachau. It was a sad evening as we could not forget our family and friends who were killed during the war.

I looked around the room where we sat and I saw the pictures of my family, a picture of my brother, Irena's family pictures as well as the pictures Dodik had brought with him.

After having spent some time together with a few celebratory drinks, we felt that the 'missing' people were still sitting with us at the table and participated in our joy of reunion and our joy of survival of this terrible period of our lives. We cried together about the destruction of 95 per cent of the Jewish community in Lithuania and our missing family members, our classmates and the fact that with the destruction, the culture of the Jewish Lithuanian community was gone forever.

The next morning, at my request, Irena took us to see the house where she and my parents had lived from 1945 to 1960.

I remember my parents telling me – many years later – how, early in the morning during the Soviet occupation, a fire broke out in that very building. The fire department arrived in a short time, but they could not enter any of the apartments. Everyone was afraid of a visit from the KGB, the Soviet secret police, and had locked and bolted their doors.

My father ran from one apartment to the other crying, 'Neighbors, neighbors, please open the door. It's only a fire.' It was such a strong statement that I have never forgotten it. It mirrored the fearful life the Jews lived under Soviet occupation.

Irena showed us the staircase. She asked if we would like to see the apartment where my parents had lived. She knew the people who were living there now, but I was not eager to see the apartment. I did not want to meet the people who had no past relationship to my family's existence in Vilnius.

We walked and toured the area where the ghetto used to be. The plaque indicating, 'This is the site of the previously existing ghetto' did not mean too much to me. Most of the area was very built up and there were no reminders of the terrible pain and sufferings the inhabitants of the ghetto in Vilnius had been exposed to at the time they lived there.

We had dinner in a small restaurant. Some of Irena's Lithuanian friends joined us. They were extremely pleasant and interested in my background. I felt that their knowledge of the destruction of the Jewish Lithuanian community was limited. On the way home, we both agreed that there had not been enough educational effort in the Soviet period to teach the story of the Holocaust. Although since the fall of Communism in 1991 there had been some effort to inform young people, the need for a documentary film seemed even more urgent as an educational tool.

The next morning we got up early and by 9:00 a.m. we were already at the office of the Vilnius archives, as planned, to meet Herb Krosney and his film crew. It was an unbelievable experience to visit this office. It contained all the collected surviving documents from the Kovno Ghetto.

We all spent several hours going through the documents. I was mainly interested in the documents related to the medical health system, which were well catalogued and filed.

I found several letters of my father's and other documents with my father's signature. I was able to obtain copies of these papers. There were many pictures in the archives that had been found after the ghetto had been destroyed. Herb Krosney found several photographs and other documentation that he used in the film.

It was an emotional experience to find these letters and documents written and signed by my father. I believed they had been destroyed in the ghetto.

Afterwards, in the late afternoon, we all drove to Kaunas (Kovno). The road from Vilnius to Kaunas was a beautiful highway, a far cry from what I remembered. In less than two hours, we arrived in Kaunas. Irena drove us directly to Santakus Hotel, on Gruodzio Street, where we had reservations and we checked in. We planned to stay in Kaunas several days. It was still light when we arrived, and I asked Irena to drive for a while through the streets of Kaunas. It felt strange to be here finally, after fifty-three years.

Kaunas looked to me as if it had shrunk. The houses looked smaller, the streets were narrower, and the people looked different. We drove through Laisves Alleju and when we came to Presidento Gatve where I used to live we could not get through because the street was closed to traffic. It had become a pedestrian mall.

That evening, Sir Martin Gilbert arrived. It was comforting for me to be surrounded by friends and familiar faces. It took away some of the pain that I had anticipated by returning to Lithuania. The next morning, we got up early and had breakfast in the hotel dining room. I found the people, from the concierge to the secretaries, as well as the waiters, to be well dressed and most helpful to us and the other guests.

The Santakus Hotel was a small, beautiful hotel. It was only a half a block away from the house where I had lived. Only the next day did I realize that I knew that street well. It was the street where the Yavna Girls School existed before the war. It was the concierge of the hotel who confirmed that before the war there had been a Jewish school here and the hotel had been built using part of the Jewish school. On the other side of the street, one block away, there were Jewish orphanage signs on the wall. The building was empty and abandoned.

There was about an hour before we would have to leave the hotel for the ghetto, to start filming. Joyce and I took a short walk to Presidento Gatve, now called Vilnius Gatve. On the right-hand side I could see the house where I had lived.

It was the first time in more than fifty-three years that I saw the house where I had spent my youth. It had not changed. It looked the same. I saw the same pharmacy that had been there when I was a child.

As I looked up at the balcony on the second floor, I remembered the day the war started.

I crossed the street and entered the house where we lived in Kaunas before the war, where the twenty-four steps leading to our apartment had been. It had not changed. It looked a little more dilapidated. It did not have the luster and the beauty I remembered. I entered the house and I went up the twenty-four steps but did not go to the apartment. The local inhabitants become very defensive thinking that when people revisited their old apartments their intention was to reclaim them. Also, I did not want to add additional memories to my past by meeting people whom I had never known and who were now living in the apartment where I used to live. They would intrude on my memories.

I also looked at the courtyard where I used to stop every day. Everything looked so familiar except that it was so small and so old. I never forgot these twenty-four steps that we did not take, steps that drastically changed our destiny during the war.

2 The Ghetto

The sun was showing its rays, accompanied by loud explosions. I went out on the balcony. It was still early in the morning and the streets were empty. It looked like a usual Sunday, but this was a special day, the day the war began, 22 June 1941.

Father had telephoned home the previous night from Vilnius and advised us that he was going to finish his paper-work, and that the epidemic of typhus abdominalis in Vilnius was officially ended. He was coming home in the morning.

In late April 1941 an epidemic of typhus had broken out. The drinking water was contaminated by sewage. The Minister of Health appointed my father to be in charge of fighting and containing the epidemic. About 4,000 residents were affected. Schools were transformed into hospitals. Approximately two months after the beginning of the epidemic, on 21 June 1941, my father declared the end of the epidemic in Vilnius, and the next morning he telephoned to say that he was on his way home to Kaunas.

That morning, during the train ride, my father was not aware that the Germans had crossed the Soviet border and that war had started between Germany and the Soviet Union.

In Kaunas, the sounds of explosions gradually diminished and the sun continued its ascent.

When my father arrived in the late morning, he brought home the news that the German Army had crossed the border and was on its way to Kaunas. He learned this from the taxi driver who picked him up at the railroad station and had tuned in, early in the morning, to the BBC, broadcast from London. The taxi driver also stated that early that morning the airport in Aleksotas was bombed. As soon as my father reached us, we turned on the local radio broadcast and heard military marches continuously. There was no mention of any war.

There were constant speculations and rumors. Our main concern was what was going to happen to the Jewish population?

In the afternoon, the news broadcast from the local radio station advised that the heroic, invincible Red Army was on its way to the Soviet-German border to repel the German aggression.

The picture from our balcony was different. I looked out at the street and noted that small units of soldiers were moving in the direction of the Soviet Union, away from the Soviet-German border.

I listened to the radio, and then went back to the balcony and tried to explain this to myself, but could not. There were no troop movements in the direction of the border. All the movement of the Soviet troops was back towards to their homeland.

I concluded that the Soviet generals were engaged in a tactic of deceit to confuse and deceive the German generals; they definitely confused me.

The day passed and a new day started. Father received a phone call from the Ministry of Health. He was advised to get ready to be evacuated with his family to the Soviet Union.

A car with a driver arrived and parked in front of the house. There were twenty-four steps to descend down the staircase from our apartment to the car. My parents discussed the situation. Father felt that it was immoral to leave his patients in the hospital unattended, and wanted the rest of the family to leave without him. Hours passed in discussion. Finally my father told the driver that he had decided against being evacuated. My mother would not leave without him, and my brother and I could not leave without our parents.

Our family did not descend the twenty-four steps that would have lead us to be evacuated to the interior of the Soviet Union and would have offered us a completely different destiny in the years to come. I always wondered what my destiny would have been, if my father's decision had been to descend the twenty-four steps and be evacuated to the Soviet Union.

I called my friend, Dodik, who with his family, was waiting for the car to arrive to evacuate them. My call was not answered. Dodik and his family had already left for the Soviet Union.

When I returned to the hotel, our group and the film crew were ready to leave for the ghetto. A car had been rented. Vytautas, our driver, had been born and raised in Kaunas. He stayed with us the whole nine days we were in Lithuania. He was in his 20s, and was well educated. I felt very happy that my effort in reviving my Lithuanian language prior to visiting had paid off. I felt very comfortable conversing with him. We were ready to leave. There was Herb Krosney and his wife, Mary Stewart; Irena, my adopted sister; Tina Lunson, from the United States Holocaust Memorial Museum in Washington; Uri Barak, a film photographer from Israel, as well as Joyce and myself. Shortly afterward Martin Gilbert arrived with a driver and another car. We split up into two cars and left for the former Kovno Ghetto.

To get to the ghetto in Vilijampolė, also known as Slobodka, we had to cross the bridge over the Neris River. Again, it looked to me as if the buildings had shrunk. Here and there were some new buildings. The traffic was not too heavy and we arrived at the bridge.

In the middle of the bridge, we heard a loud noise and the car stopped. Vytautas jumped out, checked, and told us that we had a problem. An axle had broken and he had to go and call to get a substitute car.

This bridge had played a significant role in my life: a dramatic role

In 1941, in the early weeks of the German occupation, an area was designated for the future ghetto. The German authorities, together with the Lithuanian authorities, had decided to move the Jews into the ghetto. The maps for the ghetto were drawn and redrawn almost every day, with the Germans allocating more territory to the Jews and the Lithuanians trying to reduce that territory as much as possible.

The area finally designated for the ghetto already contained 6,000 residents; 4,000 of these people were Lithuanians who would have to be relocated, and 25,500 Jews would have to move into the area where 2,000 Jews were already living. Under the German plan, 27,500 people had to live in an area where previously 6,000 people had lived.

To avoid confusion and disorganization, young people – including myself – volunteered to go to the future ghetto site to measure and record the footage of every room in every house, every kitchen space and every bathroom space. It was then submitted to the special housing committee which was formed by the Jewish Council. The Council was an elected one, formed to represent the Jewish community. It would assign people their living space prior to moving, so that the move of the Jews into the ghetto would be organized and orderly.

Every morning I got up and walked to the ghetto where I met my friends, and together in pairs we drew the outline of each house and measured its square footage.

One morning in 1941, on my way to the ghetto, I was at the same place where our car had just stopped on the way to filming. Suddenly, both sides of the bridge had been closed by Lithuanian so-called 'partisans', whose cruel game was to find Jews and to kill them. Everyone who was arrested was taken away by them to the Fourth or Seventh Fort, never to return. These 'partisans' stopped traffic on the bridge, having set up barricades on both sides. I was trapped. I knew that once I was arrested for being there I would have to pay with my life.

My face must have shown my desperation because a Lithuanian farmer with his horse and wagon, on his way to the market to sell cheese, waved to me to jump into his wagon. I did not hesitate, and jumped in. He gave me a blanket that I used to partially cover myself. He went straight to the end of the bridge leading back to the city. I was worried that the sound of my heartbeat might betray me. We passed the checkpoint without any problem. He had a very nice face with a short beard and I can never thank him enough for having saved my life without being asked. Once we left the bridge and were back on the street, I asked him if we could stop at my house, which was actually on the way, and he agreed. When I got to the house I told him that I would get my mother, with the intention of having her pay him for saving my life, as well as for the cheese that he had given me which was so difficult for a Jew to buy. You see, Jews were allowed to enter the market and food stores only after a certain hour – by which time the food supply was already sold out.

I ran upstairs, but by the time I came down with my mother, he had gone. However, I still remember his face. Even today as I stood on the bridge, I could see the impressive face and the goodness it radiated.

It took two hours to get the new car and we then continued toward the ghetto. It was an incredible experience for me when the car stopped in an area where the gates of the ghetto used to be.

There was a plaque at the beginning of Krisciukaicio Gatve, which was one of the streets that crossed the ghetto. But the plaque was not the only thing that reminded me of the area where the gate was. There were also my memories, which immediately returned, about the significance of the gates in the ghetto.

Beginning in the last week of July 1941, and ending on 15 August 1941, the Jews from the city and suburbs had to move to the ghetto. I still remember vividly the line of horse-drawn carriages that carried people's belongings to the ghetto. There was one line entering the ghetto, full of basic necessities like beds and other belongings that could fit into the single rooms to which families had been assigned. The other line was of empty carriages leaving the ghetto. It was a sad scene, ending

7. A line of carriages laden with belongings entering the ghetto, Kovno, 1941 (courtesy Avraham Tory).

the era of the Jewish inhabitants in the city of Kovno and their transfer to Vilijampolé, with an unknown future.

The only consolation of this move was that finally the Jewish population would be protected by barbed wire from the inhumane treatment of some of the Lithuanian population – the hooligans who tried to take advantage of this terrible situation.

On 15 August 1941, the gates were officially closed. The final count was 32,000 Jews in the designated area of the ghetto with a living space of 1.5 meters by 1.5 meters for each person. Surprisingly, this transition and the settling of the Jewish people in the ghetto were well planned by the Jewish Council and there were no major incidents. The life of the Jews in the City of Kaunas prior to moving to the ghetto had been very dangerous. Many Jews had been killed, people were robbed and their apartments ransacked.

Unfortunately, after the gates were closed on 15 August, the terror of life in the ghetto continued. Every ten days someone was shot and killed. In addition, the entire ghetto population experienced food rationing and the lack of proper food. Tragedy was enacted on a daily basis. The Jewish population gradually decreased. The barbed wire did not protect us.

The Jews continued to try to make their life as normal and as human as possible. There were lectures by different people. Physicians gave lectures to their colleagues. Lawyers and engineers gave lectures. There were also many musicians in the ghetto and there were periodic concerts. All this was done to try to save our minds and our ability to think.

My father made a series of notes on medicine in the ghetto, which he presented as a lecture. Later, I used my father's notes, translated by our dear friend Irene Lyons, to prepare a talk at the Yivo Institute in New York: I gave the talk on 4 November 1996.

Every morning people in the ghetto assembled at the gate of the main entrance. They would go there and meet their own working groups. Some then went to the airport for construction tasks. Some went to different working locations or different factories. One group went to Gestapo headquarters to clean the premises.

Jankele Werblowski was one of the Council appointees who worked at the ghetto gate to let the people out and receive them back on their return from work. His job was to make sure that the number of people who left and returned was the same. Jankele Werblowski was about 30 years old – a very sharp, very alert person. If a few people wanted to leave the ghetto for one reason or another and the number in the brigades increased by two or three people, the end count leaving the ghetto was always the same as the work force when he counted. If, however, a brigade leader returning from the city advised Jankele Werblowski that five people had left, or had escaped, or for some reason did not return, or that some people had returned from their hiding places because of changed circumstances, the brigade was either larger by the number of additional people or less by the number of people who had stayed in the city. With fast-talking Jankele Werblowski, the count of the returning brigade was always correct. He was an extremely important factor in keeping the entrances and exits of the working brigades of the ghetto smooth.

The main goal of the people who went to work was to bring food back to the ghetto. They traded their clothes or anything they had to trade: a watch or jewelry that was still kept hidden from the Germans. The big question was how to carry this food into the ghetto, as it was prohibited by the German army and carefully watched by the Lithuanian guards. With the help of Jankele Werblowski, however, the guards were distracted or bribed. He was very active. Most of the time he succeeded in helping people to smuggle in whatever they had with them. Occasionally, somebody was caught. Again, it was Jankele Werblowski who talked and negotiated with the German and Lithuanian guards, saving the Jews from beating or incarceration.

This gate and the activities at the gate were an important factor in the mosaic of life in the ghetto.

On reaching the former ghetto area in 1997, I immediately recognized the Lithuanian police station that was located near the gate. When people were searched and found to be in possession of food, they were always detained in this police station.

It was amazing how the houses looked the same. They had not been rebuilt. They were all wooden houses except for the brick police station.

The presence of our two cars on Krisciukaicio Gatve and the film equipment which had been set up on the street caused people to stop. They were not concerned about the filming. Their only concern was: Were we here to take back their property? Every person who stopped to talk to us advised us that the Lithuanian government had given them these houses to live in, and had reassured them that this property would never be given back to the Jews. In spite of our reassurances to them that we had not come here with any intention of getting the property back as we all lived abroad, I do not think we convinced them until they saw us leaving.

Then they were relieved. That happened to us in every place we stopped in the ghetto. People living there approached us, some friendly, some not so friendly, and the main thing they told us was that we were not getting the property back. Actually, I would never like to live in a place like that again.

One elderly lady told me to visit the monument where the Contagious Diseases Hospital used to be. She said that every week she put fresh flowers at the monument.

When we finished the filming I had to take a moment to absorb the impression that this visit made on me. Returning to the same place where the ghetto stood for three years was incredible. It was a place haunted by episodes of torment, fear and murder, but also by the ingenuity and bravery of the people in sneaking in food at the risk of their lives.

We continued on Krisciukaicio Gatve and made a left turn towards Airiogalos Gatve. We made another right turn on Paneriu Gatve. Paneriu Gatve was the street that divided the large ghetto from the little ghetto. Between the large ghetto and the little ghetto there was a wooden bridge. In the little ghetto, the Contagious Diseases Hospital was located. We came to the spot where the bridge had been and walked to the area where the hospital was. There was a plaque stating that this was the area where St Vincent de Paul Society's old-age home had been, and that in 1941 it was transformed into a contagious diseases hospital.

This hospital was not designed to be a contagious diseases hospital. It did not have any isolation facilities, but there had been no choice. It was the only facility that was more or less adaptable for starting a contagious diseases hospital. On 14 August, a truck brought patients from different hospitals and elderly people from Jewish old-age homes in the city to the ghetto hospitals. When the truck arrived, the contagious diseases patients were immediately put in the house selected for the future contagious diseases hospital. Actually, the house was empty; it did not even have any beds.

As I walked, I vividly remembered the collection of things we needed to establish a contagious diseases hospital.

Immediately after 15 August, with the closure of the ghetto gates, we started our collection process. Young people went from house to house to solicit donations – like an extra bedpan, an extra sheet, an extra pillow, a bed, or some blankets, for the Contagious Diseases Hospital and also for the General Hospital which was to be established a few blocks away.

In a very short time the equipment of the Contagious Diseases Hospital had been collected, the beds were brought in, and the hospital was opened within a week after the ghetto gates were closed.

An X-ray unit was donated by one of the physicians, brought from his office in the city, and installed in the General Hospital. It was the generosity of the people that helped establish the hospitals. But on 4 October 1941, only after two months in operation, the Contagious Diseases Hospital was burned down. I looked at the plaque before me. It was a cold reminder of what had happened. Fresh flowers were placed around the monument by some of the local inhabitants.

It was early in the morning, about 6:00 a.m. on 4 October 1941, when my father and I began our walk to the Contagious Diseases Hospital. At that time, we lived in the large ghetto and we had to cross the bridge into the small ghetto.

I was employed as a hospital clerk in the Contagious Diseases Hospital. We were supposed to start working in the hospital at 7:00 a.m.

An elderly gentleman approached my father and asked some questions. This encounter delayed our arrival at the hospital by about ten minutes. As soon as we got to the bridge to cross from the large ghetto to the small ghetto, we saw that the small ghetto was surrounded by Lithuanian policemen and that the bridge was closed. We were able to see a fire truck parked not far from the Contagious Diseases Hospital.

We knew that the doctor and the patients were inside the building and that the windows and doors were nailed shut. We could feel the desperation of the people in the Contagious Diseases Hospital who could not get out. After a while, the hospital was set on fire and sixty-two people including the patients; the physician, Dr Davidovitch; and two nurses perished in the fire. The firemen stood by the fire trucks and watched as the fire decimated the hospital.

At the same time, the people from the General Hospital two streets away were removed, as well as the inhabitants of the little ghetto. They were all taken to the Ninth Fort, where they were killed. I asked my father who the gentleman was who had stopped us and delayed our arrival at the bridge – an event that saved us from being burned alive in the Contagious Diseases Hospital. My father knew most of the people in the ghetto and had a very sharp memory, but for some reason, he could not recall the person who stopped him and asked him the questions that delayed us. It was this ten-minute delay that saved both our lives.

I was standing there on this visit fifty-three years later, and all the emotions I experienced that day, 4 October 1941, returned to me as if the clock had stopped. I could see the hospital on fire with the windows and doors nailed shut and the patients and doctor and nurses trying to get out. I remembered how their screams got weaker and finally it was quiet. The fire department was there to make sure no other buildings were burned by the fire that had been set to the hospital. The scene of the burning building with people inside trying to get out, and the Lithuanian guards making sure that no one would escape this horrible death, played through my mind. The horrible drama and tragedy continued the next day when people were removed from the little ghetto and taken to the Ninth Fort. After the people were removed, the little ghetto was liquidated. Everything was gone except my memories, and a single plaque at the site of the tragedy.

The Germans and the Lithuanians spread the rumor that there was leprosy in the hospital. They used this as an excuse for the destruction of the patients and the burning of the hospital. The truth is that there were no leprosy patients in the hospital. As soon as the rumors began to spread, my father tried to discharge as many patients as he could, but the people would not leave as they felt more secure on the hospital premises. It

8. The remnants of the Contagious Diseases Hospital, destroyed by fire, 4 October 1941 (courtesy Esther Lurie).

was my father who decided that the words 'contagious diseases' would be taken out of the diagnostic vocabulary, and no more contagious diseases were reported to the Lithuanian and German authorities. A new contagious diseases hospital was never built. The General Hospital, however, needed to be built in the big ghetto. Again, the hospital was built from the generosity of the people who each contributed from their meager belongings to the creation of the new general hospital.

I was overcome with sadness as I walked through the streets of the old little ghetto.

After having spent some time photographing the surroundings, we continued walking along Paneriu Gatve, where we made a right turn and found the Democracy Square. It appeared smaller than I remembered. I looked around and my memories came back. I saw that there were three and four-story apartment buildings outside the

Democracy Square that were apparently built during the Soviet occupation after 1945.

The cameras were set up and Sir Martin Gilbert walked around the square followed by the camera. During his walk around the square, he narrated the story of the action of 28 October 1941. While he was talking and recalling the history, again my memories and emotions were awakened.

It was a few days before 28 October 1941 when Master Sergeant Helmut Rauca, who was in charge of the ghetto at the time, ordered the Jewish Council to put up notices that on 28 October at 6:00 a.m. everyone was to head for the square, where the people would be counted. The Council immediately called on Rabbi Shapiro, our Chief Rabbi, and asked him whether the Council should put up notices for the people to assemble, as ordered by Rauca, or ignore the order. After two or three days, Rabbi Shapiro gave us his Rabbinical Judgment (*Din*) that we should all follow the German orders, because if one soul could be saved by putting the notices up and avoiding chaos, then it had to be done. The notices also advised that anybody found remaining in the dwellings would be shot.

At 6:00 a.m. on a chilly day, 28 October 1941, people started assembling. There was a place where Rauca stood and the columns of the people were directed to pass him. He directed the human traffic by sending some people to the right and others to the left. He always mixed young people with elderly people, so that it was impossible to figure out which was the good side – life – and which was the bad side – death. Everyone was prepared for the worst since no one believed the Germans could come up only with something good. Most of us present believed we faced sinister deceit and that probably some people would be killed.

Actually, during the course of the selection, 9,200 people were sent to the Ninth Fort to be killed. Those on the right were carefully watched and surrounded by Lithuanian police. That was enough to give us a clue that the side that was guarded by the Lithuanian police would be the unlucky side.

9. People walking up the Hill to the IX Fort – the Germans called it *Der Weg zum Himmelfahrt*, the way to heaven (courtesy Esther Lurie).

10. Entrance to the IX Fort, 1997

Our assumption was correct. These people were taken out and marched to the Ninth Fort. We could see them from the ghetto, walking up the hill leading to the Ninth Fort. The next morning, they all were shot.

This road was called by the ghetto inmates the 'Via Dolorosa'. The Germans, however, called it the 'Way to Heaven' (*Der Weg zum Himmelfahrt*).

The Germans had intended to remove 10,000 people from the ghetto to be killed. By some miscalculation, however, they removed only 9,200. This miscalculation saved 800 lives. I remembered how our family passed Rauca. My grandmother, Rosa – my mother's mother – was with us and she could hardly walk so my father lifted her on one side and I lifted her on the other side. We had given her a scarf to cover and disguise her aging face. We passed by Master Sergeant Helmut Rauca. He looked at us and directed us to the side giving us life.

As Martin Gilbert kept walking around the square and talking to the camera, I could see the faces of the people; I could hear the voices of the people.

Even today, I still wonder what Master Sergeant Helmut Rauca was thinking at the time he moved his finger deciding our fate – 'To live or not to live'. Did the sandwich he was eating taste good, or was it that he recognized my father and felt that the ghetto needed him as a physician, or was it *bashert* (destiny)?

Why and where did the German culture, and the nobility of the German people, who were so advanced in science, humanitarian education, and medicine, fail so that people like Master Sergeant Helmut Rauca could sit and eat a sandwich and, while he ate, direct people to life and to death? My father recalled his life in Germany: going to school there was a beautiful experience. He finished medical school at the University of Cologne in 1922. He described the family where he rented a room and the lady of the house who had her own two children and took care of my father as if he was her own son.

He could not understand where people like Rauca were

hiding at the time because during his stay in Germany, my father did not feel any anti-Semitism nor see outbreaks at the university or among the local population.

I remembered that after the 'selection' on 28 October 1941, we returned mentally and physically exhausted to our dwelling in the ghetto. It was a large three-story apartment building where we lived on the second floor. We had three rooms. In one room, Dr Blumberg and his family of three lived, in another room our family of four lived as well as my grandmother, and in the third room, Jacob Lomas and his family of three lived. One of Dr Blumberg's sons, Bubi, was a close friend of mine. I went to my corner of the room and cried. I did not cry for myself because I felt lucky that this time I survived, but I cried for my friends whose families were taken away. I cried for the elderly people who were taken away and for the sick and the young people who were mixed in with the group of elderly people for the simple reason that the Germans tried to disguise which side was the better one (selected to live) or the worst one (selected to die). I lost several of my classmates as well as people I worked with.

Sir Martin Gilbert finished his presentation and the filming stopped. There was a tremendous silence in the square except for the occasional passing of a car in the street, temporarily disturbing the tranquility in this place. I was the only person who was in that square more than fifty years ago – half a century – and it is amazing how vivid the memories were.

I also remembered the hate that I felt towards Sergeant Rauca and the German officers who surrounded him, as well as the Lithuanian police officers who were guarding the people with such expressions of delight on their faces. It was like their goal had been achieved. Finally, they were getting rid of the Jews.

Lunch was brought in for the crew and all of us, but with two such emotional experiences on the same day, I could not eat. I was not even hungry. I started walking in the area with which I was so familiar during my three years living in the ghetto. I walked through the little streets where some friends of mine used to live. Some residents who saw me became very suspicious and I felt very uncomfortable even talking to the people. They had only one thing in mind – was I there to get their dilapidated buildings back from them? I returned to the Democracy Square to a little coffee shop, where I nibbled on something, and then walked again with Joyce, Martin, Herb and Mary Stewart.

We walked the streets and filmed some of the buildings. On one street a woman came out and said that she had dug in her vegetable garden and dug up a few spoons. She wanted each of us to have a spoon. The spoons were most likely buried by a Jewish family when they felt threatened, hoping to recover them some day. We thanked her. Tina, who represented the National Holocaust Memorial Museum in Washington, DC, took one and said she would deliver one of the spoons to the museum.

It was heartbreaking to go through the streets and to think how depressing life had been there during the time of the ghetto's existence. Everybody was gone. Occasionally, we would see a dog running. A few people who saw us coming closed their doors and shutters. Others came out and greeted us out of curiosity to find out the purpose of our visit. I wanted to visit the ghetto cemetery which was near the river, and so we walked down there.

To my surprise, there was a small plaque saying that the ghetto cemetery, with all the corpses, had been moved to a Jewish cemetery in Aleksotas, which was across the river next to the airport. After her death, my grandmother, who was buried there, had been uprooted and moved to another cemetery. In the area around the cemetery was a place that the Jewish Council had designated for growing potatoes and cucumbers, to supplement our food supply. Everything was now overgrown with weeds.

The final stop of the day was a house on Krisciukaicio Gatve, where the only survivor of the Kovno Ghetto still lived. We went to see him, but unfortunately, he was still at work, although he arrived shortly after we did. The most interesting thing was that when we moved into the ghetto in 1941, every house had its own well which supplied water for the house as well as an outhouse. The distance between the outhouse and the well had to be a minimum of twelve meters. About ten years before our visit, during the Soviet period, running water was introduced to the houses and the outhouses were removed, but there was still a well at this house. Again, my memories flooded back to our living with the wells: how every morning I had to get up and fetch two buckets of water for our household to use for washing ourselves, for the meager cooking that we did, and for washing our clothes and other things. I asked Sir Martin to relate the story of the wells, and the epidemiological aspects, and I took a picture as a memento of the existence of the well in the ghetto.

The woman of the house was extremely gracious and showed us every room, apologizing for still having to live in the ghetto area. Living in this poor area was an economic necessity. As compensation she and her husband had a little garden which was beautifully cultivated. They had chickens, and the benefit of additional food for their present humble way of life.

It was an emotional day for me, to relive part of my life and to recall how close to death I had been without realizing it. Destiny had guided me in the right direction. It was late in the afternoon when Herb Krosney advised that filming was finished for the day and that we would return to the hotel. Our two cars left Vilijampolė and moved slowly through the old city to our hotel.

On returning to the hotel I climbed up to the third floor where our room was. I was exhausted psychologically and physically. It had been very difficult for me to summarize the day and to try again to understand the challenges – to be or not to be – that I had to face during my three years in the ghetto, and how difficult it must have been for my parents to raise two children in those circumstances. It took me several hours to distance myself from my emotions and enter the present again.

The crew, Sir Martin, Joyce and I went out for dinner. I am still grateful that on that day I was not alone. I know that it is impossible for a normal being to understand the inhuman conditions and circumstances that I was exposed to living in the ghetto. I needed people with me. It was extremely comforting having Joyce and Sir Martin there with me, and I do not know if I could have done it without them. Our conversation at the table consisted of trying to understand the human life in the ghetto and the inhuman conditions imposed by such a previously cultured society.

Another day began. It was a beautiful day with the sun shining. The two cars left again for the ghetto in Vilijampole. The purpose of the second day's journey was to photograph different locations in the ghetto to be used in the film.

As soon as we arrived in the ghetto for this second visit, Joyce and I separated from the group. I wanted to share with Joyce a walk through the streets of the ghetto and reflect on my life in that time period. After a short walk, we came to the monument where the Contagious Diseases Hospital was burned in 1941. According to my mother, when she returned from Stutthof Concentration Camp, she met Dr and Mrs Chaim Ipp. Dr Chaim Ipp was my father's assistant. My mother and Dr Ipp both went to Kaunas and visited the ghetto and the place where we lived. During our detention in the ghetto, I made a tin box where all our documents and the remnants of our valuables were put; then it was soldered shut and buried next to the outhouse. My mother and Dr Ipp were fortunate to find the box.

Among the things that were in the box was a lecture that my father had prepared for his colleagues, with the title, 'Medicine in Kovno Ghetto'. This original lecture is deposited in the Holocaust Memorial Museum in Washington. It gives a very detailed picture of medicine in Kovno Ghetto.

After a short walk through the labyrinth of the streets in the ghetto, Joyce and I found Paneriu Gatve without any difficulty, and crossed into the previously existing boundaries of the Small Ghetto. Again without difficulty, I found the plaque indicating the previous site of the Contagious Diseases Hospital. We found a patch of green grass and I sat there reflecting on my life in the ghetto.

To really understand the tragedy, we have to try to reconstruct the mosaic of life at the time.

The key to preventing an outbreak of any disease is cleanliness. The inhabitants of the ghetto were deprived of the basic necessity of a shower or bath for years. The fact was that the water had to be brought bucket by bucket from the well to the house, and very often, as in our case, to the second floor. It was necessary to construct urgently an *Entlausung Anstalt-Bath* (Delousing Bath) in the ghetto for the inhabitants. It had two purposes: firstly, personal hygiene for the person, and secondly, killing lice in clothing.

On 20 May 1942, the Delousing Bath was opened. Rabbi Ephraim Oshry was appointed by my father as its manager. Rabbi Oshry was a former student of the Slobodka Yeshiva and taught Talmud classes in the ghetto for the adults after working hours. He also introduced the children to the Torah in these clandestine classes. Rabbi Oshry was well educated and had a great personality and sense of humor. He often visited my father and I felt privileged to enjoy his friendship. I often exchanged thoughts and ideas with him.

On 8 September 1942, an announcement had been issued about the ban of pregnancies in the ghetto. From then on, the Germans declared that pregnant women would be killed on the spot. An episode which is still very vivid in my mind occurred in May 1943. Rabbi Oshry was in the hospital visiting the patients. A German officer had noticed a woman in the advanced stage of pregnancy. The German felt that the woman had violated the German orders against pregnancy and shot her on the spot. She was brought immediately to the hospital but was dead on arrival. The gynecologist set up the operating room for a Caesarean section, with the hope of saving the baby. Rabbi Oshry advised the gynecologist that according to the Halakah (the Written Jewish Law) it was all right to proceed with the Caesarian section and that the attempt to save the baby would not desecrate the dead mother. But worst of all, the same German officer came to the hospital, found the baby and, with his bare hands, killed the baby who had just been saved by Caesarean section.

We discussed abortion with Rabbi Oshry and felt that in view of the fact that by German decree any woman who was found to be pregnant would be killed and, therefore, two lives would be lost, with an abortion at least one life would be saved. We also discussed the topic of suicide with Rabbi Oshry. Fortunately, the number of suicides in the ghetto was minimal. According to the Halakah, Jews were not allowed to commit suicide. In a way I agree, because as my father always said, 'When there is life there is always hope.' In my own family, mother wanted to have a cyanide tablet that would allow her to escape when she came to one of the difficult moments of life. My father, who had an optimistic attitude to life, was against it. Fortunately, my father prevailed, and in spite of the indescribably horrible situations and circumstances that he and my mother were in, they did survive.

I learned from Rabbi Oshry some very interesting aspects of the Jewish religion, in the interpretation of the Talmud in a distressed life such as the Jewish life in the ghetto. That gave me a lot of hope and confidence during the difficult years I was going through and it reinforced my trust in God.

On my visit to the archives in the city of Vilnius, I found several letters written by Rabbi Oshry to my father, reporting to him the names of the people who had missed their appointment for a bath. My father added to the letter a short note to the Jewish police, advising them to find the people and bring them to the bath.

Since my father was responsible, he could not afford the outbreak of an epidemic in the ghetto. He knew that reporting the cases of louse-borne typhus (exanthematous fever) would mean the destruction of the entire ghetto. He knew that in the Russian prisoner of war camps, the existence of one louse-borne typhus patient led to the annihilation of the entire prison camp. He was willing to risk his life in not

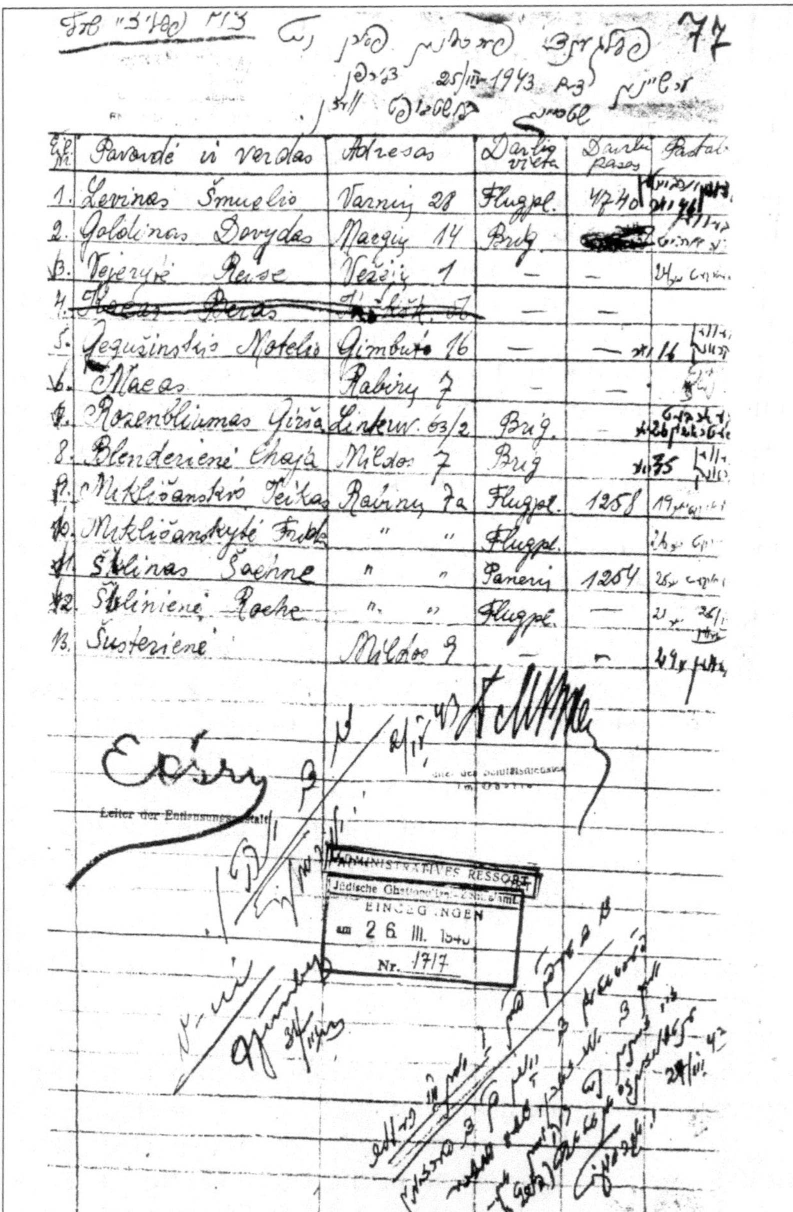

Eil. Nr.	Pavardė ir vardas	Adresas	Darbo vieta	Darbo pasas	Pastab.
1.	Levinas Šmuelis	Varnių 28	Flugpl.	4240	[illegible]
2.	Goldinas Dovydas	Mackių 14	Brig.	[illegible]	[illegible]
3.	Vejerytė Reise	Vežėjų 1	—	—	[illegible]
4.	[illegible]	[illegible]	—	—	
5.	Gegužinskis Motelis	Gimbutų 16	—	—	[illegible]
6.	Macas	Rabinų 7	—	—	[illegible]
7.	Rozenbliumas Girša	Linkuv. 63/2	Brig.	—	[illegible]
8.	Blenderienė Chaja	Mildos 7	Brig		[illegible]
9.	Mikliošanskis Teikas	Rabinų 7a	Flugpl.	1258	[illegible]
10.	Mikliošanskytė Frida	" "	Flugpl.		[illegible]
11.	Šklinas Šachne	" "	Panerių	1254	[illegible]
12.	Šklinienė Roche	" "	Flugpl.	—	[illegible]
13.	Šusterienė	Mildos 9		—	[illegible]

Leiter der Entlausungsanstalt

ADMINISTRATIVES RESSORT
Jüdische Ghettopolizei - [illegible]
EINGEGANGEN
am 26 III. 1943
Nr. 1717

11. Letter by Rabbi Oshry to Dr Moses Brauns concerning the people who missed their baths in the ghetto (Archives of Vilnius).

reporting these cases and he established a conspiracy of silence. My father and his assistant, Dr Chaim Ipp, were the only physicians taking care of patients with contagious diseases. But you also have to give credit to the population of the ghetto who suspected or knew about the contagious diseases, and participated in this conspiracy of silence.

I would like you to think for yourself how you would feel about being deprived of the basic necessity of a hot shower or a bath for several years. If you are close to nature, you will see even the birds taking advantage of any collection of clean water to take a bath. The desire to survive played an important part and was a factor in the low mortality rate of contagious diseases.

On the following day, after we had had breakfast at the hotel, the cars and film crew again returned to the ghetto. The purpose of today's filming was to capture the remnant ambience of the ghetto by photographing the streets, the houses and so on. I took advantage of the filming and walked to Krisciukaicio Gatve.

I remembered that after the destruction of the Contagious Diseases Hospital, where I worked as a clerk, I went to work in a crafts school, to learn to be a locksmith. There were different departments, including carpenter, locksmith, and other trades. It was organized by Dr Jacob Oleiski. These departments were designed mainly for young people to learn a craft. To be a craftsman at that time was the key to survival. The art of the locksmith was challenging. I learned how to make keys and locks; mainly I learned to work with pieces of iron and make something from them. My choice to be a locksmith, I later found out, played a very important part in my survival in Dachau Concentration Camp.

With me in the locksmith department worked Pinia Krakinovski. We befriended each other. He was very energetic, had a positive outlook on life and I liked him. In addition, he had a great sense of humor, which was essential to survival. One day Pinia Krakinovski went to the city to trade some goods for food. He was caught and sent to the Ninth Fort. I thought I would never see him again.

It was at this period that the Jewish Council did a good deal of lobbying of the German authorities to establish a large-scale workshop in the ghetto. The purpose was to produce different items that could be of help to the German Army and make the German war machine in a way dependent on the workers in the ghetto. About 400 people were gradually employed in workshops and departments that had been established specially to repair army uniforms which had been torn after the soldiers who wore them were injured. There were brush workshops, shoemaking and shoe repair workshops, a big laundry, soap and candle manufacturing workshops, and many other workshops.

The best craftsmen in the ghetto were mobilized as leaders in the workshops and apparently the Germans controlling the ghetto were interested in the idea.

On 5 January 1942 an official permit was obtained and gradually in a month or two the workshops progressively employed more people.

A toy department was opened. The toys were made and shipped to Germany and sold for profit by the SS who were in charge of the workshops. It was a very interesting group that worked there. There were two craftsmen from Palanga, the brothers Kahn, who were masters in working with amber. They produced amber gifts like cigarette boxes, pipes, chess sets and other things with which the Jewish Council used to bribe the German officers and the Gestapo. Due to a shortage of amber, such amber products were mainly reserved for bribes. Avraham Tory, Secretary of the Council, collected these pieces of art and used them to bribe the German SS officers.

We later concentrated on producing cigarette boxes and chess sets similar to the amber ones but in different wood, with which the SS supplied us.

In addition to my skill as a locksmith, while working in the toy department I also added some knowledge of carpentry and lathe work which contributed to my survival skills in Dachau.

With those memories, I walked through the city to the area where the workshops existed about fifty years earlier. I was not surprised that I did not find anything there. There were a couple of empty buildings. Some buildings were torn down and there was no evidence that there ever had been a workshop there before. Along the way, as I looked for the workshop area, I rekindled all the memories of the workshop – of the hours I worked there as well as the people with whom I associated. One of the figures who left a strong impression on me was Esther Lurie, with whom I worked, and who was instrumental in having documented the mosaic of life in the ghetto through her drawings. Her ghetto art has been recently exhibited in the Holocaust Memorial Museum in Washington as well as in numerous museums in Israel.

I turned and walked back along Krisciukaicio Gatve to the center of the former ghetto, looking for the *maline*.

With the successful advance of the Red Army and the retreat of the German army on the Eastern Front, logic and the survival instinct told us to have hiding places in the transitional period between the German army retreating and the Red Army arriving. *Maline* (mah-lee-neh) means raspberry in Yiddish. It was the accepted slang term for a hiding place. These *malines* were built within the ghetto. Some were simple, mere double walls, with secret entrances. Others were in attics with a hidden entrance. There were even more sophisticated ones.

I will describe the construction of the *maline* in which I was involved. An old tool shack stood next to the house on 95 Krisciukaicio Gatve, facing the river. It was approximately twenty by thirty feet. Several people, including the inhabitants of the house, took the responsibility for building a *maline*. The rules were that at least one member of the family had to work, while the rest of the families were responsible for sharing the financial responsibility in constructing it.

I was happy to see that the Kelzon family was involved. The father was a man who was an agronomist prior to the war. Their son, who was a few years older than me, was an engineering student. It was his responsibility to supervise the construction. This was a complicated process.

We had to empty the shed. That was not easy because all

the junk in it had to be disposed of without attracting attention. It was done gradually. Then we started to remove the earth in an area that corresponded to the size of the room we planned to build under the shed. The earth had to be disposed of. We dug a small garbage disposal hole between the house and the shed, filled it with garbage, and dumped the earth around it, giving an illusion that the garbage disposal hole was very deep.

Several garbage disposal holes were dug in different locations of the ghetto. As we proceeded, we gradually reinforced all the dugout structure under Kelson's supervision. When the desired size of the hiding place was reached and the meticulously dug-out earth was removed and put in different places in the ghetto, we went on to dig a small well in the center of the room. Due to the fact that the river was close by, the well did not need to be dug very deeply.

Next, we dug a hole for an outhouse and moved the outhouse structure to the new location next to the shed. It was not uncommon to dig for new outhouses and move the outhouses because the Lithuanian sanitation department had refused to enter the ghetto and empty the excrement.

We built sleeping bunks. A roof was built on top of the hiding room which was still located inside the shed. Earth was then put on top of the roof.

At this point, the shed was completely removed. The earth was smoothed out and potatoes were planted where the old shed had stood. We installed pipes and brought them out a long way from the hiding place towards the river and masked them with rocks. If you passed by you would see a small potato field and an outhouse standing nearby. We used the outhouse as the entrance into our hiding place. The floor in the outhouse was on hinges and by lifting it up we were able to enter the hiding place. We immediately started using the outhouse. Its smell made it authentic.

This hiding place played an important part in the lives of different people. The first one to benefit from it was my brother, Harry. On 27 and 28 March 1944, when the Children's

Action was going on and the Lithuanian police were trying to find the children, my brother immediately went to this hiding place and hid there for the duration of the action. This saved his life. It was a terrifyingly cruel Children's Action.

Several hundred children were taken on trucks to the Ninth Fort to be killed. Can you imagine the grief the parents experienced, and the screaming after they returned to the ghetto from work and found their children gone?

I could not understand what a mental transformation the German and the Lithuanian people had undergone to be able to execute such a barbarous act of inhumanity against little children whose only mistake was to be born Jewish. I also wondered in my mind what happened to the God of the Chosen People. Did He abandon us and let little children die at the will of the assassins?

On Christmas night, 25 December 1943, the inmates of the Ninth Fort did succeed in escaping. The majority of the escapees came to the ghetto. The German Gestapo and Lithuanian police did not search the ghetto because they did not believe a prisoner who escaped from one prison would go to another prison.

The escapees who arrived in the ghetto had to be hidden. They could not be hidden amongst the inmates of the ghetto because the smell of the burning corpses at the Ninth Fort had impregnated their clothes, their skin and body. They had an offensive odor of burned flesh, which was easy to detect. Their escape, and their hiding in the ghetto, was secret. They were brought to the *maline* that I mentioned above and hidden there for about two or three weeks before they were taken out of the ghetto and smuggled to the forest to join the Jewish partisans. During their stay in the *maline*, Avraham Tory, the Secretary of the Council, interviewed Captain Vasilenko, the leader of the escape, and recorded in minute details their life at the Ninth Fort and their escape. Another escapee was Krakinovski, whom, as I mentioned before, I had befriended and with whom I worked in the workshops to train locksmiths.

Trying to find the escapees, the Germans declared martial law in Lithuania, but this was in vain.

Approximately, in mid-January, as was customary once a month, a truck would arrive from the forest with some Jewish partisans in German uniforms and with false papers. They usually picked up twenty to thirty people and took them directly to the forest. This was done for months, avoiding the casualties of the individual people trying to reach the forest. Later on this was the safest way in which the escapees from the Ninth Fort were gradually transported to join the partisans. The truck was provided by Chaim Yellin, the leader of the Jewish partisans.

On my walk in the former ghetto, I found the house that neighbored our *maline*, but, as I expected, I did not find the *maline*.

I still remember 13 July 1944, when, after hiding for a couple of days in the *maline*, we were discovered and surrounded by the German SS. One by one we were forced to leave the *maline*, as they threatened to throw a hand grenade unless everyone came out. Most likely, as in many other places where people hid, they threw a grenade into the area of the *maline*, and the ones who stayed in the *maline* died. In our case, the entire group that had been hiding there came out and was marched to the railroad station. The last day that they had a transport arranged for the inmates of Kovno Ghetto to be transported to Germany was 13 July.

Joyce and I continued to walk in the former ghetto. I was very interested in going back to Krisciukaicio Gatve again because I knew there was a house I wanted to see. It was the house where my friend Zev Birger had lived during the time we were confined in the ghetto. It was approximately halfway between the *maline* and the workshops. I returned to Krisciukaicio Gatve and found the house without much difficulty. There were people living there, but I did not go inside. My friendship with Zev began in this house. Actually we needed each other. We needed this friendship to be able to survive, not physically, but mainly in psychological support.

Life was so discouraging that encouragement from someone whom you liked and respected meant a lot. At that time, in the ghetto I had very few friends. Zev Birger was one of my friends. David Landau was another friend of mine. All three of us went to Dachau. Fortunately all three of us survived. Irena Veisaite was also in the ghetto with us, but after a short time she left with false papers to live with a Lithuanian family who hid her for the duration of the war. Marion Fratkin was also a good friend of ours. Her parents came from Germany. Unfortunately, she perished in Stutthof. Sarah Starawolski, another close friend of mine, was also part of the group. She was deported to Stutthof and survived as well. During our bad times we shared our hopes and cried together about the friends that we periodically lost.

When we walked back to the meeting place to find the film crew, I found them searching for the house of Pnina Sheinzon, who eventually married Avraham Tory. She played an important part in helping to document and save the diary written by Avraham. Both carried the diary out of Lithuania to Israel. With the help of some local people, and knowing exactly the address, we found that this house had been demolished.

With the crew, we then went to where I thought the housing blocks had been, to find the building blocks A and B, where my family and I had lived (block A). These housing blocks had been demolished and other structures were built in their place.

We toured the rest of the former ghetto area. It was very hard for anybody except me to understand the impact of walking on the streets of the ghetto without fear and apprehension. Living in the ghetto, I did not know if I would live to see the sunrise.

Vilijampolė was well known for having theological seminaries – yeshivas – before the war. They were renowned yeshivas to which Jewish people from all over the world, especially Europe, used to come to study the Talmud. By destroying the yeshivas and all that was Jewish, the Germans ensured that Jewish culture was completely destroyed in Lithuania. It had flourished in Lithuania for 500 years. The only question I had was, why?

The destruction of books and the destruction of culture have always been inflicted by people who felt inferior to the culture and were afraid to learn about what books could teach them. I still wonder what the Germans were so afraid of in the Jewish culture to have wanted to eradicate it.

The two cars with the film crew and equipment drove along the road on the hill leading to the Ninth Fort, which the ghetto inmates called Via Dolorosa.

During the First World War, the Tsar built fortifications around the city of Kaunas to defend Russia from the Germans. After the establishment of independent Lithuania following that, the same Ninth Fort was used to imprison dangerous criminals.

During the Nazi occupation, the Ninth Fort was called 'Extermination Place No. 2', a name it properly deserved. About 50,000 Jewish people were executed there. Jews, transported from Germany, Austria, France, Czechoslovakia and Holland, were brought to the Ninth Fort on the pretext of being resettled in the East. The so-called 'resettlement' was mass execution in large dug out pits. Lithuanian Jews from Kovno were also executed at the Ninth Fort. Executions were carried out by the German SS and also the Lithuanian police.

In 1943 the Gestapo, upon order from Berlin, ordered the destruction of all the evidence of the massacres at the Ninth Fort. They used Soviet prisoners of war of Jewish origin to carry out the task. In addition, many Kovno Ghetto Jews were arrested for minor offenses and sent to the Ninth Fort to help eliminate the evidence. The dead victims, who had been piled up in mass graves, had to be exhumed. Each body was exhumed and examined, regardless of its state, some being more decomposed, others less decomposed. The gold teeth were removed and the corpses checked for jewelry. The bodies were then burned on funeral pyres. The smoke was visible miles away. From the ghetto, we could see the fires, knowing that these were the bodies of the people who had been deported from the ghetto. If the wind blew in a certain direction, the smell of burning flesh reached the ghetto.

At that time, Captain Kolia Vassilenko was brought from a Soviet prisoner of war camp to the Ninth Fort. He was a captain in the Soviet Army and an engineer by profession. The idea of escape was immediately considered. Among the prisoners at the Ninth Fort was Krakinovski, who had earlier left the ghetto and ventured into the city of Kovno to trade his clothes for food. He was arrested and brought to the Ninth Fort. As you remember, Krakinovski and I had spent some time together in the locksmith trade school. The locksmith craftsmanship acquired by Krakinovski was one of the main factors in the escape from the Ninth Fort.

Also active in the escape were Alex Fitelson and Kolia Vassilenko. On Christmas Eve, 1943, all the inmates of the Ninth Fort were able to escape. It was a stormy night and the snow was falling thickly. In the darkness of the night the escapees were able to re-enter the ghetto. The underground was immediately contacted and led them to the hiding place on 95 Krisciukaicio Gatve. They were led to the *maline* which had been built by Kelson and me and several others.

Rabbi Oshry was responsible for getting the escapees to the ghetto bath, hoping they would lose the impregnated smell caused by the work at the Ninth Fort.

When we visited the Ninth Fort in 1997, Joyce and I went into the individual cells. It was a sad experience. We also found the iron door which opened into the tunnel which the escapees used. This was the iron door in which Krakinovski had been able to drill holes, to open the escape route. We carefully followed the different corridors and tunnels of the Ninth Fort and we came to an outside opening, retracing the steps of the inmates of the Ninth Fort and their escape.

On some of the walls of the cells there were still inscriptions left by the inmates. Some were in different languages, confirming the origin of some of the massacred people: French, German, and Dutch. Many of the inscriptions were in Yiddish. The inscriptions included their name and their home town. Some of the inscriptions looked as if they had been scratched only the day before.

A massive monument has been constructed on the premises of the Ninth Fort, but no words can describe what we saw, or our emotional experiences in that place. Sir Martin Gilbert narrated the story of the escape during the filming.

At the end of the day, we had tea with the curator of the Ninth Fort whose main aim is to maintain the site, as well as establish some improved roads to the area for the visiting tourists. I was surprised to hear that in the last year the number of tourists from around the world coming to the Ninth Fort was approximately 40,000 people, which is a large number of tourists for a city of 250,000 people. The massacred people are now contributing to the economy of the city of Kaunas. The visit was a painful and emotional experience for me. It also confirmed the horrible stories I had heard; now I saw for myself. It was hard to understand the sadistic brutality that the SS and the Lithuanian police exercised upon the Jews. On the way to the hotel, I tried to understand what circle of Dante's *Inferno* I had seen today.

The next day, the cars left the hotel to go to Schwabes High School, which I had attended and in which all the teaching was carried out in the Hebrew language. This included mathematics, geography, algebra, trigonometry and philosophy. In a way, it was a preparation for reviving the Hebrew language from a biblical prayer language to an active day-by-day language. We had several Hebrew high schools in Kaunas.

We arrived at the school which was beside the river Nieman. My past life was reawakened. The front door was locked, so I told everybody that we would enter the school the same way that I used to – fifty-three years earlier – through the courtyard. In the winter the courtyard was transformed into an ice skating rink. Floodlights illuminated it.

We proceeded to the courtyard. It was as if time had stopped. As I walked in I could relive my life in school. I remembered all the friends I had not thought about for many years. I could see them running around. I could still see our physical education classes carried out in the courtyard. I could remember the ice skating and how much fun we had. I think that some of the best hours of the day were in the afternoon or evening when we came to the ice skating rink. In the privacy of our school, we had the privilege of sharing the skating with our classmates.

I opened the back door and entered the school. It was a very eerie feeling. The glory of the school that I remembered was gone. It looked like an old building (which it actually was). The windows had shrunk. I remembered them to be much bigger. I walked into one of the classrooms and I did not see the same thing that I remembered. Actually, life had changed. I felt very privileged to have returned to Schwabes Gymnasium which actually was my life from the age of six until the age of seventeen. I remembered our large assembly hall where we had our Hanukkah and Purim parties.

We had an interesting system at the Kaunas city post office before the Soviet occupation in 1940. It had a savings department where you could save money. At the end of the year in every school, certain pupils received awards for being the best savers. Points were not given for how much money you saved, but rather for how many times you went to the post office and how many stamps you had recorded in your book as a saver. We used to work out a system that for every day the post office was open we would deposit at least ten cents. Once a year the frequent depositors were the winners of very fine presents, either a table tennis set, or a watch, or certain books. It was a great honor to receive this kind of reward, which was presented in front of the entire school. Basically, we tried, with great effort, never to let a day go by without depositing ten cents to obtain the most points for depositing.

I never thought about our rewards for being a post office saver until I came back and walked into the school assembly hall. It was there. It was smaller. It is true that the glamour was not there, but I felt that if I just closed my eyes I could live the excitement of being in the assembly hall either for a holiday celebration, or for scholastic honors, or for honors for being one of the best savers in school.

On the way out of the hall, I walked up the staircase. There were little buttons on the rail, similar to the buttons that were installed at the time I went to school, which prevented us from sliding down the rails instead of walking down the stairs. It is interesting that the Schwabes School – known as the Gymnasium – split up in the late 1930s. Some teachers went to Palestine, where they formed a school. This was the first Hebrew high school founded in Palestine. It was a spin-off from our high school.

In 1957, when I visited Israel, I met my art teacher, Dr Bayles. He had gone to Palestine and brought with him drawings that his pupils had made throughout the years. I went to see a small exhibition of work from the Schwabes School and, to my surprise, I saw paintings that had been done by me when I was a child. It was such a thrill for me. I thanked Dr Bayles for having the foresight to save some of the art created by young people, most of them never having survived the Holocaust.

While revisiting the Schwabes School in 1997 I looked through the window of a classroom on the second floor and I saw the river, the same river that had flowed fifty-three years earlier. I also remembered a classmate of mine who was a year older than me. He had played truant from school and went swimming in the river. Unfortunately, he drowned. Through the window I witnessed his body being taken out of the river and taken to the morgue.

We left the Schwabes Gymnasium, which has been transformed into a trade school. From there our cars went to the city where the Jewish Hospital, Bikur Cholim, used to be. It had been one of the leading hospitals before the war in the city of Kaunas. It served a large part of the Jewish and non-Jewish population. It seemed smaller now and had been deactivated as a hospital, and was being used as an old-age home.

When war broke out, it was life-threatening to be a Jew in Kaunas. The Soviet Army had left the city and the German army had not yet entered. The Jews were prey for the

Lithuanian so-called partisans who took advantage of the fact that the Jewish population was excluded from any protective law concerning the right to live. The Jews were murdered and raped and their houses were looted. My father felt that the hospital offered protection from the Lithuanian marauders. The whole family – father, mother, brother, grandmother and I – moved to the hospital.

That was where I witnessed the beginning of the Holocaust and saw the brutality that one human being inflicted upon another. Patients were brought to the emergency room with gunshot wounds and stab wounds following rapes and beatings.

I still can see the little five-year-old girl who was brought to the hospital after her parents were killed. She was shot in her arm. The towel around her arm was soaked in blood. She was taken immediately to the operating room. I tried to follow her progress and outcome after she had left the emergency room. The little girl's arm had to be amputated and a few days later she died.

To compound the tragedy, the ambulance drivers refused to pick up injured Jews and take them to the hospital for treatment. Instead, they came in either carried in a friend's arms or on little wagons wheeled by friends or family into the emergency room.

It was very hard for me to understand the brutality unleashed by the Lithuanians toward the Jewish population. For years to come, I wondered what the Jews had done to the Lithuanians that caused them to kill children or adults, especially at a time when the Jews had no protection by law.

After having spent a few days working in the emergency room of the hospital, I became very restless and decided I needed a change of atmosphere.

Bubi Bloomberg, a friend of mine, lived in the old city, just a few blocks from the hospital. With my father's permission, I went to Vilnius Gatve to visit him. We had spent a few hours together when there was a loud knock on the door. Several Lithuanians with armbands forced themselves into the apartment. Among the intruders there was a Lithuanian man who distinguished himself from the others by being much better dressed and having better manners. He was not wearing an armband. As soon as he entered, he asked where the office of Dr Bloomberg was located (all the offices of the doctors were located in their houses). He proceeded to go to that room and looked over the equipment that was there and took away an electrocardiogram and a few other things that he noticed. My impression was that this man was a physician who wanted to take advantage of the situation and probably had asked the 'partisans' to bring him to this apartment so that he could appropriate equipment he needed for his office.

In the meantime, the other 'partisans' ordered all the men in the apartment to leave. We were forced to go to the courtyard. They collected every male from the building and made us all stand facing the wall. I was frightened. My thoughts were that I would finally face death. I recalled in my mind all the pictures and tragedies that I had witnessed at the hospital while I worked in the emergency room as a clerk. I remembered the people who were brought in half dead or severely injured with gunshot and knife wounds inflicted on them by the Lithuanians. I prayed to God asking that if I was shot I would be killed, as I did not want to continue my life with a terrible disability. I also talked to God and asked Him, how He could let this happen.

Suddenly I heard machine-gun noises. I was aware that the Lithuanians did not have a machine gun – at least, I had not noticed them having one. Also, I immediately considered the possibility that they might have brought in a machine gun while we faced the wall. Another thing that was missing was the screams of wounded people. I deduced with some logic that the shooting must be coming from a nearby house, where most likely the same type of scene was occurring. The noise became louder and I heard the leader of the partisans telling his fellow accomplices that he would be back after he had investigated the situation. Then I heard him shouting that they had to leave immediately. He ordered everybody to leave the premises of the courtyard. When I turned around a few minutes later, they were gone and we found ourselves standing in the empty courtyard. As the noises got closer, we realized that they were the sounds of a motorcycles.

We returned to our apartments and immediately went to the windows to see what really was going on in the streets. What happened was that the first German Army outriders, who were to lead the army into the city, must have become lost in the labyrinth of the city. They were checking some maps of Kaunas to be certain where they were. It is hard for me to describe how excited and happy I was that their being lost in the city saved the lives of the inhabitants of the apartment house and my own life as well. I was almost tempted to go down and thank the motorcyclist for what he had done, but, on second thoughts, I felt he must have already been upset at getting lost and might get even more upset that his mistake resulted in saving Jewish lives.

I waited another hour or so before I returned to the hospital. There, everyone was in an uproar. Apparently my father had heard what happened on Vilnius Gatve and asked the ambulance driver to go and bring Dr Bloomberg's family and me back to the hospital. The ambulance driver, however, returned to tell my father that something terrible had happened there: that streets around the house where I was had been blocked off. It was a great relief when my family saw me alive.

After a while, the looting of homes by the partisans, the killing of the Jewish population, robbery, and the rape of young girls, decreased, at least for a few weeks. Posters appeared on the streets saying that any plundering would be severely punished. After the German Army occupied Kaunas, the plundering had decreased sufficiently for us to return to our home on Presidento Gatve.

The house on Presidento Gatve was sequestered by the German Army and all the inhabitants were evicted from their apartment, except our family. Our neighbors moved into our apartment and each family lived in one of the rooms. This was really the best thing that could have happened to us, because from that day on, until we moved to the ghetto, we were protected by the German Army. There was a big sign on the door: 'This house has been sequestered for the Army.' We were spared from any acts of violence carried out by the Lithuanian 'partisans'.

The German officer in charge of the army unit was extremely kind to us. He was the one who had spared us from being evicted from the apartment. He was from Cologne, and he often talked to my father and was curious to know how Cologne was at the time of my father's studies. He was pleasantly surprised at what a beautiful opinion my father had of his student years in Cologne. In addition, he and some other German soldiers brought us food. They knew that for a Jew it was almost impossible to buy some food. There were stores which opened at certain hours when the Jewish population could buy food. Usually it was at times when the food was already gone and the stores were empty.

How did the entire house survive, with five families living with us in the apartment? The German officers who lived in our house were fond of eating Lithuanian food and had no problem procuring food by going to the store and buying it, or sequestering it. They brought us their rations.

We had two more sources of food. One of the sources was a Lithuanian friend of my father who was the Chief of Police. He had been a patient of my father and appreciated my father having saved his life. He used to come to the apartment and try to convince my father to come to his house and hide there. He said that nobody would ever come to his house to check for Jews living there. My father was emphatic in saying he had done nothing wrong, therefore there was no reason for him to hide from anybody, and he politely refused his offer. This man turned out to be a very devoted friend to my father and helped us tremendously with our food supply while we were in our apartment. Later, when we lived in the ghetto, he periodically came into the ghetto and brought food packages. He felt it was the least he could do to repay my father for saving him when he was very sick.

The third and most important source of our food supply was our housekeeper, Maryte. Maryte was in her late 30s and had worked for us, taking care of our household. Every day or every second day, she used to arrive at our apartment and bring food that she had been able to buy, as a Christian, in the store or the market. It was also Maryte to whom my mother entrusted our jewelry. In spite of the beatings that she sustained from her two brothers, who tried to find out if she had received anything from a Jewish family to hide, which many people used to do, she did not betray the fact that she had our jewelry, and she returned it soon after mother returned to Lithuania from Stutthof.

I mention this to bring out that people can be kind-hearted. Unfortunately, there were more people who expressed their hatred for the Lithuanian Jews, than those who devoted themselves to do all they could to help the Jews.

In the meantime, the date of 15 August was set for the Jewish move into the ghetto. A patient of my father who lived in the part of the city which had been designated for the ghetto came to us and offered his house in exchange for the apartment. We were very happy and felt that it would be a good exchange. As the time passed, however, this gentleman and his wife issued new demands and finally the exchange fell through. We all were very disappointed, because the uncertainty of where we would live was a large factor, especially for a teenager. My father always said, 'You never know what is for the best.' My father was right. If we had concluded the transaction of moving to the house of this Lithuanian family, which was located in the Small Ghetto, we most likely would not be alive. On 4 October 1941 most of the people who lived in the Small Ghetto were taken to the Ninth Fort and killed. Most likely our family's fate would have been sealed in the same way.

I learned that what happens today can have a positive or negative effect on you in years to come. It was impossible to tell at that time if this move was really good or if we would have perished on 4 October, as did all the inhabitants of the Small Ghetto.

In the years to come, in 1943 and 1944, some German officers would go home to visit their families and some were killed during the Allied bombing of Germany. For months to come, you never knew if it was good for the Jews if they were killed or bad for the Jews. It depended on the man who took his place and what his personality would be. Gradually I became a fatalist in my thinking.

Good things cannot last forever. Between 10 and 12 August, we moved to the ghetto. When I lived in the apartment on Presidento Gatve, I decided not to leave the house. I was scared to leave the house because of past experiences and because I knew that young men walking on the streets disappeared. Their fate was eventually known. They had all been taken to different forts and shot.

The Germans took tremendous pleasure in humiliating people. Very often I wondered why one person would try to humiliate another person. I came to the conclusion that most likely they felt threatened by the Jews: an inferiority threat. The Jews were not allowed to walk on the pavement and had to walk in the streets alongside the horses and wagons. I never could understand how such a progressive people, as the German nation was before the Second World War, could allow the humiliation of other people, because basically they humiliated themselves by doing so.

Sarah Starawolski was a good friend and classmate of mine. She was very brave and never felt a threat as a woman walking on the street. Sarah used to come to the apartment where I lived and we spent the days together. We had a great time sharing our thoughts, philosophies and past experiences being in school together. Sarah was deported from Kovno Ghetto to Stutthof, where, fortunately, she survived. I met her for the first time after the war in New York, after she was married. It was like meeting a sister. We spent many hours finding out from each other what had happened in our lives and how she had survived the horrors of Stutthof. She was excited to learn that Zev Birger and David Landau survived.

During our visit in 1997 Joyce and I walked to Valancius Gatve and visited the first house that I remembered living in, in the city of Kaunas. The building, which still stands in front of the church, looked unchanged. Many memories of my childhood returned, including when my mother brought home my newborn brother. After having walked a little on Valancius Gatve, we slowly walked back through Vilnius Gatve to our hotel. The street was one which I had often walked. Many of my friends lived in this area, which was part of the old city of Kaunas. We slowly returned to the hotel. Nothing much had changed in the old city of Kaunas. By the time I got back to the hotel, I was mentally and physically exhausted.

After taking a shower and relaxing for an hour or so, Joyce and I met the rest of the crew and we all walked together to a restaurant. It was Friday night. We asked the waiter for some wine and candles because we were celebrating Oneg Shabbat, the meal on Friday night to welcome the Sabbath. Just before he brought out the food, he brought some candles which he lit and then he tried to pour the wine. We advised him that we would be lighting the candles ourselves and we would also pour the wine ourselves. I wondered what he was thinking. This waiter had never known and would never know the beautiful Jewish tradition of Friday night, because the Jewish culture had been destroyed before he was born.

Mary Stewart blessed the candles for the Shabbat, I did the blessing of the wine and Martin did the blessing of the bread. It was a wonderful evening, one of the most memorable evenings of my stay in Kaunas. It brought us the flavor of a vanished Jewish tradition.

On Saturday morning there was no filming. I suggested to Joyce we visit the Choral Synagogue which was open, and maintained for the worshipers.

It was a short walking distance from our home to the synagogue. Our family used to attend services there on holidays for many years. At the synagogue, during our visit in 1997, we found several people gathered in the courtyard. I told them that

I would like to have an aliyah to be called to read a portion of the Torah during services. They were excited to see me, in spite of the fact that they had never met me, and were very accommodating. They lent me a prayer shawl and after joining for the Saturday morning prayers I was called for an aliyah. It was an eerie feeling to be in the synagogue where I grew up and to sit in the same seat where I had sat always between my father and my brother – but they were not there. I looked up in the synagogue where the women used to sit. Nobody was there.

I became very emotional and had to leave. I went out into the courtyard and, to my surprise, there was a beautiful monument dedicated to the Jewish children who had perished. My thoughts went to my brother.

After the morning service, I spoke to the people who were there participating in the prayer. To my surprise, none of the people were Lithuanian Jews. They were all Russian Jews, who during the Russian occupation had settled in Lithuania and whose children grew up in Lithuania. However, I was very pleased that in Kaunas there were two synagogues that were still open for worshipers.

At lunchtime, I left the synagogue with Joyce and walked back to the hotel, where we met Herb Krosney and Mary Stewart. The four of us took a long walk. We passed the post office where I had been a frequent visitor before the war, and we kept going until we came almost to the railroad station. Just before the railroad station was an open market. It was interesting to me to watch the people of this generation who were shopping there.

In the evening we stopped at a restaurant on the way home. I am glad that following the experience in the synagogue, I was able to spend some time with the Krosneys. It distracted me from the memories and started the bond of a very close friendship.

In the summer of 1938 our family went to Palanga for a vacation. We always stayed at Gutman's Pension (room and board). It was a place where some of the people from Kaunas used to spend their vacation. The Rabinovich family usually stayed there, and upon our arrival they were already there, including my two friends, Nomi and Osia Rabinovich. Nomi was my classmate and we had a great time together. We used to get up early in the morning and, together with his brother, Osia, go to the beach to collect amber. The best harvest of amber to be collected was early in the morning. It usually washed ashore during the night. At four o'clock in the afternoon most of our schoolmates would get together in our classmate Jodidio's summer home for a table tennis game.

In the middle of our vacation the weather changed. We had rain for an entire week. Nomi, Osia and I were bored and did not know what to do with ourselves. The dining room was next to the main building. It was very easy to get on to the roof and to walk from there to the roof of the dining room. It was customary at that time to collect the rainwater from the gutters into buckets. One of us had the bright idea – I really do not know whose idea it was – to take a few buckets of rainwater and pour them into the chimney of our dining room. Needless to say we created havoc. We got the punishment that everyone felt we deserved. We were excluded from the dining room for a day or two – for a teenager to miss his food was a very big punishment.

My father always used to say, 'For good deeds there are good rewards. For bad deeds, there is punishment.' It is interesting that my father also said, 'There is payment for every deed, especially for the bad deeds.' I remembered that all my life.

I have mentioned my father's Estonian friend, Jaan Lattik, with whom he had grown up in Viljandi, in Estonia, and for whom he cherished a deep friendship. Lattik was ordained as a Lutheran minister. In 1930 he went to Palestine, engaged in theological studies at the Hebrew University of Jerusalem, and learned Hebrew. By the time he returned to Estonia he was fluent in Hebrew. He was also active in the Estonian National Party whose leader and secretary he became. A few years later he became the Minister of Education in Estonia. Being fluent in Hebrew, he was instrumental in founding the first Hebrew high school in the Estonian capital, Tallin. His daughter married the President of Estonia. After Lattik's wife died, he was appointed Consul General of Estonia to Lithuania.

Lattik spent many evenings in our house. After dinner my father and Lattik discussed the Talmud and the interpretation of the Talmud. I often joined them and found them extremely interesting in spite of going to a Hebrew high school myself.

Also staying in Palanga was the Balkin family. They had two daughters about my age. They had come from Chemnitz, in Germany, to get away for the summer from the harassment that they had to endure during the Nazi regime. During our stay in Palanga, the stories of horrible discrimination and humiliation that the Jewish residents of Chemnitz had to endure stuck in all our minds.

At one of these dinners, my father told Lattik of his impression of the sufferings of the Balkin family. Lattik immediately made arrangements to instruct the Estonian Legation in Berlin to issue a visa for a temporary residence in Estonia for the Balkin family. It usually took five years to get an affidavit (visa) in order to emigrate to the United States of America. It was decided that it would be wise for them to wait for their United States emigration visas in Estonia.

On their way to Estonia, the Balkins stopped at our house for two weeks. Lattik spent an evening together with us. He was saddened by the stories of the treatment of the Jewish citizens by the German government. While they stayed in Kaunas, Mr Balkin went to the United States Embassy, where he learned that finally his visa had been granted. However, another problem occurred. As war had broken out between Britain and Germany, it was impossible to cross the Atlantic from Europe to the United States. It was Lattik who suggested a way round the problem. He would discuss the matter with his friend, Sempo Sugihara, who was the Consul General of Japan, in the hope that he would issue a transit visa to go through Japan, from where they could then go on to the United States. Lattik wanted Sugihara to come to our house, where Balkin, Lattik and my father could discuss the story of the Balkins and the treatment of the Jews in Germany.

Within a week this meeting took place. It was an interesting evening at which I was a participant. Again, the harsh and humiliating treatment to which the German Jews were exposed was described.

It was the first time that I had ever met a Japanese person. I immediately liked Sugihara. He was a kind and sensitive man. The main thing from my point of view was that he treated me like an adult. In the few minutes that we talked together, he asked me about my schooling and my future plans. He told me that I must always strive to fulfill the goals that I believe in. I never forgot those words.

There was no problem for the Balkins. After they went to the Japanese Consulate they received their transit visa and, shortly afterwards, were on their way by the Trans-Siberian railroad to Japan. While they were in Japan, the Pacific war broke out. All the Jews were transferred to Shanghai and lodged in a special area of the city, where they were protected. After the war, the Balkins eventually reached the United States and settled in New York.

On 8 February 1995, I was co-chairman for an event honoring the late Sempo Sugihara in Los Angeles. It was then that I met his family, Mrs Yokiko Sugihara and her sons, who related the hardship that the family had to endure from the Japanese Government because Sugihara refused to obey the original order not to issue visas. He was dismissed from the Japanese Foreign Ministry and his pension was revoked. He was lucky that his fluent knowledge of Russian allowed him to find a job at the Japanese Trade Fair in Moscow.

In 1968, Sempo Sugihara was honored by the Israeli government and its survivors in Israel by nominating him as a Righteous Gentile. A tree was planted for him in Jerusalem. His son Nobuki received a full scholarship to the Hebrew University in recognition of his father's deeds.

During my visit to Kaunas in 1997 I watched the filming in front of the main entrance of the building where the Japanese

Consulate used to be before the war. There I listened to Sir Martin Gilbert's description of Sugihara and how he saved more than 6,000 Jews. The Honorable Sempo Sugihara will go down in history as being one of the biggest heroes and one of the few Japanese heroes who saved Jews during the Nazi regime.

I am convinced that during the meeting in my house in Kaunas with Sugihara, Lattik, my father, and the Balkin family, their emotional narrative of the treatment and the persecution of the Jews in Chemnitz left a great impression on Sugihara. He was a sensitive man and a true humanitarian. This meeting, followed by the arrival of hundreds of Jewish refugees pounding on the consulate door asking for visas, influenced Sugihara to pursue his humanitarian feelings.

In the summer of 1944 fighting was gradually getting closer and closer to the city. The German Army was retreating and the Soviet Army was advancing. Then came the order to evacuate the ghetto.

This was a signal that the time had come to go to the *maline* and hope that the German occupiers would leave Lithuania and that the Soviet Army would liberate us. We went to the *maline*. We hoped we would not have to stay too long there. We had water from the well which we had constructed. We also had a food supply for about two weeks. Our destiny turned out to be different.

The German SS had sent a unit to search the ghetto for the people who had avoided deportation. On 13 July 1944, with the help of dogs used by the SS, we were discovered. This was the last day of deportation. A special convoy of cattle cars that had been assembled by the SS was waiting for us at the railroad station. In a way, we were lucky. Everybody who was discovered by the SS after 13 July was taken to a big warehouse, locked up, and the warehouse set on fire, with all the people inside being burned to death.

It was one of the heartbreaking experiences of my life to be found in the hiding place by the SS and their dogs. The front line was gradually shifting towards Germany. Instead of the Germans worrying about finding transportation for their retreating troops, they directed all their efforts to finding Jews in the ghetto and arranging for their transportation to concentration camps inside Germany.

The really sad thing for me was to think that in spite of spending my whole life in Lithuania, being taken away now, there was no door that I could knock on and receive shelter and help. There were people standing on the street watching us being marched over to the railroad station. I saw their hateful faces.

While walking I scanned the area, but there was really no way for me to escape and find a shelter, as I was surrounded by the guards. I knew that even if I escaped and knocked on a door, I would not be welcomed. In the faces of the people who were standing lined up in the streets, watching us being taken away to the railroad station, I could see only hate, and pleasure that finally they were getting rid of the Jews. I can still see it – the hate.

As we walked to the railroad station, we looked back to the ghetto and saw many small fires that had been caused by grenades that the SS tossed into the houses. At that time, I was not aware that my good friend, Nolik Ben-Zion Schmidt, had perished during one of those fires.

I had known Nolik Ben Zion Schmidt since kindergarten. We both went to Schwabes Gymnasium. It is very interesting that in all the years I went to school, I always sat with him on the same bench in school. We developed a close friendship. I spent a lot of time in his house, and I remember his dog, Rex, and how we all played together. The greatest influence that Nolik had on my life was the fact that he was an artist who was tremendously interested in art and visited every art exhibit in Kaunas. He always invited me to go with him and we shared the experience of different artists. That led to my interest in art and my understanding of art, even if I never had the gift of drawing myself.

When the ghetto was formed, Nolik got a job in the art

12. Relocation of the inmates from one part of the ghetto to another, watercolor by Ben Zion (Nolik) Schmidt (courtesy Avraham Tory).

department of the ghetto, preparing all the signs and orders given by the Jewish Council. This was the way of communication between the Council and the people in the ghetto. In addition, the art department was actively involved in helping Avraham Tory, the Secretary of the Council, in documenting the events of the ghetto. Another friend of Nolik's and mine was William Mishell, who worked with Nolik in the same art department in the ghetto. After he was discovered by the SS in a *maline*, he was deported to Stutthof, then to Dachau, and survived. We met in Dachau, when he told me that my good friend, Nolik had been with him in the same *maline*. Nolik died when a hand grenade was tossed into this hiding place because he refused to leave.

It was 13 July 1997, between two and five o'clock when we arrived and photographed the area of deportation. As soon as we arrived at the site, my heart stopped. I looked around and recognized the place. Nothing had changed, except that the line-up of cattle cars assembled for deportation was missing. The rails were overgrown with grass. It was fifty-three years

13. Deportation site, railroad tracks overgrown, 1997.

to the hour when we had stood in the same place waiting to be deported.

I could see the assembled people with desperation in every face. I could see my father, my mother and my brother. I also remembered the incident when Dr Shlomo Nabriski was led to the cattle car and, because he was not walking at the speed required by the SS, a soldier hit him with a rifle and kicked him with his foot. I never forgot this episode and it came to life for me when I stood there in 1997. Dr Nabriski had graduated in medicine from the University of Berlin and was the chief of the gynecology and obstetrics department of the Jewish Hospital in Kaunas. He survived the war.

My 1997 visit was coming to an end. The film was nearly done. It was early afternoon when the Lufthansa plane took off for Frankfurt. It was about the same time in 1944 that the cattle car left, with us locked in it, for the journey to Stutthof and an unknown destiny. During the flight, in thinking about our trip, I could hear the voice of Vytautas, who had been our driver for ten days, driving us from one killing-place to another for the photography to be used in the creation of the film, *The Buried Secrets of Kovno Ghetto.* He was an intelligent man who supplemented his income in order to continue his education by driving us around. I could hear his voice asking me the question: 'What did the Jews do to the Lithuanians that we Lithuanians had to kill them?'

PART II

From Stutthof to Dachau Concentration Camp

3 Deportation to Stutthof, 14 July 1944

I woke up from a deep sleep, looked around and tried to recollect the day before. I did remember the traumatic episode of being found in the hiding place by the German soldiers, dragged out and marched through the streets of Kaunas from the ghetto to the railroad station. There were people lined up on the sidewalks to watch us. The saddest thing was that I saw a group of women standing there and shouting, as they shook their fingers at us: 'You, the ones who killed Christ, will be paying now. Hopefully, we will get rid of you for good.'

I remember running to board the railroad cars. If our speed did not please the guards, we were helped with a few kicks and hit on the head or on the rest of our body with their rifles. I looked around the car and saw the desperate faces of the people, some who were sleeping, and some lying in the cattle car. I felt comfortable having my father, mother and brother with me. But that day the pain that showed on the faces of the people, including my parents and my brother, was indescribable. I will carry these pictures in my mind for the rest of my life.

The sun penetrated through the little window at the top corner of the cattle car. The air was contaminated by all kinds of odors from the bucket that was put in the corner of the railroad car. I asked my father if we had moved while I was sleeping. He told me that the train had been stationary since we boarded it the day before.

The explosions were closer today than they were the day before, suggesting that the front was moving closer to Kaunas, and our hope glimmered. Maybe the railroad tracks had been damaged and they would not deport us. Maybe the Soviet

Army had blocked the passage of the train. Other hopes entered our minds. But all our hopes suddenly disappeared when the door opened and one of the SS soldiers entered the car and sat down, suggesting to us that he had been assigned to watch us. The quality of the air was gradually improved by the door being opened and then only partially closed.

Close to noon, the train started to move. A few minutes later we saw through the open door the bridge we were traveling over. We knew then that we were on the way to Germany. We did not know our destination, but our hopes like candlelight flickered and died. I looked at my parents and the other people (approximately fifty) in the car and I wondered what would be the fate of these Christ-killers? It was a pathetic picture. The scene of the women shaking their fingers at us, screaming and accusing us of being Christ-killers left a very big impression on me. I could see the hate in their faces, but I could not understand it. In 1985, Claude Lanzmann made a film called *Shoah,* a documentary. He visited a small village in Poland where 50 per cent of the population were Jews before the war. At the time he was filming, all the Jews were gone from there. All had been killed. He put the camera at the entrance of a church. When the villagers came out of Sunday mass, he interviewed the people and asked how it felt to live in a village where 50 per cent of your neighbors, with whom you had lived for several hundred years, were gone – killed. Those interviewed looked straight into the camera and said, 'After all, the Jews killed Christ, so there is no sin in killing a Jew.' This took place exactly thirty years after the Second World War. The hatred and the thinking has not changed: at least in part of Poland it has not changed.

The train gradually gained speed. It was not until after midnight that the train stopped at a small railroad station. We were ordered to leave the cattle cars and were given a kind of soup for our nourishment. This was the first time we had received any nourishment since we had been discovered in the *maline* and taken to the railroad station for deportation.

The German organization was incomprehensible. They

were trying to mobilize as many cars as they could to evacuate their troops from the advancing Soviet troops. Yet they still found a train and cattle cars to transport us to Germany.

After having spent a little time at the station, we were ordered back in the same cars and our journey continued. In the early morning the train stopped at the railroad station, Tiegenhof. It was a very clean, meticulously-kept station and we were ordered to leave the cattle cars. It was a beautiful day and the sun was shining. We were now in forbidden territory in Germany and there was no hope for us to escape. I could not imagine myself knocking on the door of a German farmhouse and expecting some encouragement to hide. We would have been immediately taken to the Gestapo.

After a short walk, we boarded open wagons, which were smaller cars without any rooftops. The wagons were loaded and the train started moving again. In a short time we knew our destination. It was Stutthof Concentration Camp. It was the first time that I saw a German concentration camp. We were put into rows and counted and walked through the gates. It said on the gate, 'Arbeit Macht Frei' ('Work makes you free').

We were taken to a large open space which later turned out to be the *Appellplatz* (the main assembly area). We were counted again and the men were separated from the women and children. My father and I were together and my younger brother was with my mother. It was the last time I ever saw my brother and I still remember his big, sad eyes. Even without speaking, they were saying, 'What will happen to us and will I ever see you again? I will never forget nor forgive.' I was separated from my mother at that time and it was sixteen years before I saw her again. I never saw my brother again.

The men were marched to a large warehouse. The warehouse was full of mounds of clothes. We were separated into groups of fifty people and the fifty people had to get undressed and leave everything they had (shoes, clothing) piled in a heap. All of the jewelry, watches and wedding rings had been taken away in the ghetto.

Then groups of fifty people were led out and the door closed behind them. However, nobody ever came out of that room. This caused great apprehension among those of us who were waiting, about what happened to them and what our destiny would be.

Finally, our turn came; naked, we walked through the door into another warehouse where there were barbers waiting to shave our heads. It did not take too long to shave the heads of the fifty people. After we left the pre-bath area, we were forced to go to the bath house. To our biggest joy and surprise, we noted there was actually water coming from the shower heads. Our luck held. In the ghetto, rumors were circulating that in the extermination camps, shower heads were connected with lethal gas.

We received a small piece of gray clay-like material that was supposed to be soap. After the shower, we went to another room where we each received a striped garment and a striped hat worn by the inhabitants of the concentration camp. The real problem for most of the people was not the clothes but the shoes. We had to find a pair of shoes that fitted our feet. I was very lucky and the first pair of shoes that I found fitted my feet. Most of the people got shoes that were either too small or too large. This became a great problem in their survival.

When we left the warehouse, I looked at the people. I recognized that not only had dignity been stripped from us, but also, our looks were altered by putting on these clothes. Each of us received a bowl and a spoon for our meals. These were the most important two utensils in our survival. We were then marched to some barracks where we were assigned a sleeping place. People shared bunks. For five days we did not work. At the *Appellplatz* we were counted and then we had to march all day. We were taught how to take the caps off our heads and how to put them back on, to salute a German regardless of his rank.

During this time, we saw the most horrible sight: 'walking skeletons'. I learned that these people were called musselmen and they had been at Stutthof for some time. Looking at them, you knew they were skeletons with a piece of skin stretched over their bones. These people were in the final stage of starvation prior to death. The German war machinery did not have to waste their bullets to kill them. They would die from starvation, which is a horrible death.

In my own thoughts, I felt that a bullet, which would be a bigger expense to the Third Reich, would be much more humane than letting people starve to death. But being exposed to the horrors of the camp played an important part in my determination against all the odds to survive, and during the subsequent year in the concentration camps, to do all I could to outlive the Third Reich.

On 21 July, the first rumors spread that an attempt on Hitler's life had been carried out. A day later, the rumors came again saying that Hitler had survived the attack. I was very disappointed, heartbroken even, to hear that the effort to kill Hitler had not succeeded. We did not know then how near to Stutthof he was: Rastenburg in East Prussia, a mere eighty miles away.

A day or two later, we found out we would be shipped from Stutthof to a different camp. There was speculation about where we would go from here. Would it be to a working camp or to an extermination camp? Speculation was a way of life; our uncertainty was a fact of life. A day later we were ordered back to the warehouse where we had to return our new camp clothes. We had to pick some clothes from a heap of used clothing that some prisoners of war had left.

I had become used to the striped garments. I felt violated again in having to put on some clothes that were used and some of which were unfortunately contaminated with lice, but we had no choice. This time it was much more difficult to recognize the people with the new clothes. I was also lucky that I did not have to change my shoes. A few people who had shoes that were too small or too large had a second chance to pick shoes from another shoe pile to improve their 'shoe status'.

In the late afternoon of that day, we were marched back to the open wagons and they brought us back to the railroad station at Tiegenhof. We were ordered to climb onto cattle cars. A few hours later, we were on our way to another concentration camp. Questions went through our minds: what camp will it be: extermination or working camp?

The mood of the people was despondent: despondent because there was no escape. There was no German soldier sitting in the car with us guarding us. The cars were locked tight. They felt that there was no chance for us to escape anyhow, as we would not be able to survive without help from the German farmers, who were not predisposed to help any Jews.

We spent a few days in the train without knowing and without seeing where we were going. Occasionally we saw a station through the little windows in the cattle car. We knew that we were very deep in Germany. It took about three days before we finally reached our destination.

4 *Dachau*

Hungry and exhausted, we arrived at a small railroad station called Kaufering. It did not take us very long to orient ourselves and we learned that several divisions of Dachau concentration camps (labor camps) were located in Kaufering.

Landsberg is a well-known city and was publicized during the Nazi regime. This was mainly because Hitler wrote his book, *Mein Kampf*, there in 1924, while in prison.

One of the guards advised us that we had reached our final destination – Concentration Camp Dachau. What he failed to explain was that around Kaufering were located a dozen 'Dachau' camps for prisoners working on construction.

Dachau was the first concentration camp created by the Nazi regime, in 1933. Its main purpose was to punish and silence the opposition to the National Socialist Party.

As soon as we left the cattle cars which had been our home for several days during the transportation, we were assembled in columns. We started walking toward our destination. The road was surrounded by forest and we saw how beautiful nature is. The walk was long and it seemed even longer due to the fact that we were walking toward an unknown destination. Looking back at the marching people, I saw a pathetic column. Many of the people who had started walking had removed their shoes and were walking barefoot due to the fact that most of the people had shoes that did not fit.

This column gradually moved in silence down a small side road from the main road leading into the forest.

Suddenly, the serenity of the landscape changed as we entered the gates of Kaufering – Dachau Camp 2 – which was designated as a working camp. There were no signs there that said, 'Arbeit Macht Frei' (Work makes you free) or 'Work can kill you too'. What we learned later was that we did not need a crematorium to be killed. Working camps can kill you too.

The beautiful forest that we had walked through suddenly changed to barbed wire with high observation towers and armed guards. The gates were opened and we entered our new habitat. At the gate entrance and a little further down on the right side, there were some prefabricated wooden buildings. After we passed the prefabricated buildings, we found ourselves in a large empty space which we later learned would be our daily assembly area, the *Appellplatz*.

Further down there was row after row of greenish tents designated, as we learned later, to be our sleeping places. We looked around hoping that our long trip had ended in an actual working camp, not an extermination camp. Each of us received a towel, a blanket, a bowl and a spoon. For our meal, we had to form a long line. When my turn came in the line, I received a little warm soup with a few floating cabbage leaves and about 200 to 250 grams of bread (about two slices).

We were later assigned to our tents. Every tent contained about twenty-five people, who would sleep on the floor of the tent with a few pieces of straw which was their bed. The straw was so scarce that it did not even cover the ground. When we were able to lie down in the tent, I remembered the sardine cans where sardines are laid one next to the other. Fortunately, at the top of the tent there was a special opening which was constructed in the form of a small umbrella to prevent the rain from coming in, and did help to ventilate the air in the tent. In spite of the small and crowded sleeping arrangements, I fell asleep.

It was the 'get up' whistle that awakened me in the morning. I took extra time to wash myself with the cold water. We had received a little soap which was sandier than any soap I had ever seen before.

After having stood in line for an hour or so, we were given another 200 to 250 grams of bread for the day and a bowl of warm brown water. It was supposed to be our breakfast. Following breakfast, we found ourselves back in the *Appellplatz* standing for hours. This became a normal routine during my stay in Camp 2. We would stand for several hours in the morning and several hours at night. This first day was a special day. After having been counted and recounted, registration occurred and we lost our identities as human beings. Our names were taken from us. We were given numbers. 84481 was my new identity. Unlike at Auschwitz, the numbers were not tattooed on our forearms, just printed on tags attached to our jackets.

I could never understand the harsh behavior of the people in charge of Organization Todt. Fritz Todt (1891–1942) was the founder of the Organization Todt Construction Company. It was one of the main users of slave labor.

The first dehumanization had started as soon as the Germans entered the city of Kaunas in 1941. The Jews were not allowed to walk on the sidewalk. We had to walk in the streets along the area where the horses with carriages and cars were supposed to go. A Jew had to take off his hat to salute every German or Lithuanian in uniform. Dr Gerber, a physician in Kaunas, was shot on the spot for not saluting a Lithuanian officer. He either did not notice the officer or was too slow to remove his hat.

At the same time, as already described, the Jews were notified that they could shop for food only during certain hours, usually starting in the late afternoon when most of the food had already been sold to the Christian people.

The Germans did not talk to us; they screamed and cursed. I often wondered where all the SS learned to massacre the German language. What happened to German culture, to Schiller, Goethe and the other great German writers?

I was thinking about the humiliation that occurred in Dachau Kaufering. I stood in the *Appellplatz* as 84481. I wondered what culture the Germans came from that produced people who had nothing else to do during a time of war, but to humiliate and dehumanize people. I thought that the inferiority complex had to play a very important part in their behavior. I recently came across a quote from the renowned Austrian psychiatrist Alfred Adler: 'We should interpret loss of temper as a sign of inferiority.'

Here I am, 84481. I felt that if I should die in Kaufering it would not be Jascha Brauns who died here. He no longer exists. Who would ever know that he was number 84481 except for me? Who would cry out to the world that I was alive or that I had died here in this camp?

That afternoon, a middle-aged man in an Organization Todt uniform with several SS officers came to select some people for work. One of the SS men from the camp called out, 'We need two carpenters with experience.' A young inmate, Joseph, stood next to me. He was about my age and I had worked with him in the ghetto workshop. We both stepped forward. It was not natural in the ghetto years and, I am sure, in the Dachau years, to volunteer for anything. But after having seen the tragic sights in Stutthof, I felt that it was time for me to take my destiny in my own hands. I remembered that at my bar mitzvah I had received a book written by Dr Ernst Rothe: *Gluck Haben-Ubungssache*. This means that having luck is a question of exercise: in other words, you are the master of your life. During my difficult years in the ghetto, as well as in Dachau, I always tried to recall the things that I learned from this book, which was mainly to depend only on yourself.

I guess Joseph and I were the only volunteers. The Organization Todt man looked us over and asked me how long I had been a carpenter. I said since I was able to work, I had always worked as a carpenter, thinking if asked to include the time I spent in the toy department in the workshop as well as my experience as a locksmith in the locksmith school. I do not know what he thought about me. He looked at me and said, 'Tomorrow when you come with the working brigade, come to the carpentry department in the working place and I will meet you there.' He gave the same instructions to Joseph. Several other people were selected in different fields, but not many volunteered. From experience, we knew that volunteering was not always a good experience. It was like the lottery; very rarely did you win.

In the late afternoon, I saw my father, who had been appointed as the physician at the small infirmary and hospital with thirty-six beds for patients. With him, he had two of his old friends, Dr Shlomo Nabriski and Dr Aharon Percikovitch (Peretz), who were both gynecologists. I told him about my volunteering as a carpenter. When I finished relating my experience that day, my father said he too had had a very interesting experience today. He met and spent some time with Rottenführer (Senior Lance Corporal) Helmanowitsch, who was in charge of the camp.

I had seen Rottenführer Helmanowitsch standing in the *Appellplatz*. He was very energetic, running around giving orders in a loud voice. He looked familiar to me, but at that time I could not recall him as part of my past life.

In 1937, an ambulance brought Helmanowitsch's wife to the Jewish Hospital, Bikur Cholim, in Kaunas, which had a large department designated for contagious diseases. It was the only civilian hospital with a contagious diseases department in the city of Kaunas. My father was in charge of the contagious diseases department and Mrs Helmanowitsch was admitted with a diagnosis of typhus abdominalis with the complication of intestinal bleeding. Mr Helmanowitsch was employed at the local brewery as a coachman.

The family was of limited means. Finally, Mrs Helmanowitsch was discharged and my father continued to see her when he made house calls. The Helmanowitsch family lived in Aleksotas. My father utilized a local taxi service that took him to make his house calls. I always volunteered to accompany my father on his house calls. I had the opportunity to meet Mr Helmanowitsch several times and always enjoyed seeing him because of his extreme courtesy and the respect he always showed my father as well as me for coming to visit them. In spite of their limited means, he never failed to prepare tea for us with some sweets.

In 1939 the German army occupied the city of Memel (Klaipeda). The Germans intended to use it as a military seaport as it was on the Baltic Sea. The Soviet Union and Germany signed the non-aggression pact which had a provision that all Baltic Germans could leave the areas occupied by Soviets to go to Germany. Mr Helmanowitsch and his family left for Germany. He did not have a profession that he could use in Germany to provide a livelihood for his family, so he joined the SS.

In 1944, when my father and I came to Kaufering, Mr Helmanowitsch was Rottenführer Helmanowitsch and second-in-command of the camp. He recognized my father, apologized for the situation and promised to do what he could to help. He also was aware that Dr Nabriski and Dr Percikovitch who were in the camp were very well-known physicians in the gynecology and obstetrics department of the Jewish Hospital in Kaunas. He pledged to help in any way he could. The man in charge of the camp was SS Sturmführer (Second Lieutenant) Haffner, but Rottenführer Helmanowitsch was the man who ran the camp.

I heard the story from my father; I recollected my trips to his house in Aleksotas and remembered the tea and cookies that I had been served during the visits.

My father showed his optimism, saying that maybe with the help of Helmanowitsch we would have a better chance to survive and turn destiny a little in our favor. He was more concerned about my mother and my brother being in Stutthof.

Joseph and I spent a little time together before we retired to our tent and discussed how we would approach the elderly gentleman in the Organization Todt uniform and convince him that we were true carpenters. The big advantage which helped was my fluency in German. I felt by being fluent in the language, I would use my charm to convince him that both of us were worthy of him taking a chance on our knowledge of carpentry.

I crawled back into my little sardine space. During my time in Dachau, the nights belonged to me. At times it was very difficult to fall asleep. The 'bed' was not very comfortable. The only blanket I had was light and skimpy. There was no heat. I was very hungry. It was at that time that I was able to create the most wonderful imaginary dinners, by remembering both the festive and non-festive dinners that our family shared together before the war.

During the summertime before the war, my father used to take a whole month off and we went to visit my mother's family in Riga, Latvia, or my father's family in Viljandi, Estonia. In 1939, we visited Helsinki, Finland. I tried to relive each trip many, many times during the long nights in Dachau. It is very interesting that in reliving our family trips I was able to reconstruct almost everything, but I wished I had pictures, either still pictures or movie pictures, that would help to refresh my memories of such important events in my life.

In the tent and in spite of the severe hunger that crept up, and in spite of the uncomfortable conditions, I soon fell asleep. I had some dreams during the night. The dreams consisted of being very hungry and in search of some food, then consuming a large meal with our family. It was interesting because when I woke up, I still felt as hungry as when I had gone to sleep. I realized then it was only a dream.

I was awakened by the sound of the whistle. My first duty of the day was to clean up. I had been indoctrinated by my father who believed that 'cleanliness was the key to survival'.

Then I joined the line waiting for early 'coffee'. It did not taste like coffee, but it was brown and in spite of being whatever it was, it was pleasant to have early in the morning.

At that point we were assembled in the *Appellplatz*, where the 2,000 prisoners were counted – and counted again – until the number of prisoners from the night before corresponded to the number of prisoners in the morning.

After the counting we were assembled in columns of five and we started our journey to work, leaving behind the grim scenery of the camp. The road wound through the beautiful forest. I had always enjoyed the forest. The sun was shining and the birds were flying. I envied their freedom. I looked at the big trees and knew that they had survived many storms and I always hoped that I would be able to survive the storm I faced at that time in my life. I also knew that the forest was very generous and a lot of food could be harvested from it. The road was at a higher elevation than the valley and we could see the whole construction site that suddenly appeared in front of us. After four miles of marching, we reached the valley. There were no trees in the valley. They had been replaced with construction cranes.

There were two railroad tracks at the outer border of the construction site. As we gradually descended, the cranes became larger and larger. We noted that part of the floor of the construction site, a quarter to half a mile, had already had cement poured on it. On the floor of the construction site, there was an outline of a narrow rail system which was used for small wagons pushed by hand to distribute the material arriving by railroad to the working site. Prisoners from different Dachau camps were working at the construction site. I did not realize at the time the role these small wagons would play in my survival.

On the construction site, there were prefabricated structures which housed workshops. We were told where the carpentry workshop was located. As we left our column and walked towards the carpentry workshop, we were met by the man responsible for selecting us the previous day. He greeted us and asked us to follow him. He explained to us the function of the workshop; it was to repair the small wagons that were used extensively at the construction site. He showed us the location of the circular saw, the band saw and the new material, as well as where to place discarded wood. He also showed us the stove. It was a circular, tall stove and on top of it there was a pot of warm water with another pot inserted in it. This contained glue. He explained to us that the stove was to keep the water warm which kept the glue warm and ready to be used. Surprisingly, it would be an important part of Joseph's and my survival in Dachau.

After a few minutes, the Organization Todt man took us to one of the small wagons that had to be repaired, and advised us how he wanted to have it repaired. We listened carefully and put all our knowledge of carpentry into action and did our best to repair the wagon. After an hour or two we finished the wagon and proudly went to the man, advised him we were finished, and walked back with him to the wagon. As he walked around the wagon and inspected it, he had a little smile, but did not make any comments except that after inspecting it he told us, 'Good luck. You will be working under my supervision from now on.' He was extremely polite and asked if we would like to have a cup of coffee to start the day. It was the first time in any of my experiences that any German official had given me anything else but curses. We accepted the coffee as he apologized that it was not real coffee as compared to the coffee before the war. It was ersatz (substitute) coffee that was then used in Germany. It was the color of coffee and for us it really tasted like strong coffee – exceptionally good. We had succeeded in charming the man and, hopefully, we would do a good enough job to survive Kaufering with working conditions that were more acceptable.

The man introduced himself as Hans Schmidt and said that he was a Volksdeutscher, which meant that he was German who lived outside Germany: in his case, Yugoslavia. He had been drafted by the Organization Todt. He also informed us that the man in charge of the whole carpentry department was Otto Jager, and he took us to meet him. Jager was a stern-looking man who gave us a severe look. It was very hard for me to assess at that time what kind of person he was. We also met the third carpenter, whose name was Max, who was a veteran of the German Army, but had been discharged from the army after he had been wounded in the head.

My apprehension gradually subsided and I started to evaluate our working conditions. I also inspected the area to see how many wagons were lined up to be repaired. I tried to learn how many he expected us to do on a daily basis. Joseph and I discussed it and decided that we would work together on each wagon. We felt this was the ticket to our survival if we could stay in this place for the duration of our time at the camp.

This first day came to an end and we were ordered to march back. We were tired and the distance back appeared much longer.

We returned to camp 2 and, after more than an hour at the *Appellplatz*, we were dismissed and again had to stand in line for our daily ration: 200 to 250 grams of bread and a liquid soup which contained two to three leaves of cabbage, but only if you were lucky. We returned to our tents and crawled into our little sardine boxes where, in spite of the sleeping conditions, I fell fast asleep. This was our first day at work.

Joseph and I used the little skill that we had to repair these wagons. After having assessed the workshop and seen the jobs of other people who had to carry the bags of cement and other heavy material, we felt that we were blessed to work in the carpentry department. We would use all the skills that we were taught in our limited experience as carpenters to do our best.

I think as time passed our skill and craftsmanship improved. We became friendly with Hans and he apparently became comfortable with us. After a week or two he started talking to us and expressed the tremendous dislike he had for the National Socialist Party. He would give us some sandwiches that he was able to take from his own ration and always said, 'This is more important for your survival than for mine.' We never refused them. Joseph and I shared them with gratitude.

One day Hans was in the mood to philosophize. He told me that Hitler was sent by God. He felt that the attempt on Hitler's life had failed because it was God's will to continue punishing the German people for the sins that they had committed toward their European neighbors as well as to the Jews. He asked me then if I knew what Hitler meant. Telling him that I did not know, he said, 'Then I will tell you. HITLER means: (H) Hinter (I) Ihre (T) Tuehre (L) Lauert (E) Eine (R)

Revolution, which meant, "Behind the door is lurking a revolution".' Unfortunately, the revolution did not succeed at this attempt. After hearing that, I said, 'Maybe we can all hope that the next time the revolutionary forces will be more successful.'

Hans was a devout Catholic. He thought even the Germans had to work seven days a week, including Sundays. Hans still went to church for mass every Sunday. I felt that we had become comfortable with each other. and I felt the compassion that he had for our faith. Hans brought us an apple that Joseph and I shared. It was the first apple we had had in a very long time.

The man in charge of the workshop, Otto Jager, was a sterner individual. After he learned of my fluent German, he often engaged me in conversation, mainly about politics and the outcome of the war. He tried to convince me of the achievement of the German Army and the magnificent things Hitler had done for the German people. I felt that by talking to me, he hoped to create a controversy in discussion.

I was apprehensive of him and I was cautious about expressing my opinion, always claiming that it was impossible for me to know – having been deprived from reading a newspaper for a long time. I tried to avoid having a meaningful discussion with him. One day he advised me that he would bring a newspaper every day for me and put it in a certain place which he showed me. He asked me to put it back in the same place after I read it so, that he could dispose of the newspaper. I felt that I had reached the peak of his trust.

At this time, the Allied Air Forces dominated the skies and bombed Munich daily. Usually, they started the bombing around noon and finished an hour or two later. During that period of time, Jager used to run to the nearby forest. When the sirens advised that the air raid was over, he would return carrying mushrooms, which he collected in the forest during that period of time.

Before the war, when I visited my grandmother in Viljandi, I used to go to the forest to collect mushrooms. I learned from my grandmother the skills to differentiate edible mushrooms from poisonous mushrooms. I shared with Jager my knowledge about this.

Gradually, Jager and I developed a relationship of mutual understanding. He began to feel compassion for Joseph and me, and started to bring a small amount of food that he could gather from his rations. The key to my friendship with Jager was my fluency in the German language. It was actually my mother tongue, as we had spoken German at home.

After seeing that the other men were giving us some remnants of their food, Max, the third German carpenter also started giving us food. Every time he gave us food, he used to say, 'Well, I had enough for today. You can have the rest of it.' He did not feel our tremendous necessity for food: rather, it was mainly that he had eaten enough for that meal and the rest should go to us. I do not know if he even knew exactly the hunger that we experienced. We always thanked him and never refused his generosity.

When I walked into the construction site, I saw the other inmates who worked for Holzman and Moll, and the abuse that they received from their supervisors, who were not members of the SS. These poor people could hardly stand up. They had to carry fifty to one-hundred-pound bags of material that was unloaded for the construction. If they did not move fast enough or to the liking of their supervisor, they received a severe a beating. These beatings were a contributing factor to the deaths of many inmates. Many inmates were from Camp 1 and were also deportees of the Kovno Ghetto.

October 1944 passed. We got hungrier and the weather worsened. It would rain and the temperature fell. We had to walk to the working place during the rain. Joseph and I had the opportunity to dry out near the stove in the workshop, but if it rained on the way home, the problem was really great because there were no stoves or heating facilities in the camp, and we had to crawl into the sardine boxes to sleep in our wet clothes.

Because of the brutality of the foremen of the Holzman and Moll Company, the death rate increased. It showed itself in our sleeping facilities. Our sardine boxes suddenly became bigger because in every tent a few people had died.

One day, when we arrived back from the work place, Dr Nabriski was waiting for me at the gate. I always appreciated Dr Nabriski's smile as well as his optimistic outlook. In the time spent with Dr Nabriski, he became a second father to me. He told me not to get upset or worry, but that my father was not in the camp, and he asked me to follow him to the infirmary. We stopped outside the infirmary and he told me the story.

When the first inmates in Camp 2 died, my father wrote the death report and certified in the report that the cause of death was starvation. This report had to go to Dachau main camp on a weekly basis, where the top German physician in charge of all Dachau camps had to review it. The specific day when the report arrived, the chief physician, who was known to be an alcoholic, was not in Dachau and the report was sent on to Berlin. It was a big surprise in Berlin that the death certificate stated that the inmates in Dachau had died from starvation. This was not accepted by Berlin, which insisted that the rations were all calculated and provided for survival, not for death.

A few weeks later a committee from Berlin arrived to investigate how a prisoner or inmate could die from starvation. What they did not know, and I do not know if they even wanted to know, was that more than half of the food assigned to the camp was taken by the SS and sold on the black market, with the income being pocketed. When the committee from Berlin left and the German physician returned to camp 2, he was obsessed with the desire to kill the man who had written the report – my father. He did not know my father personally, directly or indirectly. To save my father, Rottenführer Helmanowitsch came to the camp and took my father away to his own home. He felt that it would be safer for my father to be there until the storm calmed down.

Dr Nabriski had been entrusted with that secret and promised to advise me about my father. A few days later my father was returned to the camp and continued his work.

In November the weather worsened. Nor did the continuous feeling of hunger make our life easier. The mood of the camp inmates worsened. In spite of the optimistic news from the front and the progression of the war, the weather as well as the hunger left imprints on our mood and our thinking.

The German authorities decided to replace the tents with a new underground 'habitat'. The new structure consisted of a trench dug in the ground which was the corridor. The earth on each side of the trench was covered with wooden boards and a thin layer of straw, constituting the bed. The roof consisted of prefabricated wooden frames assembled like a gable and covered with sod. We were lucky: each hut had a stove.

One day, I was asked by an acquaintance of mine from school if I could make him a pair of wooden shoes. He knew I worked in the carpentry department. He remembered that I made a pair of wooden shoes for my adopted sister Irena, at the time that I worked in the workshop in the ghetto. To make a pair of wooden shoes was not so hard. I had to make sure, however, that I would not get into trouble, because I would be using wooden material that was German property. Stealing German property was punished by hanging. I discussed making the shoes with Joseph and we decided to discuss this with Hans. Hans was extremely receptive and advised us that he would take any pieces of wood usable for making wooden shoes and put then in the scrap and discard area. It did not take us very long, with the help of the electric saw, the band saw, and the other equipment that was there, to carve out a pair of wooden shoes. The next problem was the construction of the top for the wooden shoes. We had no material available that was suitable to use.

When we came to Kaufering from Stutthof, each of us received a blanket. Due to the cold weather several people cut up their blankets and used them for different clothing needs, mainly making socks for their shoes or wrapping them around their feet to keep warm. Two people were caught once and their punishment was hanging – to show the other inmates

14. Jack's habitat in Dachau Kaufering No.2, which he shared with 49 inmates (courtesy Holocaust Memorial Museum, Washington, DC).

that German property, in this case the blankets, cannot be destroyed and had to be used for its designated purpose.

We did not want to make the same mistake and be hanged, so we discussed this dilemma with Hans. The next day he brought his old pants and helped us to cut them out in shapes for the top of the wooden shoes. By the end of the day, our friend came to the workshop and picked up a beautiful pair of wooden shoes: at least, they were beautiful and essential under the circumstances.

My friend was overwhelmed with the present he received from us, and decided to repay us by telling everybody we could make wooden shoes. Surprisingly, the next day several inmates came to Joseph and me, asking if we could make them a pair of wooden shoes for them. They offered to pay something for the shoes. Money did not exist in the camp. Instead, they offered a piece of bread.

There were other exchanges going on, especially among the inmates who were smokers. Two cigarettes could be exchanged for half the daily bread ration.

We could not make more than two pairs of wooden shoes a day during our so-called lunch break, which usually coincided with the Allied bombings. The longer the bombing raids lasted, the longer was our so-called lunchtime. There were days, however, when the bombers did not arrive; that deprived us of our lunchtime. We discussed with Hans what we were doing and decided to tell the story to Jager. He gave us his blessing and told us not to worry about using the machines as long as we took the wood from the area assigned for discards.

We started with one pair a day and gradually worked up, as our skills improved, to two pairs of wooden shoes a day. We also decided, with people we did not know, that we would charge a certain amount. This would be one ration a day. We laid out a payment plan that could be paid in four instalments to make it easier for all of us to survive. We were happy and the people who received the shoes were very happy. Everyone benefited from this plan. By making only two pair of wooden shoes a day, we were not imposing on Hans, who had to supply the tops of the wooden shoes.

The man who had received the first pair of shoes always smiled when he saw us, and always pointed to the shoes. 'In saving my feet,' he said, 'you saved my life, at least temporarily.'

The situation improved a little, in that we had a small supply of food from Hans, Jager, Max, and from our 'income' for the wooden shoes. The amount that we charged was so minimal that it did not affect the other inmates' hunger in one way or another.

We never enforced the charge for the shoes. If some of the inmates did not pay, we felt that they could not for one reason or another.

Potato fields lined the roads to work. Many people were brave enough to jump out to steal some potatoes. On returning to the camp, one of the men who had potatoes unfortunately had put too many in his pockets and they bulged, and the bulge of the pockets was noted by one of the guards. He was taken to the *Appellplatz* and received ten lashes with a whip. He was a brave man and did not complain. This irritated the guard who believed that he had not felt the pain of the punishment. In spite of this 'lesson', the stealing of potatoes from the fields did not stop. The people who were brave and stole the potatoes had another problem: how to eat the potatoes. Most ate them raw.

One day I had an idea. I inspected the stove carefully. It was about five feet tall, very narrow. On the top of the stove there was an opening with a huge pot inserted into the stove to boil the water. A smaller pot was inserted into the water-boiling pot to prepare the glue for the workshop. There was a small door at the bottom of the stove where the wood was put in, to keep the fire continuously burning during working hours. After inspecting the stove, which was only a foot and a half in diameter, I felt we should put a rod inside the stove, just under the water pot, where we could hang another pot to boil some potatoes. The idea was good, but how could we execute it in the workshop with so many people present? Joseph and I discussed it and decided again to talk to Hans and get his opinion. Hans listened to us carefully and asked us to let him think about it, to see how he could construct the bars inside the stove so that we would be able to hang the pot for the potatoes in the middle of the stove. Then an amazing thing happened. In two or three days, Hans, with the help of a locksmith, prepared the iron bars that were to be inserted into the stove. A day later he called us in to show us what he had done. It was the most incredible thing: a stove within a stove. If someone had come to inspect it, they would never have been able to learn our secret during working hours when the stove was lit.

Again we went to Jager and talked to him. He nodded his head and said we had his blessing if it helped us. We decided, because of the risk involved, that we would again charge. The cost for cooking five potatoes was one potato. At least once a day, our 'clients' came with potatoes that had been stolen on the way to the working place and we cooked the potatoes.

Even the potato that Joseph and I shared contributed to our survival.

The SS periodically came to inspect the workshop, including the stoves. Jager would come out and stand before the SS and say that it was his workshop and that he was responsible for what went on there. He told them that no one here had stolen or done anything with potatoes. That was the end of the story. With the generosity and ingenuity of Hans and Jager, we succeeded in increasing our ration a little, but at that time the 'little' was a lot.

By watching the other foremen's cruelty toward the inmates, I wondered where these foremen had learned this cruelty. Even today, I cannot understand it, because the cruelty in achieving more or less work from the inmates was not necessary. With just a little better treatment, they would have done more work. The construction site at the camp was very important. The Allies had destroyed the air superiority of the German Air Force. Years later, after the war, I learned that it was Hitler's intention to build new jet fighter planes at the facility we were building. How happy I was that the construction had not been completed before the end of the war.

One day Hans came and told us that he would be going on leave and would return in two weeks. We were delighted for him to have an opportunity to see his family in Yugoslavia, but we were worried, because many Germans who went on leave never came back, due to the bombing or other accidents that occurred. Before Hans left, Joseph and I sat down with him. He told us he wanted to keep us out of trouble. He asked us to build an outdoor latrine at the edge of the forest. He told Jager that Joseph and I would build a latrine which was urgently needed. He felt that we were qualified carpenters by then. We took some paper, and with his help we designed a latrine. Then Hans left for his leave.

The first thing we did was to dig out the hole for the outdoor latrine. It was not too hard. The ground was not frozen yet and, with the amount of wood we had, it took little effort to put together this outhouse. We diligently worked on it for two weeks. In between we also repaired all the wagons that had to be repaired. This kept us extremely busy. We thought we had done a good job on the latrine and were awaiting Hans' return for him to inspect it.

Something happened, however, with the hole that we dug, and for some reason the whole latrine turned on its side. Looking at the latrine, I thought about the Leaning Tower of Pisa. When Hans came back from his vacation, we took him to see it. He broke out in laughter and said, 'This looks like the Leaning Tower of Pisa, and we will call it the Leaning Latrine.'

The month of December brought snow to the area. It was hard to walk to the working place and hard to return, especially in the driving snow without winter clothes. We returned to our sardine boxes, which were very cold. It was difficult to fall asleep because of the cold. The one blanket that we received on arriving there was no match for the freezing cold. Many people died as a result of the work, hunger and severe weather. Those who were still living prayed for the success of the Allied forces in liberating the camps.

The camp authorities decided that something had to be done with the clothes of the prisoners, since all we had was the summer clothing that we had received at Stutthof. One day the distribution of winter clothing took place. The clothes were used and contaminated with lice. Thus, lice were introduced into the camp. Fortunately, these lice were not sick with typhus fever.

On 12 January 1945 we were transferred from Dachau Camp 2 at Kaufering to Camp 7, also at Kaufering, five miles from Camp 2. Some of the inmates could hardly walk and some already appeared to be in the early stages of the musselman. We observed in the columns of the inmates that their vigor was gone, replaced by desperation. On our walk we carried with us our guests: the lice we received with the clothes at Camp 2.

Camp 7 was similar to Camp 2, so it was easy to get oriented. The inmates we found in Camp 7 were mainly from Czechoslovakia. They looked as if they were near to death.

The Jewish doctor of Camp 7 was a Czech. He was very

friendly and welcomed my father, Dr Nabriski and Dr Percikovitch. He told us that he was an internist and was concerned with the mortality rate being so high in Camp 7. He thought that many of the inmates were affected with typhus fever. This was of great concern to my father, who had specialized in contagious diseases and had witnessed the mortality rate of typhus fever during the First World War. Given the history of the illness, and having examined some of the patients, my father confirmed clinically the existence of typhus fever, while the Czech doctor reported that he had sent some blood samples to a laboratory in Landsberg for confirmation.

From Camp 2, SS Commanders Lipman and Bier were transferred to Camp 7. Sadly, Helmanowitsch was transferred to Camp 11. In Camp 7 there was a delousing oven which, unfortunately, was not functioning at the time we arrived. After having talked to SS Commanders Lipman and Bier, an effort began to repair the delousing oven. Within a week or so, this special oven began functioning and the delousing of clothing was started.

Unfortunately, it was too late for several people who were affected with typhus fever. This is how the disease is transmitted: it starts with a sick patient, and a louse that had recently bitten a sick patient. After the louse bites the sick patient, the louse gets sick, and when the sick louse bites a healthy patient, the disease is transmitted to him through the feces of the louse. At the site of the bite, the patient develops a severe itch which he scratches, thereby rubbing the virus-infected louse feces into the site of the bite. This infects the person.

The incubation time for the disease is eighteen days. It usually starts with a severe headache and high temperature. The first to become sick in our group was my father. After that, I was also infected with typhus fever. The number of infected patients increased and the camp was sealed. Nobody could enter and nobody could leave. Once a day, some food would arrive and be dropped at the gate. The people who delivered the food would then leave. After they left, the gate would be opened and the food would be brought into the camp.

The second time the camp was opened was in the afternoon, when the dead people were put on little wagons and taken to a common burial ground. Those who conducted the burial were like the people who were dead except they were still moving and still had the strength to push the little wagon carrying the dead people. Dr Percikovitch was the only one who did not get the disease. He had caught typhus fever during the First World War, which provided him with a permanent immunity. He was my father's lifesaver. Dr Nabriski had a mild case.

My savior was my childhood friend and classmate, Zev Birger. Zev and I were deported together from the Kovno Ghetto and then to Kaufering. We used to meet periodically at the construction site where he worked as an electrician. We always encouraged each other with the challenge of surviving in these difficult circumstances. According to Zev, when I got sick and was unconscious, I would wake up periodically and ask for my mother and some jam.

Zev used to come to see me regularly, encouraging me and reporting to me the status of my father's health. I really do not remember much about these days, but I know that the liquids and nourishment that Zev gave me when I was awake, or gave me when I was incoherent, were the key to my survival. And, yes, I did survive. During my recovery I learned to walk again, and, three or four weeks later, I helped Zev overcome the same disease. I feel privileged that my relationship with Zev is to this day that of the closest of friends, actually like brothers, who can attribute our survival to each other.

With the help of Dr Percikovitch and Dr Nabriski my father gradually improved. SS Commander Lipman, who was in charge of the camp, went to the city and bought some sulfonamides for my father to help him overcome the infection. Without SS Commander Lipman's personal intervention and personal journey to get the sulfonamides, my father most likely would not have survived.

The fatality rate for typhus fever was 60 per cent without any medication. There was no medication available in any of the camps. The Third Reich no longer needed gas chambers. The rations that we received at Camp 7 were about 70 per cent of the rations that we received at Camp 2, and they were not rations that were essential for recovery after such a contagious disease, but we had no choice – it was all we were given.

In April 1945 we were assembled in the *Appellplatz* and advised that we would be relocated to Camp 1 in Kaufering. This was the camp where the first deportees transported from the Kovno Ghetto had arrived. They had been sent directly from Kovno to Dachau, avoiding Stutthof.

The four or five miles that we had to walk from Camp 7 to Camp 1 were almost impossible due to our physical condition, both as a result of the conditions in Camp 2 and Camp 7, and because of having been affected with typhus fever. The people who were walking with me were a pathetic sight. I asked myself, 'where are You mighty, God? How could You allow something like this to happen?' This is a question that I asked for many years to come. The line of emaciated people finally arrived in Camp 1 where we were greeted by our friend, Dr Benjamin Zacharin, who had been a well-known and respected surgeon in Kaunas. He put my father directly into the hospital. Dr Zacharin had been a large, heavy man in Kaunas, but when I saw him in Kaufering for the first time in one year, I hardly recognized him. He had almost 'melted away'.

Dr Zacharin immediately gave us some good news and encouragement, describing the situation of the war and the advance of the United States Army. This good news gave us a tremendous psychological boost.

I met other friends there whom I had not seen for a long time. One was my classmate, David Landau. Just seeing these friends, and the encouragement that we gave each other, was a tremendous aid to our survival.

Two days after our arrival at Camp 1, an SS man came and seized me and another nine people and marched us to the gate. Among the people seized was Dr Nabriski. The SS man put us on a truck and drove us to a railroad train that had been machine-gunned and was stopped in its tracks. Apparently the train was carrying prisoners from one of the camps to the main camp of Dachau. When we opened the first door in the railroad car, we saw the most terrible scene. There were four or five people who had been machine-gunned, with blood splashed over all of them as well as over the walls of the car, and the smell in the railroad car was unbearable. I thought we had opened the door to one of the circles of Dante's *Inferno*.

The job of the ten people was to remove the corpses from many railroad wagons and load them into one wagon. The job was one of the worst nightmares I could ever imagine. The bodies were skeletons with open mouths. In order to take them out from the car, we had to lift the bodies by the waistline and when we put pressure on the abdomen air would come out of the mouth, a noise as if the person had not finished saying his last word. This was a horrible experience. We worked the whole day and through the night. Fortunately, that night there was a full moon and we had at least some light to carry out our task. We were so filthy, covered with the blood and the feces from the corpses.

When we opened one of the cars, we heard a voice. We had found a person whom we had known in Lithuania. His name was Benjaminovitch. He was not wounded, but he was exhausted and unable to move out of the railroad wagon filled with dead inmates. He was too weak and too tired to tell us what had happened with the train. We had nothing to give him except hope. We helped him out of the wagon and he rested outside for the remainder of the night, where he could breathe the air more easily than the air in the locked wagon.

Early in the morning we finished our 'job'. We were hungry. Our two SS guards told us that it was time to go back to Camp 1 and they drove us there. We took Benjaminavitch with us. To our surprise, when we arrived at Camp 1, the people in Camp 1 were all gone. Only the camp was still there. Apparently, it had been evacuated in our absence. The

SS man with us, who was himself very hungry as he had not eaten anything since we had been together, went to the SS kitchen and found food still there. He told us that he would reward us for having done such a good and unpleasant job. From the SS kitchen all kinds of food was brought out, food that I had not seen for a long time. The SS man looked at us and saw how pathetic we looked and said, 'You were pigs, you are pigs, and you will always be pigs. Therefore, you are going to eat without washing. You will eat like pigs eat – in the dirt.' The truth is that I was terribly hungry, and if I had not had Dr Nabriski sitting next to me, I would most likely have wiped my hands on my trousers and eaten whatever was edible. Dr Nabriski, however, stood up in front of the SS man and said, 'You are right, we were pigs; you are right, we are pigs; and you are right, we will always be pigs, but we are Jews and according to the Jewish religion, we have to wash our hands before we eat. This is our religious custom.'

The German officer was stunned by the fluent German spoken by Dr Nabriski – who had graduated from the University of Berlin Medical School – and was astonished that he dared to speak defiantly. So our guard regained his composure and said, 'Well, if you don't want to eat, that will be fine with me.' Dr Nabriski was sitting next to me and he poked me in the arm and said, 'You know, Jascha, we will not eat.' I was sitting there watching some of the people eating and my salivary glands were working and I felt twice as much hunger. I looked at Dr Nabriski and I decided that because I felt so close to him and respected his decisions I would not eat.

Many years later I met Dr Nabriski in Israel, where he was in charge of a maternity hospital, and he said to me, 'Jascha, do you remember the episode in the morning when we came back to Camp 1?' I said, 'How could I forget it?' He said, 'You know, Jascha, by not eating we won the war. With all the deprivation, with all the humiliation and with all the pain that we suffered, our spirit was never broken or destroyed and we actually won the war in spite of what everyone says and thinks.' He was so right. This is one of my proudest memories.

After not having eaten and watching others eat, we went to the washroom and washed whatever way we could. The SS guard returned, after a short absence, and advised us that he would take us to the place where the inmates of Camp 1 had been relocated. We joined a train that was still parked on the tracks. In the same car was Dr Nabriski, Dr Percikovitch, my father, and myself.

In the late afternoon, the train started to move. After traveling for about an hour, it was strafed by machine-gun fire from Allied airplanes. The first to abandon the train were the Germans. They ran to the nearby forest. The airplanes strafed the running people. When we noted that our guards were gone, we decided to flee, but we were unable to run, due to malnutrition, and so we walked toward the forest. Periodically some airplanes would fly over and machine gun the inmates who were running or walking to the forest.

When I saw an airplane coming, I decided to fall to the ground and be parallel to the approach of the plane. I figured if I had to get shot I would rather get ten shots since I would be very uncomfortable just lying there wounded. I would rather die than be wounded. From our group, there were several people who were so close to liberation yet were killed by Allied airplanes. The pilots could not identify the people who were running to the forest from the train.

Dr Nabriski, Dr Percikovitch, my father, and I and a few other people who reached the forest walked deep into it. We could hear the sounds of explosions. The front was clearly very close. We were hungry and tired. Dr Nabriski, my father and I had to decide what to do. Dr Nabriski decided to go to the right. As my father was very tired and unable to walk fast enough, having just recovered from typhus fever, he and I decided we would not hinder anybody else in their escape but would sit in the forest and rest, and then we would follow the same path. We spent the night in the forest. In the early morning we were surrounded by German soldiers. It was the German army. The soldiers did not know what to do with us. They talked among themselves, and one of them said that there was a train going to Dachau with other inmates. They brought us to the train and loaded my father and me on it. We were on our way to the main camp of Dachau.

Dr Nabriski and Dr Percikovitch had been able to walk to a United States Army outpost and were liberated that day.

When we came to Dachau we saw that there was chaos in the camp. There were some guards, men of 60 or 70 years old, who were not as vicious as the other SS men. Apparently they were new draftees who had been conscripted in order to guard the Dachau camp.

On reaching Dachau, we had to go through the washing and cleaning up which was a real blessing for us. After that, we received a little soup. Dachau contained about 40,000 people. Out of the 40,000 people there were only about 2,000 Jews. The rest were of many different origins: Germans who were anti-Nazi, some British prisoners, some French and some Poles. The inmates were very sympathetic to us. Their treatment had been much less harsh than the treatment of the Jews. They gave us some food in the evening, saying that what little they had they would like to share with us.

Only part of our clothing was returned to us; we received our shirts. For some reason, there were no pants in the warehouse. So the last transport that arrived in Dachau got only shirts and no trousers. We were confined to the barracks.

5 Liberation: 29 April 1945

At about two o'clock in the afternoon on 29 April 1945, the gates of Dachau were opened. After four years of incarceration, humiliation and walking on a tightrope to avoid death, prisoner 84481 was liberated and resurrected from a living hell to the life and challenges of a free man – I was Jascha Brauns once again.

As soon as the United States Third Army opened the gates of Dachau and the first soldiers arrived, there was an incredible celebration. The celebration and the emotional feeling are hard to describe on a piece of white paper with words written in ink. It was an emotional liberation, something that people had been hoping, dreaming and praying for – in my case since June 1941. Unfortunately, millions of people never lived to see the day of liberation. They had been killed and buried.

The next morning we received our pants. We went out to breathe the April air that smelled and felt so very different, breathing the air as free men.

Out of compassion and generosity the Americans gave the prisoners chocolate, other sweets and fatty foods. This caused the deaths of several of the prisoners. Therefore, in front of the gate, there was a large sign, 'Please do not feed the inmates you are visiting. We know your intentions are good, but they can be detrimental.' Many years later when I visited the zoo, I would see a sign that said, 'Don't feed the animals, it could be hazardous to their health' and remembered the day of my liberation. The digestive systems of the inmates were not geared to the heavy, calorific, greasy food. They needed a period of readjustment.

Some emotional aspects of liberation had to be faced. We

were all concerned about our families – parents, aunts, uncles, cousins, grandparents – and their fate. The facts and reality of the tragedy that had fallen on the Lithuanian Jews was incomprehensible, and at that period of time not completely known to us.

After obtaining liberty, the question arose: What do we do now? Where do we go from here? To return to Lithuania was emotionally impossible for me. It was like returning and trying to live in a cemetery. My father, however, felt that his main obligation was to return to Lithuania and to find our family. After that, we would make the decision of where we would go from there. My father and I were concerned about the fate of my mother and brother whom we had last seen in Stutthof.

The new administration at Dachau, run by the United States Third Army, was well organized and provided a progressive diet, which gradually increased the nutrients and taught the stomachs of the inmates how to return to eating normal food. With the gradual progression of food, we also felt we had progressed in our rehabilitation. In his book, *The Day the War Ended*: *May 8, 1945*, Martin Gilbert writes:

> In Dachau, several thousands of prisoners who had been liberated nine days earlier were slowly recovering under American medical help. One of them Jack (Jascha) Brauns, who had survived as a boy in the Kovno Ghetto, was still in Dachau, and in quarantine, on VE Day. He later recalled:
>
> With the sunrise, May 8 arrived and my ninth day of freedom started. The winds were sending rumors to all the corners of Dachau. The subjects of the rumors varied from some credible to some incredible situations. The rumors included what food would be served today; the different concentration camps that were liberated and the fate of the inmates; the fighting of the Allied forces and the surrender of the Wehrmacht in different locations of Europe.

My father and I were walking between the barracks to the *Appellplatz*. People were walking, talking and some were congregating in small groups where the rumors were discussed, and comments were added to the rumors. The inmates were wearing the same clothes. They were still emaciated, but their faces had changed. From the look of despair, you could see an occasional gentle smile.

My conversation with my father centered on our concern about the fate of my mother and brother. We had last seen them one year ago at Stutthof. Rumors about the fate of the inmates were discouraging, but all the information obtained was based on rumor and speculation as well as wishful thinking. We tried to console ourselves and not consider the possibility that our family might be incomplete. I tried to imagine how my mother and brother looked after enduring one year of Stutthof. We were concerned with how we would manage to reunite with them and where we would live.

But with all the turmoil that was consuming my brain, the ninth day of freedom was a special day. I received an orange from an American GI and shared it with my father. It was my first orange in four years. I will always remember May 8, the ninth day of freedom and the taste of that first orange.

I had been liberated on 29 April 1945. Finally my freedom had arrived and with it the challenges that freedom created. The quarantine was established. This gave the ex-inmates an opportunity to adjust to food. Before liberation I had learned how to survive with a lack of food. After we were liberated, I had to face a new challenge: to learn how to survive with an abundance of food. It was much easier to learn to survive with an abundance of food. It was a test of self-control and understanding the problems that we faced and the consequences that overeating would lead to.

The outside walls of the barracks were used as a bulletin board. The Red Cross provided a daily list of survivors from different camps. The list was large and was updated daily with new names. Because of the number of prisoners in Dachau, these lists were posted in different areas of the camp and were always surrounded by people. Together, my father and I watched the lists very carefully. Unfortunately, I never found the names of my mother or brother. It was agonizing not knowing if they had survived.

Many of the inmates made plans. My father and I signed up to return 'home' to Lithuania, because he felt it was his responsibility and moral duty to find my mother and my brother. Hopefully reunited, we would all decide on where we would settle.

A few weeks after liberation, United States Army trucks arrived and the ex-inmates who had signed up to return to Eastern Europe were taken to the airport. Lithuania was once again part of the Soviet Union. Early in the morning, before the trucks had arrived, I checked the bulletin board again, and, sadly, did not see the names of my mother and brother. Our apprehension grew. The ride on the American trucks was my first ride in freedom. We shortly arrived at the airport and saw thirteen American transport airplanes lined up. We spent the day at the airport, during which time we were organized into different groups designated by our destinations. Since my father was a physician, he was assigned to accompany a transport with sick people. We found ourselves separated.

That day, twelve planes left. A mechanical defect was discovered in the thirteenth plane. My destiny was not to leave. This changed my life completely. I was left in Germany, and from that moment, I was on my own. The same truck that had brought us to the airport brought me back to Dachau. I was told that in a few days I would be taken back to the airport to proceed with the plans as scheduled. However, a few days passed and then a few weeks passed and I was still at Dachau.

On my return to Dachau, I befriended two young ex-prisoners of war, Vanya and Ivan, who were from the Ukraine. We had been allocated the same plane that never took off.

They had been in the Red Army and had been taken prisoner. They were writers for the Red Army newspapers, very intelligent, and I enjoyed spending time with them. After being in Dachau for a few weeks, we were advised that there would be no more planes to take us to the Soviet Union, and that we would be transported by trucks and railroad to our 'homeland' – the Soviet Union.

I learned from Vanya and Ivan that the treatment of Russian prisoners of war had been as harsh as the Germans had treated the Jews. The Germans had no obligation to treat the Jews well. For the prisoners of war, however, there was the Geneva Convention with special specifications on how to treat prisoners of war, but since the Soviet Union had been expelled from the League of Nations in 1939, as a result of its attack on Finland, the German authorities completely disregarded it.

15. The liberation of Dachau concentration camp, 29 April 1945 (courtesy Holocaust Memorial Museum, Washington, DC).

6 *Traveling East and then South to Italy*

The day came when we were put on trucks to be taken to our homeland. We spent a few hours on the truck and were dropped off at a fenced-in compound, previously a German Army barracks. The red flag of the Soviet Union flew at the entrance of the compound. Vanya, Ivan and I were assigned to the same room. It took Vanya just a few minutes to realize that we were now in a Soviet re-education center. The purpose of the center was that all prisoners of war, as well as any other prisoners who had worked on German soil and were being repatriated to the Soviet Union, including the Soviet Republic of Lithuania, had to undergo a few weeks of political re-indoctrination. All the 'evil' we had learned from Western civilization had to be eradicated from our minds. Vanya, Ivan and I had a discussion and we decided to be obedient citizens and to be re-indoctrinated. Vanya also learned from other Soviet prisoners of war that the food was good and the treatment was gentle.

Day by day, we were indoctrinated with Marxism and Leninism and the advantages of communism compared to the capitalistic social structures in Western civilization. To Vanya, Ivan and myself, it sounded absurd, but the policy had been established by Moscow and we could not escape it. It became very depressing, but it was far better than the time we spent in Dachau before we were liberated.

One evening I shared with Vanya and Ivan the fact that I had severe abdominal cramps. It was after dinner and Vanya and Ivan insisted on taking me to the infirmary. The infirmary was already closed and we were assured by the nurse that she would call the physician on duty immediately. After a while, a highly-decorated Soviet officer came to the infirmary. Vanya and Ivan recognized that he too was a Ukrainian and engaged him in conversation. They were very interested in what happened during the war years, how the Ukraine looked today, and about the cities where they lived.

The nurse then told us that she had to leave. The doctor reassured her that he would lock up the infirmary after treating me. It took some time before he realized that he had not come to socialize, but to see a patient – who happened to be me. He looked at me and said, 'A Jew. Did I come down here in my leisure time to treat a Jew?' He looked at Vanya and Ivan and said, 'I'm glad we won the war, but Hitler should have killed all the Jews. He would have done us all a big favor.' Vanya slowly approached him and asked him to repeat what he said.

The physician repeated what he had said. At this point, Vanya, who was smaller in stature than the physician, swung his fist and hit him in the face. The physician fell to the floor. I knew we were in trouble. Vanya and Ivan grabbed me by the hand and said, 'We have to leave right away or else we will be in big trouble.' The key was on the desk. As we slowly walked out, the physician was getting up. He was cursing us in Russian and screaming, 'For a Ukrainian to hit another Ukrainian about what I said about a Jew is preposterous and unheard of – it shows the capitalistic influence.' We locked him in the infirmary.

We were inside an enclosed compound, but it was not a concentration camp. It took us only a short time to find our way out of the compound. Within minutes we were on the road, having decided to make the journey to the East on our own. A truck was passing by and stopped when we flagged it down. We asked the driver if it would be out of his way to drive us to the nearest railroad station. He smiled and said that he would be passing a railroad station within two hours and would be happy to drop us there. Approximately two hours later, we found ourselves at the railroad station.

A train was parked at the station and we were told that

shortly it would be going east. We boarded it. A few hours turned into long hours and early the next morning the train started moving. We were on our way east. We sat inside because at that time no tickets were required. The train made frequent stops at small stations and many people boarded the train. It seemed that all of Europe was moving somewhere because everyone wanted to go home. At one of the stations where the train stopped we reviewed the map and decided that our goal should be to go to Vienna and then proceed from Vienna to Budapest. In Budapest we would go east through the Ukraine and I would continue on north alone to Lithuania. I felt very comfortable with this decision and hoped that by traveling this route we would avoid the checkpoints set up by the Soviet military police for the ex-prisoners of war and survivors of the camps. However, the episode of beating up the Soviet officer-physician made me afraid. Eventually the Russian military police would be looking for us. I kept looking over my shoulder.

There was no problem obtaining food. There were many Soviet military trains along the way, often stationary, each containing a kitchen. The chefs in the kitchens of the military trains were extremely generous with their food, especially due to the fact that Vanya, Ivan and I spoke Russian.

The bathroom facilities were also not a problem because the train was more stationary than actually moving. If the train started moving, it moved so slowly that you could always catch up. After spending a few days on the train, we regained confidence in ourselves and in our plans.

At one station on our journey we were told that this was the last stop. The man in charge of the station advised us that other trains would be passing through and that it would not be a problem for us to catch a train to Vienna.

We spent a few days at this railroad station until finally a passenger train arrived. The train was packed. Many people were already traveling on the roof of the train. There was still some space available on the roof of the train and we decided we would take it to Vienna. Between each railroad car, there was a built-in ladder to climb onto the roof. We found a space for the three of us. We also received a gift of some blankets from the Russian kitchen chefs. They were very generous to us. The blankets we received were our only possessions apart from the clothes we were wearing.

That is how we became 'train roof dwellers'. The roof was flat and the speed of the train was such that there was no danger of us falling off. It was traveling very slowly with frequent stops. The three of us stayed together. When the train stopped, two of us went to get food and the third one stayed behind to protect our roof space. At each stop new people boarded. The roof dwellers looked out for each other. When a tunnel was approaching, those in the first car would warn the people in the next car that a tunnel was coming. At that point, all of us would lie down either on our bellies or our backs and hope that the tunnel would not be too long. Every train had coal locomotives and, after passing through a tunnel, very often we looked like chimney sweeps. Fortunately, we had several blankets that protected us from the smoke.

The train we were on was in contrast to the transportation which the Germans had used to bring us to Germany. At least we were free and benefited from our freedom even if we were train roof dwellers. At night, I thought about my mother and my brother and wondered if my father had found them. The insecurity and uncertainty of my future was a heavy burden on me.

The only problem we had as train roof dwellers was rainy days. Fortunately, we had blankets that absorbed some of the water, sometimes efficiently and sometimes not efficiently. Again, that was the price of our freedom.

I lost track of time. I did not know how many days we lived on the roof, how many days we had traveled. All I knew was that with every day, every mile, the train took us closer to hopefully seeing my parents and brother again.

We arrived in Vienna and found another train to Budapest. It was already completely packed. Again we found a place on the roof of the train. The train was very slow, but, fortunately, we had acquired sufficient food for the trip.

Finally, we arrived in Budapest. We went to the main railroad station to get oriented and to find out which was the platform for the trains traveling to the Ukraine and on to Lithuania.

Suddenly, I saw a group of people walking and I recognized Dr Simon Dolnitzky, who had worked with my father in the ghetto. I knew him and his family very well. With him were his wife and their little boy. I stopped him. It took a few minutes for him to recognize me. He put his arms around me and told me how happy he was to see me.

Dr Dolnitzky, his wife, Sarah and their five-year-old-son, Alik, had decided to leave Lithuania and were on the way to Palestine. They hugged me and felt badly for not having recognized me right away.

They told me they had some good news. They had seen my mother about a week ago. She had been liberated at Stutthof and had returned to Vilnius to wait for my father and me. He told me that my brother had perished in Stutthof and that my father had not yet arrived in Vilnius. They also told me transportation in Eastern Europe was treacherous and unreliable. Immediately, they advised me not to return to Lithuania.

Dr Dolnitzky told me that in Budapest there was a Jewish community which had organized living facilities for the *Bricha* in the Jewish Community Center. *Bricha* in Hebrew meant 'escape'. It was the underground movement for people to leave Eastern Europe and travel to Western Europe and eventually to Palestine. He wanted me to join them. I explained that I was not alone and was traveling with two good friends who were Ukrainians. He told me not to worry: that he would arrange for them to join us in the Jewish hostel.

After a short conference with Vanya and Ivan, we decided we would follow Dr Dolnitzky's advice. He also talked to them and reassured them. We would spend a day or two in Budapest to get oriented and then make future plans. It was not easy after liberation: dilemmas, decisions – all on my own.

The Jewish Agency had arranged for a truck to come to the railroad station and take us to the Jewish Center.

It was a large multi-story building. Here we received sleeping accommodation as well as food provided by the Jewish Agency. I felt comfortable having with me Dr Dolnitzky and his wife Sarah because they were close friends of my parents. I felt that with their help I could do something for Vanya and Ivan, who had done so much for me.

The week that I spent in Budapest changed my life completely. Dr Dolnitzky kept trying to convince me not to return to Lithuania. My father had done many things for his family during the difficult ghetto years. Dr Dolnitzky told me that if he could convince me not to return to Lithuania, it would repay part of the moral debt that he owed to my family.

I was greatly relieved to learn that my mother was alive and that she lived in a small apartment in Vilnius. I was saddened about my little brother. I could not get him out of my mind and I was worried about how he died.

Budapest had not been damaged too much by the war. Life was gradually returning to normal. Food was easily available at the Jewish community. For the first time, I received a small amount of money which was given to every survivor for their daily necessities. One day, as I walked down the street, I noticed a photographic store and went inside. I paid the small charge and left the store with a picture of myself. That was actually the first picture taken of me since I had gained my freedom two months earlier: in fact, the first picture of me for more than four years.

I was continuously looking over my shoulder. Budapest was filled with Soviet military police and I had the undying fear that they knew of our escape and were looking for me.

One day I noticed a young man following me. A few minutes later I noticed that he was walking next to me. He asked me, 'Amcho?' (member of the tribe). I answered, 'Amcho' (Yes, I am a Jew). He told me he was from Vilnius and had stayed some time in Romania, and with the help of the *Bricha* was now going to continue his trip from Budapest to Italy and finally to Palestine. I looked at him. He had a slight beard with a nice face. I did not know if I could trust him. I

16. Photograph of Jack, taken a few months after liberation from Dachau, Budapest, 1945.

was paranoid and felt that everyone was chasing me. I tried to figure out how I could verify that what he was telling me was the truth. I decided that if he was from Vilnius, he must speak Hebrew. I asked him if he spoke Hebrew. 'Certainly', he said. The conversation shifted to Hebrew. I walked faster, hoping to lose him, but he kept up with me. Finally, he figured out a way to gain my confidence and said, 'I'm traveling with some people from Kaunas, maybe you know them.' It was a very ingenious way for him to inspire confidence, provided I knew the people. He named a man, Jonna Rochman, whom I knew very well from our stay in the ghetto. I thought to myself, Jonna Rochman would not work for the KGB. I knew him well enough to know his political affiliation. I told the man, 'Yes, I am from Kaunas and I know Jonna. If you can put me in touch with him so that I could have a conversation, I would feel more comfortable talking to you.'

We made arrangements to meet the next day. He would be

standing at a specific place waiting for me with Jonna. Discretely, from far away, I evaluated the situation and noted that it was Jonna who was with him. It convinced me that he was telling the truth. Jonna and I embraced. We both had tears in our eyes. We had not seen each other for over a year. The young man now introduced himself as Zev Gdud, later known as William Z. Good. We walked for a long time. I tried to get all the information about his life.

The *Bricha* was a logical and well-organized plan to help the East and West European Jews to reach Italy, and from there sail to Palestine. This was what Simon Dolnitzky was trying to tell me before. Sometimes it takes two people from two different sources to get a clearer picture of the situation.

One afternoon Vanya, Ivan and I became bolder and decided to see a movie. None of us had seen a movie for years. On the billboard of the movie theater there were two familiar faces: Laurel and Hardy. So we decided to indulge ourselves. One of Vanya's acquaintances explained to him how to enter the movie theater without paying. We were to go through the back door and then enter the movie from the rear of the theater. We followed the instructions that Vanya's acquaintance had given him. Within a short time we were sitting in the movie theater watching our first movie. In my case, it was the first movie I had seen in four years. Suddenly the lights went on and it was announced that the military police were at the door and would be checking everyone's papers. They were looking for Soviet citizens who avoided the re-indoctrination camps.

As soon as we assessed the situation, the three of us walked calmly to the rear of the theater. There was a door behind the screen that led us to the outside, the same way we had entered. Within minutes we were on the street wondering what would have happened to us if we had entered the theater the regular way, paying for a ticket and not knowing how to leave without passing the control of the military police. All my survival instincts re-emerged and again I looked over my shoulder, always thinking that somebody was going to follow us and arrest us.

Vanya and Ivan decided to leave Budapest the next morning on a train to the Ukraine. They asked me if I would like to go as far as the Ukraine with them and then continue on to Lithuania on my own. It was a big decision. My greatest insecurity was being on my own from the Ukraine to Lithuania. I was being continually indoctrinated by Dr Dolnitzky not to return. He told me repeatedly that it was my mother's wish that I should not return, but stay in the West. She had to stay in Lithuania pending my father's arrival and she was still hopeful that my brother would be alive somewhere and return to Lithuania. Also having met Zev Gdud and Jonna, I felt my only choice would be to go to Italy with the *Bricha*.

While I was still in Dachau, after our liberation, my father had reiterated to me that in 1930 he took out an educational insurance policy of $2,000 in Italy with Assicurazione Generali of Trieste. He believed that it was a very large insurance company, very reliable and trustworthy. He told me that all the premiums had been paid, in dollars, until the outbreak of the war, and that Generali did not require premiums to be paid during wartime. The policy would mature at the end of 1945. This was another important factor in my decision to join the *Bricha* and go to Italy. It would give me the financial security to pursue my educational goal.

The next morning I saw Zev Gdud and Dr Dolnitzky and told them that I had changed my mind and would not be returning to Lithuania; I would continue with the *Bricha* to Italy.

I saw Ivan and Vanya and explained my decision to them. They understood and were very happy. They felt it would be suicide for me to continue on my own from the Ukraine to Lithuania, especially after our experience in the Soviet rehabilitation center in Germany. We all felt that the Soviet military police still might know enough and would still be looking for us.

Dr Dolnitzky and his wife were ecstatic. They felt they had fulfilled their mission and my mother's wish. Vanya, Ivan and I hugged, and with tears in our eyes we said goodbye, wishing each other the best and hoping to get together sometime. Not having an address to exchange, I never saw them again. Very often I think about the two friends to whom I became so close, who helped me on my journey to freedom.

A few days later, I was advised by the *Bricha's* leaders that the next transport would be leaving Budapest in the morning on a train to Austria. Dr Dolnitzky's entire family, his wife, Sarah, and his son, Alec, age four, as well as Zev Gdud and his group, were on the same train. We received documents from the *Bricha* stating that we were refugees from Greece on the way home to Greece. We all spoke Hebrew. The only problem would be if we met real Greek people, who would argue that Hebrew is not Greek! Fortunately, we did not meet any Greek travelers. We avoided any confrontations.

We arrived in the town of Villach, Austria, which was at the border in the mountains. We had to cross this border on foot in order to leave the Soviet Zone of occupied Austria for Italy. The border was heavily guarded by Soviet soldiers. I wondered if we would really succeed since we had with us both elderly people and some children.

We slept in Villach in a hostel. Early in the morning we were guided across the border through the mountains. Our guides were twin brothers, Julius and Ignacy Marek. We were told that a few days earlier a whole group had been guided through and had had no problems. We knew that thousands of refugees had crossed the mountains that were heavily guarded by the Soviet Army. I tried to find out what the key to success was. None of the group carried valises. Our possessions were few and the backpack that I received from the *Bricha* more than accommodated my belongings. The only new acquisition that I received in Budapest was my newly acquired photograph of myself and a blanket, which I substituted for the old blanket that I used on the train on the way to Budapest. We were told the blanket was our security in case we should be detained at the crossing and had to spend the night in the mountains, which got cold even in summertime.

The Marek brothers were very intelligent, energetic and

knowledgeable in their job of guiding people through the mountains. They tried to dispel our fears, explaining to us the secret of their previous successes. Hopefully this crossing would be a success too. Every soldier guarding the frontier was bribed. The bribe was a watch. For every person who crossed the border, each soldier received a watch. Occasionally, they received more than this, but a watch was the usual payment for the crossing. Unfortunately, I did not have a watch. Marek reassured me that the *Bricha* would provide a watch for each soldier to pay for my crossing.

In spite of the reassurance that we received from the Marek brothers, I was apprehensive. Every step I took in the treacherous crossing, I expected that a Soviet soldier was hiding behind each large rock or tree and that at the appropriate moment he would jump out. We were cautioned to be silent, but how could we be silent when we had little children with us? The weather, which is usually unpredictable in the mountains, was very favorable. By the end of the day, as the sun began to hide behind the mountains, we were told we were in Italy. Again, we spent the night in a hostel. The crossing, the accommodation, and every detail had been arranged in an incredible way. I often thought about my father and mother and wondered if my father had reached Vilnius. I still hoped that my brother had survived and was reunited with my mother. I knew this was wishful thinking, but it is easier to live your life by thinking wishful thoughts.

Early in the morning, two trucks that belonged to the British Army and were a part of the Palestinian Jewish Brigade – Jewish soldiers of the British Army – arrived. It was wonderful to see the young Jewish soldiers who came to pick us up. In an hour or two, we were in Tarvisio. We were taken to a mountain lodge where we were greeted by big banners: 'Welcome Survivors'.

For the first time in the two months since my liberation, I felt wanted. Nobody questioned my right to survive, or was disappointed that I did survive. It was like arriving at a celebration ball. This lodge was run by Jewish soldiers, who were exuberant in their feelings for our survival and wanted to do everything they could make us feel welcome. The food that the Jewish Brigade prepared for us was superb. It was a transit stop where most of the refugees stayed for a day or two and were then transported by the same trucks to southern Italy. After looking at me – I must have been one of the first Dachau survivors who had arrived there – they decided to extend my stay for ten to fourteen days so that I could benefit from the food and build up my strength.

Tarvisio was a beautiful place. We had a lot of free time for walks in the mountains. It gave Zev Gdud and me time together to learn about each other. I learned from Zev Gdud how he had been taken to the death pits at Ponar, outside Vilnius and shot at on 13 July 1941. He fell into the mass grave prepared for the victims, a split second before a bullet would have hit him. He lay there amongst the dead and the wounded. During the night he escaped. After his escape he spent three years hiding in the forest, finding assistance from different Lithuanian farmers. Unbelievably, he found his father in the forest and together they both survived. Unfortunately, his mother and a younger brother were killed at Ponar.

In my discussions with Zev Gdud, we decided that our future was in medicine. We would stay in Italy and enroll in the Faculty of Medicine. It truly was a dream, and I guess it was because of the low concentration of oxygen in the high mountains that it was easier to dream the impossible: applying to the university without having any papers, without knowing the language, without any financial backing, and graduating with a degree in medicine in this new country. The ten days that we spent together in Tarvisio were the foundation of a close friendship between Zev Gdud and me that has continued until the present time.

The days passed quickly, and finally the day arrived when we were taken by truck to Milan and Rome. Zev Gdud and I decided to proceed with our plans. We each would work on them and continue to keep in touch with each another. I was to go to Milan and Zev Gdud to Rome, to explore the possibilities of enrolling in medical school in the different cities.

I was dropped in Milan at the Jewish Community Center at Via Unione No. 5. It was used by the Jewish community as a hostel for the *Bricha*, as well as for Italian Jews returning either from the partisans or from the different internment camps. I stayed at Via Unione about ten days. It was located in the center of Milan and gave me a wonderful opportunity to explore the city.

The first step in our plan was to find a temporary residence while pursuing the feasibility of entering medical school. My stay at the Jewish Community Center offered me exposure to many different people. I met several Italian Jews who had previously been students and who told me the requirements for entering an Italian university. Ten days after my arrival in Milan, a Jewish Brigade soldier, Abraham, arrived looking for a refugee willing and able to teach Hebrew to children from five to fifteen years of age at an orphanage located in Turin. After speaking with him for fifteen minutes, I convinced him of my fluency in Hebrew and my eagerness to teach for at least several months.

The next day Abraham picked me up and we drove in his jeep to Turin. He had an apartment at Via Morosini 19 and offered to share the apartment with me. Just across the street was the Jewish orphanage. For teaching at the orphanage each day, he offered me ten dollars a month and food that was provided by the orphanage. I felt delighted that my first goal had been achieved – temporary residence including food and ten dollars a month for my efforts.

Abraham was an understanding and compassionate man who made every effort to make me very comfortable. Periodically, he would take me to the British soldiers' club. At that time, the only clothing I had was a British army uniform without an insignia. It was easy for him to take me there.

Next, I had to learn Italian. I browsed in a small used-book store and found a few books that enabled me to learn Italian. The books had been prepared for German soldiers during their occupation of Italy. My main methods of learning Italian were by reading a daily newspaper, meeting people and going periodically to movies. I also relied on the children to whom I was teaching Hebrew to teach me Italian. It was a symbiosis beneficial to both.

Following liberation, my mother had been hospitalized at a Red Army hospital with a broken ankle. On her return to Lithuania, most of the Jewish survivors were living in the city of Vilnius. My mother moved into a small, fourth-floor apartment – without an elevator. This was a hardship for her after her recent injury.

Only a few survivors appeared in the city. They confirmed that the Lithuanian Jewish community had been destroyed and that almost no survivors were left.

It took my father several months to return from Dachau to Vilnius, where he joined my mother. There, they learned that my brother had been killed at Stutthof.

A few months after settling in Vilnius they received a larger apartment and asked Irena Veisaite to join them. Irena's parents, Isidor and his wife, Sonya, were old friends of my father. In the first days of the war, Irena's mother was brutally killed at the Fourth Fort. Several forts had been constructed around Kaunas by the Tsarist Government for defense during thr First World War against the Germans. In 1941 the Lithuanian Government used these forts for prison facilities and killing grounds. Her father was living outside Soviet Lithuania when the war started. He survived the war and later moved to the United States. My parents were delighted to have Irena live with them. It made the post-war survival easier for all of them. It was a beautiful arrangement; everybody needed the spiritual uplifting that occurs by forming a new family. Thus, Irena became my sister.

7 Admission to Medical School

The new academic year of 1945/46 was approaching. I spoke with different people from the Italian Jewish community and many of them advised me to see Professor Giuseppe Levi, professor of anatomy. He was an internationally renowned scholar and humanitarian, and was well liked in the Italian Jewish community of Turin.

I did not call for an appointment, but went straight to Professor Levi's office, which was on the second floor of the Institute for Anatomy at the university. As soon as I entered his office, I felt his paternal smile and welcome. He gave me the confidence that I needed. He was very interested in finding out about my life, my family and the circumstances that had brought me to Turin. I knew enough Italian to explain my predicament.

After we had spoken for two hours Professor Levi asked me what he could do for me. I told him of my desire to enter medical school and asked him many questions about the requirements. He was silent for a few minutes and then he said, 'To tell you the truth, I don't know the answer to any of your questions. However, Professor Mario Allara is the Dean of the Medical School and he is a very good friend of mine and I will call him and introduce you to him. It might be prudent for you to visit him and ask him these same questions.

I thanked Professor Levi for his compassion and wanting to help me and left his office. I did not yet fully appreciate how much he was doing for me by introducing me to Professor Allara and by restoring my self-confidence.

A week later, I went to see Professor Allara. Again I was received with open arms. Professor Allara knew everything about me. I was sure he had obtained the information from Professor Levi, who had kept his word and introduced my dilemma to Professor Allara, who was very much to the point. 'The academic rules in Italy are very simple,' he said. 'Everybody can go to a lecture at any university in any field and this applies also to medical school. Unless you are a student and unless you have passed all the exams, you cannot graduate with a degree. However, due to special circumstances – and hopefully you will obtain your high school documents to enter medical school – I will arrange for you to become a conditional student. What is a conditional student? A conditional student is a student who participates in all the lectures and also takes all the exams.'

This status would be applied to me for a year or two, and by that time I should have obtained all the required documents. As soon as the documents were obtained and verified by the Ministry of Education in Rome, they would provide a clearance for me to enter medical school, and all the exams and colloquiums would become official records and would be entered into the log of my education.

I spent about a half an hour with Professor Allara. When I left his office, I felt that I was walking on air. I had obtained

17. Irena Veisaite with Dr Moses and Basia Brauns, Vilnius, 1948.

two of my first goals and succeeded in establishing my status as a conditional student, a status which gave me some time to get my documents.

In early September, as soon as the doors opened in the different lecture halls, I was to be a student there. A big problem was the cost of buying the books that would enable me to follow the classes. I visited different book stores and found used books for my first year of medical school. It took me very little time to adjust to being a student. My Italian improved every week and I felt very comfortable mingling with the Italian students.

One day, when Abraham returned from his base in Milan, he mentioned that he had two important things to talk to me about.

The first was that his commanding officer, Captain Joseph Zarchin, had asked about me, and asked Abraham if we could make an appointment on Saturday to visit him in Milan. He was very eager to see me.

The second thing that Abraham told me was that it was decided eventually to move the orphanage to a different location. As long as the orphanage stayed in the same house, I would be teaching. He did not know, however, how he could provide financial support for me after the orphanage was moved with its students to a different location.

Not knowing exactly where I would be living, I went to the post office and rented a post office box. Finally, I received a letter from the Jewish community office in Vilnius: a reply to my request for my parents' address. I started corresponding regularly with my parents. My father had returned to Vilnius and together with my mother rented an apartment. Unfortunately, he confirmed that my brother had perished in the concentration camp at Stutthof.

My father mentioned to me in a letter that he had found the metal box where he had put all our documents – his diplomas and educational documents, my mother's documents, my educational documents – and they were all there. He advised me that he had found the policy with Assicurazione

Generali of Trieste (it was policy No. 332) and that the money would be available, according to the policy contract, in October 1945. He also advised me that he had entrusted an officer of the Polish Anders Army to deliver my high school diploma to England. I was very excited about it.

The academic year 1945/46 ended. I had completed all the examinations and I was still a conditional student. In the first week of July I found in my post office box a registered letter from London. It had been posted by a friend of my father, a Polish officer, who took my high school diploma to London and sent it to me from there. This dramatically improved my mood. That evening I telephoned my friend, Zev Gdud, who was then in Rome, and shared the good news with him. He told me that some months earlier the Lithuanian Embassy at the Vatican had arranged the translation and authentication of his high school documents. Afterwards, the embassy delivered them to the Ministry of Education in Rome.

The following week, I was on my way to Rome. I stayed with Zev Gdud for a few days and I visited the Lithuanian Embassy at the Vatican. Stasys Lozaraitis was the ambassador. He represented the pre-war Lithuanian government. Before the war Lozaraitis was the Foreign Minister of Lithuania. I made an appointment with him and he saw me immediately. He remembered my father well. Interestingly, in 1939 he had made the arrangements for my father to fly from the resort where we had been staying on vacation in Palanga to Kaunas for a consultation. President Smetona had fallen ill and an infectious disease was suspected.

Ambassador Lozaraitis was upset, and I could see the pain and tears on his face when he spoke about the fate of the Jewish people in Lithuania. He also told me that he had earlier met Avraham Tory, the former secretary of the Jewish Council in Kovno, who had survived the war and made his way to Palestine. It was from Tory that Lozaraitis had learned for the first time the details of the fate of the Lithuanian Jews.

I discussed with Lozaraitis the purpose of my visit. He reviewed my documents and he told me he would be more than happy to take care of things. The documents would be translated into Italian, authenticated and submitted to the Ministry of Education. Mr Macevicius was in charge of this function. Ambassador Lozaraitis introduced me to him, and I left my documents at the embassy.

I spent a few more days with Zev Gdud in Rome. We were both very concerned for our economic security for the next five years, in order to be able to complete our medical studies. Zev Gdud had met an Italian engineering student, Luciano Coen, who felt that if we wanted to negotiate with any organization, we had to be somebody. He advised us to form a Jewish student organization and to speak on behalf of the organization, even if the organization had only a few members. Zev Gdud put an announcement in the Jewish refugee newspaper in Rome, in Hebrew and Italian: 'Jewish student organization in Italy has been established. If interested in continuing your education, contact the secretary, Zev Gdud.'

At that time the American Jewish Joint Distribution Committee (known as the Joint) was granting a ten-dollar a month scholarship for living expenses for students who were enrolled at the university. Medical students were excluded from the ten-dollar scholarship, due to the fact that most of the refugees would go to Palestine, and there were already too many physicians there. Many of the physicians already there were doing manual labor in the kibbutzim.

One Saturday Abraham and I drove in his jeep to meet Joseph Zarchin in Milan. Zarchin was then a captain in the Jewish Brigade. It was an emotional encounter. Zarchin had first appeared in my life when I was about fifteen years old. He was my Boy Scout leader in Kaunas. I was enrolled in the Jewish Boy Scouts, a division of the Lithuanian Boy Scouts. We had weekly meetings. Many of my classmates were Boy Scouts. The most exciting thing that I remember was our summer camp. There were only Jewish Boy Scouts there, and Joseph Zarchin was our Boy Scoutmaster. On Saturday afternoon we met Joseph and went out to dinner together. Seeing him gave me a lot of excitement and pleasure.

In 1939, Zarchin had been accepted as an archaeological student at the Hebrew University of Jerusalem. Lithuania was not then at war with Germany and he received all his transit papers and went by train from Lithuania through Germany to Italy. In Venice he embarked on a ship for Palestine. When the Jewish Brigade was formed, he enrolled in it and, having been a lieutenant in the Lithuanian Army, was promoted captain in the British Army.

Zarchin was eager to learn about the fate of his family in Lithuania. We both reminisced about our Boy Scout days and camping experiences together. I was sorry to give him the bad news that most of his family in Lithuania – they were well known textile merchants – had perished. He was eager to learn about me, my fate and my future plans.

I felt the time had come to change my economic status. I had been living on ten dollars a month, and the cost of tuition, laboratory fees and books made for a disastrous situation. The books and my supplies for medical school had to come from the funds for my food. This presented a very difficult situation for me after having lived for four years in different camps.

I discussed with him a problem that was on my mind. My uncle Heinz, my father's brother, lived in Johannesburg. My father had said to me, in Dachau: 'Count on him.' One day a chaplain from the South African Army unit, who had been looking for me, located me in Turin. The chaplain invited me to dinner and told me that it was my uncle's desire, as well as an obligation to his older brother, my father, to help me to pursue my medical studies.

There were problems in accomplishing this. In South Africa, there was a ban on sending money abroad and the total amount of money that a South African could send was ten pounds maximum, and only to countries that were in the British Commonwealth. Italy was not in the British Commonwealth. I had to figure out how I could overcome this obstacle: how would I get ten pounds monthly to help my education? Zarchin thought a little about my dilemma and said, 'Jascha, I think I have a solution. It will take me a couple

צו אלע יידישע סטודענטן אין איטאליע

מיר טיילן מיט אלע יידישע סטו=
דענטן אין איטאליע, וועלכע זעצן
פאָר זייער שטודיום אויפן וועג קיין
ארץ=ישראל, אז ס'איז אָרגאניזירט
געוואָרן א יידישער סטודענטן=פאר=
באנד „אגודת הסטודנטים העברים
באיטליה", וועמענס ציִלן עס זיינען:
פארייניקן אלע יידישע סטודענטן אין
איטאליע, זיי פארטרעטן אין די ציוו=
ניסטישע און אנדערע מוסדות, האלטן
א שטענדיק קאָנטאקט מיט דער
„התאחדות עולמית של הסטודנטים
העברים" אוי דער ארץ=ישראלדיקער
סטודענטשאפט;

דער אדרעס פון דער מזכירות
פון פארבאנד איז:

Roma, Via Cairoli 31, int. 8
צו דעם מזכיר Gdud Sew

שריפטלעך ביטע מיטיילן דעם
נאָמען און פאמיליע=נאָמען, וואָס און
אין וועלכן אוניווערסיטעט מען שטו=
דירט און פינקטלעכן אדרעס.

אגודת הסטודנטים העברים
באיטליה

18. Advertisement in the Jewish newspaper in Rome regarding the formation of a Jewish Student Organization and enrollment procedures, 1945 (courtesy Dr William Z. Good).

of weeks, but I will have an answer for you if I can arrange it.' He did not discuss with me how the problem would be solved, but I had confidence in him. I hoped that my financial problem would finally be solved.

Avraham and I returned to Turin late at night. Abraham, knowing that my job at the orphanage might end, tried to cheer me up and encouraged me. I greatly appreciated Avraham and his concern for me.

About two weeks later, Joseph Zarchin came to Turin and he was very excited. He said, 'You know, Jascha, I think I have solved your problem.' He then explained the arrangement to me.

In Turin there was a well-known Jewish industrialist, Mr Leonello Segre, who was the owner of a large pharmaceutical company. His sister was living in Israel, and was good friends with the Zarchins. Joseph arranged for my uncle Heinz to send the ten pounds to Segre's sister in Tel Aviv. Segre would then give me every month the ten pounds in Italian liras. It was a good plan and he hoped within a month or so that I would be getting my first money from Mr Segre. He introduced me to Mr Segre. It was a great pleasure meeting him.

He was a wonderful person, much involved in Jewish life. In fact, he offered all his land to be used by the *Bricha* to house the refugees prior to their departure to Palestine.

I became a monthly visitor to his house and I was often invited for dinner with his family. My uncle would finally be able to send me ten pounds every month. That definitely tilted the scales in my favor. I became more independent and I could enjoy a student's life better without always having to skimp on food to pay my expenses for books and laboratories.

It was very interesting that ten pounds a month made my student years extremely comfortable. I am grateful to my uncle Heinz and to Joseph who had the idea to transfer the money regularly into my hands through the Segre family.

The security that Joseph had arranged for me and the closure of the orphanage prompted me to look for a room. Avraham and I had to move. Work in the orphanage came to an end at the same time the house we lived in was to be renovated.

I was fortunate enough to find a room at Via Pinelli 45. The Carlino family was well known. The owner of the apartment, General Carlino, was a general in the Italian Army. The Carlinos had a twelve-year-old son, and due to the economic situation in Italy, they were happy to rent the room and provide some food for ten dollars a month. The general's wife, Antoinette, was extremely wise and concerned for my well-being. She tried to do whatever she could to help make my life easier. I finally had a room with a desk, and a light on the desk so I could study late at night. I found the Carlinos, like every other Italian family I met, to be gentle and understanding. It was a considerable walk from their house to the university but it always invigorated me. Only in bad weather did I take the streetcar.

Very often I corresponded by mail with Zev Gdud and compared notes. Our economic security was still shaky. Would the International Refugee Organization (IRO), which had provided a small sum each month – not enough for our studies – suddenly stop the payments, and would we be able to finish our studies? In spite of my insecurities and apprehension, I was happy and the time passed quickly.

It was late spring when I received a letter from Zev Gdud telling me that he had just met another student from Lithuania, Paul Geleris, who was on his way to Turin with some interesting ideas for our financial security. I was anxious to meet Paul Geleris.

A few days later, Paul Geleris arrived at the railroad station and I was waiting there for him. I had discussed his visit with my landlady, Mrs Carlino, who graciously said she would let my good friend from Lithuania stay with me in the same room for a week or two. So I brought Paul Geleris to my rented room.

Paul was a fascinating person with unbelievable energy. Before the war, he had been admitted to medical school in Kaunas, and had finished two years, but his studies were interrupted by the war. He was determined to continue medical school and to finish his education in Italy. Paul had all his documents and his transcript from the medical school in Kaunas. He had carried these from Lithuania in the soles of his boots. When he was in Rome, he had applied to medical school there. However, the registrar in the office advised him to apply to any medical school but Rome, as Rome was already overcrowded and he would have difficulty in being accepted at the University of Rome. At Zev Gdud's recommendation he decided to apply to the University of Turin.

Economically, Paul Geleris was in the same situation as Zev Gdud and I. We had to work out how to assure our financial security. We spent some time together discussing all our options and the possibilities of surviving the next five years in order to complete our studies. Prior to undertaking the trip to Turin, Paul, on Zev Gdud's advice, met Mr Macevicius at the Lithuanian Embassy at the Vatican and – as I had done earlier – gave him his documents to be processed.

The day after Paul Geleris' arrival, we went together to the Registrar of the University of Turin Medical School and I introduced him to Miss Jona, the secretary to the Registrar. We told her that the Geleris documents were already at the Ministry of Education in Rome.

It was summertime and Paul Geleris and I went to the Italian student hostel. Commendatore de Benedetto was the director-manager of the student hostel in Turin, which was designed for Italian students. We tried to see if we could enroll in the Italian student hostel. He was extremely hospitable and understanding of our problems and our desires, but explained that according to the by-laws of the student hostel, no foreign students could be admitted. It was designed during the war for students who were mainly officers in the Italian Army. He arranged, however, for Paul Geleris to stay there during the summertime as there were only a few students during the summer. It was Paul's intention not only to find a place to live, but to learn the functional structure of a student hostel.

At the student hostel, Paul met Dr Ivo Mattuci, the Administrative Director of the University, who later played a very important part in helping foreign students to be transferred to the University of Turin from other universities.

Before the beginning of the next academic year, Paul Geleris returned to Rome and, together with Zev Gdud and a Jewish-Italian engineering student, Luciano Coen, formed a strategic plan. They went to the headquarters of the Joint in Rome for a meeting. Paul was a very well-organized person, and an excellent and persuasive speaker. I can only say if not for Paul, we would not have a Jewish student hostel.

They were introduced to Dr Gelbart, from Omaha, Nebraska, who was the Director of the Joint in Italy. After several meetings, they were able to interest Dr Gelbart in the idea of having a student hostel exclusively for student Holocaust survivors.

I was assigned the task of finding suitable housing for fifty students to be located not far from the University of Turin. One of my classmates, Cesare Reyneri, and his brother, Paolo Reyneri, were close friends of the son of Count Raimondo Balbo Bertone di Sanbuy, whose father was a former Mayor of Turin. The family owned an abandoned villa situated on the hill overlooking the river Po and within walking distance of the university. Raimondo's family was very compassionate and interested in helping the students who were survivors of the Holocaust to study. He agreed to lease the villa.

Dr Gelbart traveled by train to Turin to inspect the location, as well as to sign the contract leasing the villa. Prior to his arrival we met with Raimondo Balbo Bertone di Sanbuy and explained to him our vital interest in spending at least another five years in Turin, and asked him for compassion in signing a lease with the Joint for not less than five years. When Dr Gelbart arrived, Raimondo told Dr Gelbart that he would not lease the villa for less than five years. After negotiations, however, the contract was signed leasing the villa for four years.

The Casa dello Studente for student survivors of the Holocaust was established at Corso Moncalieri 167. It would house students studying medicine, engineering, chemistry, architecture, music, law, pharmacy and political science.

An administrator, Mr Lesman, was hired. He stayed with us for two years (Mr Kapize took his place until the closure of Casa dello Studente). The administrator of Casa dello Studente hired a cook, Mrs Rimer, and a groundsman who maintained the gardens of the estate.

Mrs Rimer was originally from Lithuania and was knowledgeable in East European cooking. She often surprised us often with specialties that we had learned to appreciate in pre-war times with our families. I will never forget her cholent. This is a traditional, East European Jewish dish prepared and put in the stove on Friday to be eaten on Saturday, thus avoiding the task of cooking on Saturday.

Casa dello Studente became our new family for the duration of our studies and helped us in the transition into society as free men and women. It helped us to enter a free society with all its challenges and benefits.

The students maintained a good grade average and were greatly respected in the university circles.

We shared all the household responsibilities. We were

responsible for the maintenance of our rooms. We made a schedule and shared the responsibility of serving at table in the dining room. In the evening, when the doors were locked, we were available to unlock the doors for late arrivals.

The dining room was used for our meals as well as for the gatherings that we periodically had with our Italian colleagues from the university. We invited several professors from different academic disciplines who gave lectures at Casa dello Studente, and we invited our student colleagues to join us.

Eventually fifty students were enrolled. All of them finished their studies.

The most beautiful thing was that we became a family. We lived like one family, with all its pleasures and frustrations. We celebrated all our scholastic achievements and birthdays together and sympathized with one another about our problems. Life in Casa dello Studente was exciting. We organized excursions together on our holidays. We had several acres of land where we made a volleyball court. Some of the vegetables we ate had been grown by us. We had on goal in common: to prepare ourselves through education for a constructive life. Our benefits were a roof over our heads as well as food on the table for the duration of our studies, and the most significant achievement was the security that we would be able to finish our studies.

In 1950 the Casa dello Studente was closed. The students went on to become professionals in their respective fields. Today they live in many countries, mostly in the United States, Australia, Switzerland, and Israel. Some became researchers and inventors, all prominent in their own fields.

The day started like any other day, but it was an important day – it was the day I met Cesare. After having attended the lecture on anatomy by Professor Levi, on my way out of the Anatomy Institute, I met a student in my class. We introduced ourselves. I learned that his name was Cesare Reyneri. We walked slowly and talked and tried to learn about each other.

19. The students of Casa dello Studente, Turin, 1946.

After we reached Via Roma in the center of the city, we sat down in a coffee house to continue our conversation. The meeting with Cesare Reyneri – our conversation as well as the time spent together in the coffee house – changed my life. After having spent several hours in the coffee house and learning about one another's philosophies of life, studies, and so on, Cesare asked me if I would like to study with him in the evenings to prepare for our upcoming exams. It was not only a lucky break for me, but it also started a lifelong friendship that we both enjoy to this day.

Cesare's parents, Antonio and Ada Reyneri, had four sons: Giorgio, Paolo, Cesare and Marco.

Cesare's and Paolo were actually raised by Ada Reyneri's sister, Olga Teppati, and her husband, Dr Ferdinando Teppati. Because Olga and Ferdinando did not have children, Ada Reyneri arranged for two of her sons to live with the Teppati family and to be raised by her sister. The Reyneri family and the Teppati family did not live far from each other.

Almost every day I visited Cesare at Via Re Umberto 8. There was always pastry and coffee available to make our studies more pleasant. Frequently, I was invited by Dr and Mrs Teppati to join them for dinner. Cesare's brother, Paolo, was also in medical school, two years ahead of us.

The two brothers often went on ski or bicycle vacations. They never left on vacation without inviting me to join them. There was always a pair of skis or a bicycle available for me. Every time we went on a trip, there was always a picnic prepared to take along, and I was included. In other words, I was adopted by the Reyneri and the Teppati families.

My new relationship did not alleviate my longing to see my father and mother, but it made my life much easier to live. We also had some tutoring help. One of the toughest exams in the first year of medical school was the examination given by Professor Durio in chemistry. Mrs Reyneri, who had a doctorate in chemistry, tutored Cesare and me in preparation for the chemistry examination. I was pleasantly surprised at how easily I passed the toughest exam of the year.

I finally felt comfortable with my life. It was the first time since my liberation that I felt surrounded by a family who radiated such love and compassion for me. I had received help indirectly or directly from the Reyneri and Teppati families, as well as from other Italians who played such an important part in my life, like Professor Levi and Professor Allara.

It was October 1945. I felt that my knowledge of Italian had markedly improved and I decided to take a trip to Rome to visit Assicurazione Generali of Trieste, which had an office in Rome. I brought with me a note from my father advising me that the educational policy number was 332. He did not feel comfortable in mailing the policy to me at that time.

The Italian railroad had special tickets that were free of charge for refugees: still being a refugee, I qualified. I received a free ticket and embarked on my trip to Rome. It was very easy to find Piazza Venezia. It was the same piazza with the balcony Mussolini used for all his speeches. Across from the balcony was a big building that housed Generali. I went there and was received with true Italian hospitality, which included coffee and biscotti. The man in charge of the office looked me straight in the eye and said that he was very sorry to tell me that he had no records and no indication that Generali ever wrote a policy, in the Baltic States. I told him that I did not have the policy No. 332, dated September 1930, but my father had the policy and he would not fabricate a story like that. The man in charge of the office was very cordial and very sympathetic to my feelings and promised me that he would look into it personally. As soon as he found anything out he would write to me in Turin. I never heard from him.

I was very sad when I left the office. I was sad because the policy was my real hope of having the financial security for finishing medical school. I also could not understand the attitude of Generali: my father had advised me about the insurance policy of $2,000 that he personally took out, and given me the policy number. There was a flaw that at that time I could not understand. I returned to Turin.

When I was in Rome I stayed with Zev Gdud and we spent some time together. We both had worked very hard to achieve our goals. He was enrolled in the University of Rome Medical School.

The year 1945 passed quickly. To celebrate the New Year in 1946, Cesare invited me to go skiing in Salice d'Ulce. It was only an hour away from Turin by train. We found a farmer who offered us his stable as sleeping accommodation. I was very excited the first time I went to ski in the Alps and I did not mind sleeping in the stable on straw. The most exciting thing was that early in the morning the cow that shared our sleeping quarters with us delivered a calf. The farmer was instrumental in helping the cow to deliver its calf. It was the first time that I had seen a calf being born.

In the morning we went skiing in Sestriere, which was an elite ski resort. The cable car took us to the top of the mountain. Suddenly I found myself on top of the mountain, scared to death. I was a good cross-country skier, but never had been exposed to downhill skiing. With the guidance of Cesare and Paolo, however, my backside took all the blows inflicted by the descent. Cesare and Paolo were my teachers. After several trips back to Sestriere, I became a downhill skier.

One day, I received from my uncle, who was still living in South Africa, some fabric for a new suit. It was Mrs Reyneri who took me to their family tailor and supervised the making of a suit for me. I felt very privileged to receive the motherly love she shared with me and her children, love of which I was so deprived. Finally, I had a suit and a new pair of shoes, and when I bought some shirts I felt integrated into Italian society.

In the second week of September 1946, I went to my post office box and found a letter from the Ministry of Education informing me that I was admitted to Medical School. It was thrilling and exciting finally to receive the letter from the Ministry of Education confirming that I was being admitted as a regular student. The problem, however, was that I was admitted to the first year. I felt in my mind that because of my lack of admission documents I should not be penalized and have to repeat the first year. That would be an additional disaster to my economic situation.

I decided to visit the Dean, Professor Allara, who had always demonstrated friendship to me, and always had a good solution for every problem. I visited him and showed him the letter I had just received. He smiled and said he had watched my grades for the year and was happy that everything worked out for me. At this point, I discussed my dilemma in having to repeat again the first year of school. He thought for a few minutes and then straightforwardly told me: 'I have an idea how to solve your problem.' He agreed with me that theoretically I should not have to repeat the first year in medical school, especially being a conditional student and with the grades I had received. He advised me to return in the next few days and bring to him a letter addressed to the Academic Senate. I should put it on notarized stationery.

The Academic Senate was going to meet in the next two weeks and he would need in writing an explanation of my

20. Jack preparing for an exam, Turin, 1946.

dilemma. He would then take it and personally present it to the Academic Senate meeting. Within a few days, I brought my notarized letter as requested and gave it to Professor Allara's secretary. The secretary told me to return on a particular date to see Professor Allara. This happened to be one week after the Academic Senate meeting.

When I returned two weeks later for my appointment as scheduled, Professor Allara saw me immediately. He had a big smile on his face and said, 'We are in luck. The Academic Senate, prior to adjourning, voted to admit you directly to the second year of medicine. Congratulations. I always had confidence in you and I think you will make the most out of your education. Your status as a conditional student has changed to a regular student of the University of Turin, Faculty of Medicine.' He shook my hand and said, 'My best wishes. I don't foresee that you will have any additional problems.' I left the office of the Dean, delighted. Finally, I had achieved my goal, to be a regular student in the Faculty of Medicine at the University of Turin.

I do not think I could have done it by myself without the help of the extraordinary Italian people who went out of the way to help me, like Professor Mario Allara and Professor Guiseppe Levi.

The other person I went to see that day was Professor Levi. Being a member of the Academic Senate, he already knew all about my application and my admission directly to the second year of medical school. He smiled and said, 'Congratulations. As far as I know, you may be the only student who has been directly admitted to the second year of medicine in medical school.' I thanked him very much.

In 1948, a few months after the creation of the State of Israel, the European Jewish Student Organization sponsored a two-month trip to Israel. We were guests of the Israeli government. Several of the members of Casa dello Studente joined the trip including Zev Gdud and me. The boat from Marseille was a small boat. After having survived very rough seas near the island of Crete, we saw the shores of Israel and a glimmer of the golden roof of the Bahai temple in Haifa.

We received VIP treatment while traveling through Israel. Our first stop was the Technion in Haifa, a well-known institution. After having slept the night in the dormitory of the Technion, we were taken to a kibbutz, Kfar Hahoresh. It was a kibbutz that for several months during the War of Independence had been surrounded by the Syrian Army. It was finally liberated by the Israeli Defense Forces. Most of the buildings of Kfar Hahoresh had been destroyed and we slept in tents. It was my first experience in a kibbutz.

After staying approximately one week in the kibbutz, I decided to hitchhike through Israel. Kfar Hahoresh was in northern Israel and the town of Afula not far away. I knew that Dr Nabriski had settled in Israel and was in charge of the gynecology and obstetrics department of the hospital in Afula. I went to visit him. He was very excited to see me and insisted that I stay with him in his apartment. Dr Nabriski was like a father to me. He reminded me of the time when we were taken back to an empty, evacuated camp. I recalled vividly the speech Dr Nabriski gave to the German SS who insisted that we eat without washing our hands. We drank an extra glass of wine to celebrate this episode.

During my stay with Dr Nabriski I discussed my future – settling in Israel. He was very positive in suggesting that I should not come to Israel until I had completed my surgical training. He felt that if I had an opportunity to specialize in the United States or in Sweden, it would be the best option I could give myself.

Armed with a piece of paper on which Zev Birger's address was carefully written out, I took the bus from Afula directly to Haifa. I criss-crossed Haifa and after finding the street, I found Zev Birger's apartment on Hanezirot Street. The apartment was located below street level and when I walked in I found Trudy and Zev. The emotion that I experienced was hard to describe. I had not seen Trudy since the ghetto and I had lost track of Zev Birger during the liberation of Dachau. It was a Friday afternoon and the Sabbath arrived with the sunset. Trudy surprised us with a magnificent Sabbath dinner that she prepared. We talked about our past, that was always associated with some pain, but the three of us also talked about our future. Our conversation continued until the early morning. In the morning, all three of us went to see the Bahai botanical gardens. Haifa is a very beautiful city and the garden provides its visitors with a panoramic view.

Sunday came very quickly. Soon I was on my way to Hadera and Tel Aviv. I was thinking about my reunion with the Birgers and came to the following conclusion: with people like Trudy and Zev, I was confident that Israel had a future. Zev had joined the customs administration and was already in charge of the customs house in Haifa. Six months later he was appointed as Chief of Customs for all of Israel.

After leaving Haifa, I went to Hadera to visit the Gdud family. I was with them for only one week, but it left a lifelong impression on me. From Zev Gdud's father, Rabbi Gdud, I learned the teaching of the Talmud and its philosophy, and was impressed with its implementation in his daily life. Through the years of my close friendship with Zev Gdud, I felt an enrichment of my daily life by following the Talmudic teaching.

Subsequently, I went to visit my friend, Joseph Zarchin,

who was already a major in the Israeli Defense Forces, and his wife, Emmy. He was very generous in hospitality and offered me their house while he was away in the army.

It is hard to describe all the events of my experience hitchhiking through Israel, but there is one episode that I remember with pride. It was the last Friday night we spent in Israel before the Sunday afternoon on which we were to depart from Haifa and return to Marseille. Three of us were hitchhiking, Zev Gdud, and I and another Casa dello Studente resident, Stella. We found ourselves on Friday night in Haifa. At that time, to eat in a restaurant in Israel, you could eat only one meal. If the portion was not satisfactory, you would not be given a second portion. If you wanted a second portion, you had to leave the restaurant and come back later and be treated as a new customer. It was our last night in Israel and we went to a small, family-run restaurant. We got to know the owner, who was also the chef and cook of the restaurant, and we told her it was our last night in Israel. After we had told her how good the food was, she went to the kitchen and brought us each another portion.

When the time came to pay, she would not accept any money because it was too late on Friday night and the Sabbath had arrived. She told us to come back on Sunday in order to pay our account. We smiled and said, 'We are leaving on Sunday by boat from Haifa.' She said, 'In the thirty years I have owned this restaurant, I have never had one person who did not pay. I always eventually get paid.' So on that Sunday morning, our last day in Israel, Zev Gdud and I ran to the restaurant and paid our bill. I felt it was one of the finest experiences that I had while I was in Israel. I feel that there are still some people who take their religious observations seriously and I have faith in people.

We made it back to the boat in time and sailed back to Marseille. Zev Gdud, Paul Geleris and I were sitting in a train compartment on the way to the farewell party we planned to give for Paul, who would be traveling to Naples to embark on a ship to New York.

We chose to have our party in a small restaurant, Santa Lucia, overlooking the waterfront. In spite of its modest prices, which we could afford, the food was excellent. Naples was famous for its seafood. After having enjoyed our food, we philosophized about our futures and were very excited that Paul had finally found a way to the United States, where he would be able to continue his education to build up his life. Italy was such a beautiful place and its people had helped us so much to forget our past and regain our sanity as dignified human beings.

At this point, Paul took out an envelope and simply said, 'Before I leave, I have something to give you.' Paul had relatives living in the United States, and during the years he periodically had received a modest amount of financial support to continue his studies. He saved every penny he could and lived a very modest life. Because of his modest lifestyle, when we opened the envelope, we found that he had left for Zev and me $850 for our security to be able to finish our medical studies in Italy. It is difficult to describe how speechless Zev and I became. It was an enormous amount of money then and if you convert it to the present value of the dollar, it was an incredible amount. The only thing that Paul said was, 'You would have done the same thing for me if the cards had been in reverse.' The friendship that developed in the years that we studied together and came to know each other continued for a lifetime, as well as transmitting itself to our families, wives and children.

The academic term at the university had already started and I was enrolled in the fifth year of medical school.

One day, two letters arrived from the American Consulate in Naples, one addressed to Edmund Bass and one to myself. Edmund Bass was my room-mate and a student in veterinary medicine. Both of us had been approved for emigration to the United States. Prior to the issue of all the necessary papers, however, we would need to go to Naples to complete the emigration application.

Edmund and I felt very privileged and special at being the

first students to receive such a letter. We soon worked out that it was because our last names started with a 'B'. Within a week, we were on our way to Naples. The process of emigration was to be carried out in a suburb of Naples called Bagnoli, where we found a room in a small local hotel. For the next five days, we were 'processed'. The processing included a review of our past history, our present history, as well as our intentions for our life in the United States. Finally, we had a medical examination. The medical emigration officials were focused on making sure that we were not infected by tuberculosis.

It was wonderful that I was with Edmund. He was a photographer and the proud owner of a camera. During our free time, we took advantage of the beautiful scenery of the area and took many pictures. One night, the sky gave a lightning performance. It was spectacular, and Edmund taught me how to take and capture the flashes of lightning. It was spectacular due to the fact that the sea reflected the lightning. I still have the picture that we took that night.

The week passed quickly and we were already on our way back to Turin. We returned to the university and to our studies.

This was an interesting year which involved mostly clinical medicine. Six to eight weeks later, we again received a letter from the American Consulate in Naples congratulating us for passing all the requirements and advising us that our emigration papers for the United States were complete.

I had qualified to be one of the emigrants for the bill that President Truman had signed allowing in 100,000 'intellectuals'. The intellectuals included teachers, professors and scientists as well as students who were studying in different fields at universities. It bypassed the overloaded affidavit quotas in the American immigration rules. We were also advised that we had to depart on a certain date by train to Bremen where we would be embarking on a ship called USS *General Sturgis*. In life, usually with every joy, there is also pain. The joy of sailing to the United States was great, but at the same time there was no way to postpone the trip and graduate prior to my departure.

I went to the American Consulate in Turin and asked for more details about how long it would take for me to get a green card and obtain the permits to return to Italy. I was told that I could expect to be in the United States for two to three months, where my papers would be processed. At that time, I would be able to return to Italy to complete my studies. I had no choice but to accept the consulate's decision.

The next step was to visit Professor Allara, the Dean of the Medical School, to see how I could interrupt my studies for a few months. He was extremely kind and understood the situation fully. He advised me to go to the United States and then return later to complete my studies. He also advised me that he would make arrangements to give me a two-month leave of absence, which it was in his power to do. He called in his secretary and told her of his decision. When I left Professor Allara's office I felt once again as close to him as to a father, giving me guidance and suggestions for my medical school curriculum.

At the specific time, Edmund and I were both ready. My main luggage consisted of a few textbooks for the current year's classes, that I took with me with the intention of keeping up with the class work during my absence from the university. The day came and both Edmund and I took the train to Germany from Turin to Bremen.

As I was sitting in the train, it was a dream come true. But with every dream you have to face reality. How would I be back in Italy within two months to complete my studies? My goal in life was to graduate with a medical degree. The Korean War had already begun and I was advised by the American Consulate in Turin that to leave the United States I would have to obtain from the draft board a postponement of my draft into the United States Army. In evaluating the situation, I decided that it was not a problem, but rather a challenge, to achieve my new goals in as short a time as possible.

The train journey to Bremen was my first trip to Germany since I had been liberated in Dachau in 1945. It was difficult psychologically for me to work out if I was comfortable being back in Germany or not. The people we encountered on the train were surprised at Edmund's and my fluency in the German language. It was often customary in the small compartments of the train to try to share their hospitality with fellow travelers. I did not feel that I was in Germany.

After arriving in Bremen, we were taken to a German army barracks, Camp Grohn. There were several houses there which during the war had been barracks for German officers. We had to wait for the next ship to arrive. We spent two weeks in Camp Grohn waiting for our ship to arrive. We took advantage of the time and visited the surrounding areas. We also took a special trip to Hamburg, a large pulsating city where the busy post-war construction had erased most of the visible scars from the war.

The two weeks passed quickly and finally the USS *General Sturgis* arrived. It was one of the liberty boats used during the Second World War for troops and was crewed by the United States Navy. We boarded the ship. The passage from Bremen to New York was pleasant. What made my passage even more exciting was that I was asked to work in the infirmary, which was run by a Navy nurse, Angela. She was of Italian descent and spoke fluent Italian. In the ten-day passage, crossing the Atlantic, I had the opportunity to learn a lot a great deal about life in the United States.

The thing that perplexed me most on the voyage was the usage of paper cups. It was very difficult for me to understand that the purchase of disposable paper cups was economically cheaper than washing ceramic cups. I learned many other aspects about the United States; this was the beginning for me of learning and understanding life in the United States.

We arrived in New York on the eve of Thanksgiving. We could not disembark and so we had a Thanksgiving Dinner on board. It was my first Thanksgiving Dinner.

The next day we disembarked. To my pleasant surprise, Paul Geleris came to greet me on my arrival. With him were my cousins, Eleanor and Julius Kase. I had corresponded with them when I was in Italy. To meet them finally after so many years was a great pleasure. In the years to come I learned what great people and humanitarians they were.

Paul proudly showed us the new car he had just purchased. In the excitement of my arrival he forgot to turn off the radio. When we were ready to leave, his car battery was dead. Eleanor and Julius took me home to their house and that evening we went to visit Eleanor's mother and father, for a repeat Thanksgiving Dinner. They had two young children, a girl, Nina, and a boy, Peter. One of the most exciting moments that I had was looking at the pictures that Julius, Eleanor and her mother, Emma, gave to me as a surprise welcome gift. All of the pictures of my family had been gathered by Eleanor and Julius from our relatives and presented to me. It was the most thoughtful present.

Paul Geleris surprised me with an arrangement he had made. He arranged for me to be a junior intern in St Elizabeth Hospital in New Jersey. A few days later, Paul picked me up and took me to Elizabeth, New Jersey where I met Dr Veigel, who was in charge of the intern program at St Elizabeth Hospital. It would give me the opportunity to get acquainted with American hospitals and American medicine.

After returning from the hospital, I explained to Eleanor and Julius my plans. They were very eager to have me stay with them during my time in the United States. I decided, however, that I would start my junior internship as soon as I straightened out my papers and the Draft Board in preparation for my return to Italy.

My first step was to go to the immigration office in New York and fill out my application. Eleanor volunteered to come with me to help with the application. A few days earlier I had learned how to ride in the New York subways. I was proud to show Eleanor how efficient I had become in using the subways. We arrived at the main immigration office in New York and were directed to a middle-aged lady. We sat down at her desk and before she even started processing the application I explained to her my problem, to find the fastest way to obtain all the papers and to return to Italy in time to graduate from medical school. She listened and as I finished she asked me if I had a phone available where the transaction of my papers could be carried out.

Eleanor immediately volunteered to put her phone in use for the transaction. The lady looked at me and told me that now that I had a phone I could return in two days and all my papers would be processed and ready. Within a week I would be able to return to Italy. She also mentioned to me that because of my age I would have to get permission from the Draft Board to leave the country. I told her that if she could arrange it I would be forever grateful. Unfortunately, I cannot recall her name today, but what she had done for me was unforgettable.

I returned two days later to see her and proudly she took out the envelope with all my processed papers, congratulating me for now having the green card and all the necessary papers required to leave the country. She also gave me a list of the Draft Boards. On my way home, I told Eleanor that I felt another miracle in my life had happened.

We immediately needed to start my transportation arrangements to return to Italy. The trip to the Draft Board was uneventful. I presented my case and within fifteen minutes, I was granted a deferral for the United States Army until after obtaining a medical degree followed by one year of internship.

Two of my important goals in the United States were completed. My third goal was to make arrangements to return to Italy and complete medical school. After spending some time in the office of the Cunard Line, I was able to obtain a ticket on the *Queen Mary*, leaving New York three weeks later. I cabled my Uncle Heinz who had volunteered to pay for my passage. Within a few days my uncle deposited the fee at the Johannesburg office of the Cunard Line and I was notified by Cunard that my ticket had been purchased and that I should pick it up. In one day, I obtained from the French consulate a transit visa through France and an entry visa to complete my studies from the Italian Consulate. I was also very eager to spend at least two weeks as a junior intern at St Elizabeth

Hospital. It would still put me in the time frame of my leave of absence from the university.

The trip on the ocean liner *Queen Mary* was an exciting experience. Within five days of crossing the Atlantic to Southampton and a few more days by train, I arrived in Turin. I had a lot of work to do to catch up with my studies, but at my first opportunity I went to see Professor Allara to thank him again for all the arrangements and to tell him that I had managed to return to the university within the two months allowed by him. He was delighted to see me and wished me the best in continuing my studies.

After returning to Turin, I felt very comfortable knowing a little about the arrangements for my future life. I spent my free time with Cesare and Paolo going skiing or visiting other cities and becoming even better acquainted with Italy. I never saw enough of the beauty and the richness in art and culture that Italy has to offer to its population, as well as to visitors.

Finally, I completed all the exams of the fifth year of medical school and started the sixth and last year of medical school. The contract of Casa dello Studente was ending and the few remaining students, mainly medical students, had to move out and find other accommodation. I went to see the Bachi sisters, Octavia and Matilda, from whom Paul Geleris had rented a room during his stay in Turin. I knew them fairly well and the room was still available, so I immediately rented it.

Octavia and Matilda Bachi were the daughters of the former Rabbi of Turin. The sisters, who were in their early seventies, were delighted to take care of me. I used to eat my meals with them. The Bachi sisters had very interesting stories. During the war, the chief of the Italian Police used to send a police officer to notify them when he would come to inspect or check on them, ordered to do so by the Fascists. He always used to ask them not to be in the house during his visit. He wanted to be able to write on the report that he had been unable to contact them.

When the Germans occupied Italy, the police chief again sent a police officer to notify them that he would be coming with a German police officer, and advised them to go to the country as soon as possible. As planned, on his arrival with the Gestapo, he did not find them. The apartment was sealed. The two sisters were already on their way to the country to hide with some acquaintances. At night the neighbors broke the seal on the apartment and emptied the apartment of all its contents. The contents, including even the toothbrushes, were put in storage in the neighbor's house. A few years later when Italy was liberated by the Allied forces, the two sisters returned to their apartment and all the contents that had been removed, including toothbrushes, had been put back in the apartment as if nothing had happened and nothing of theirs was missing. This is a beautiful example of the humanity of the Italian people.

The year passed quickly. The subjects at the university were all exciting. There were clinical lectures with exposure to the patients. I had the opportunity to do my doctoral thesis with Professor Mario Dogliotti, professor of surgery at the University of Turin. I had the opportunity to meet him personally, and told him my life story. He mentioned to me that he had spent some time in the Mayo Clinic and knew everyone there. After my internship, if I desired to have my residency at the Mayo Clinic, he would help me.

In 1951 the International College of Surgery held its meeting in Turin. The graduating class of the medical school hosted the delegates. I had the opportunity to meet Professor Zondek from Jerusalem. I met Professor Blalock from Johns Hopkins as well as Professor Thorek from Chicago. The lectures and presentations by the guest speakers provided another opportunity to become acquainted with American medicine and also to become acquainted with the professors themselves. The senior students who spoke English had the privilege of taking them shopping or accompanying them to different events.

On 12 July 1951, I graduated and received the degree of Doctor in Medicine from the University of Turin. I was Dr Brauns – like my father. The day after I received my doctorate,

I went to see Professor Allara to thank him again for having played such an important part in helping me to achieve my dream of graduating with a medical degree. He replied that his effort was only guidance, but the achievements were all mine.

He congratulated me and wished me all the best. I never wanted to lose contact with him. I told him that I would return to visit him again in the years to come, but when I did so I would not come to him with my problems. He laughed and again wished me all the best. I also visited Professor Giuseppe Levi to thank him for his assistance in my life.

After graduation, I spent a lot of time with the Reyneri family, especially with Cesare and Paolo. The biggest surprise was that they wanted to leave Italy and join me in the United States. We discussed all the possibilities and options, and, before saying goodbye to the Reyneris, with tears in my eyes, I promised them that I would see how I could obtain an internship for both of them, which included a roof and food on the table and twenty-five dollars a month as compensation for being an intern.

To receive a return passage back to the United States was very difficult. The third class was sold out. I worked out that it was cheaper for me to go second class than wait for a passage for a third class. Again, it was my Uncle Heinz who helped me. I boarded the ship in Genoa and for ten days I had time to contemplate my future life.

Embarkation was to begin in the late morning, and I was there on time. I could not afford to miss the ship. To avoid this, I arrived in Genoa the night before embarkation, and slept in a small hotel not far from the embarkation pier. The next morning, as I walked slowly to the pier, the magnificent silhouette of SS *United States* came in sight. It was the pride of the American transatlantic shipping fleet. The band was playing popular music and a large crowd was gathered at the pier. What a beautiful day it was – and the weather cooperated.

A portable gangway connected the pier to the ship. As I crossed it an episode of my past flashed back: 1945, when Zev Gdud and I were discussing our future. We decided that our future was in medicine. We would stay in Italy and enroll in the faculty of medicine. It was a pure dream, and I guess that because of the different concentration of oxygen in the high mountains, it was easier to dream the impossible: applying to the university without having any papers, without knowing the language and without any financial backing, and daring to dream of graduating with a degree in medicine in a new country.

That morning in Genoa, as I walked with my head held high, with proper clothes on, I blended into the crowd around me. I did not look like a refugee or displaced person. I was going 'home'. In my wallet, I had my green card, giving me the right to a permanent residency in the United States. I had graduated from the University of Turin with a medical degree. I had the medical diploma and certification in my suitcase.

As I boarded the ship, I took with me the incredible memories of my experience in Italy and carried them safely locked in my head – memories which I had accumulated during my six year stay. Memories not just of an extraordinary landscape, but also of the people who were responsible for having given me a wonderful stay in Italy, built on understanding and compassion. They built a bridge which made it easy for me to cross now from Dante's *Inferno* to a normal life with a future.

After a few minutes of the official procedures to board the ship, I was ushered into a large reception hall with a huge crowd of passengers and well-wishers who had come to say good bye to the passengers. As I looked around, I saw so many people, everyone smiling and well dressed. I did not see any recognizable refugees. I was alone, but I felt very good not being a refugee anymore. I felt liberated from the status of a refugee.

A siren sounded and the visitors were escorted off the ship. The ship moved slowly out of the harbor. I was leaving Europe and I wished that my parents had been with me. I would have had so many memories of Italy to share with them.

I found my cabin, and the suitcase that I had brought with me was there in the cabin waiting for me. Shortly afterwards, we were advised that a buffet lunch was being served in the main dining room. A dining room seat was assigned to me for the second sitting. This would be my table for the duration of the voyage.

We were out in the open sea when the time came to return to the dining room. I found my table and, to my greatest surprise, a young Italian lady was seated next to me. She was a graduate of the university and was on her way to the United States to join her father. This was Miss Fermi, the daughter of the Italian nuclear physicist, Enrico Fermi. Although we spent some time together, due to her modesty she never mentioned the role her father had played in achieving the end of the Second World War. I was fortunate to have been introduced to her as a dining companion. It was also fortunate that we had a lot in common: our love for Italy and its people.

After passing the Rock of Gibraltar we steamed into the Atlantic Ocean. Beautiful weather and a calm sea was the present we received as a bon voyage from nature. A few clouds accompanied our ship.

Having walked from the promenade deck, I found a secluded deckchair with a beautiful view of the sea. I was eager to organize my thought and ideas. I always felt that understanding the past is essential in planning the future. My thoughts wandered to my parents left in Europe and my brother who had perished in Stutthof concentration camp. I recalled the memories of the time we spent together. I only wished that I could have had my brother on this voyage with me, as well as my parents. I thought about my mother and how grateful I was to her for having always encouraged me to study languages with an emphasis on English. It was almost as if she had the intuition that one day I would be sailing to the United States of America.

How I missed my father with all his wisdom. How, after graduating and becoming a physician, I would have benefited from his wisdom and knowledge of medicine.

I recall that in my last year of medical school I wrote an article on twins. I had it printed and posted it to my parents.

My mother wrote to tell me how excited my father was to read it. She also explained her own concern: 'Women are a beautiful creation. Don't spoil it by becoming an obstetrician-gynecologist.' She did not have to worry about that, as my mind was set to continue my education and study surgery.

I always remembered the walks that my father and Dr Zacharin had together in Palanga where we spent our summer vacations. During these walks he described to me the art of surgery. I was also fortunate that in my last year of medical school I met Professor Mario Dogliotti, who was the sponsor of the thesis I prepared for graduation. Just before I left for the United States, I went to say good bye to him and he told me to keep in touch in case he could help me in the future.

I left Italy with feelings of nostalgia, especially thinking about the friends I had left behind. I knew that Zev Gdud would be taking his exams. With my departure, the money that Paul Geleris had left for our studies was left with Zev Gdud so that he would have the financial means to finish his studies, and within six to eight months follow us to the United States. On the other side of the ocean I was also aware that Paul Geleris was waiting for me. In the meantime he had arranged an internship for me at St Elizabeth Hospital.

New dreams appeared. The two main ones, most vivid in my thoughts, were to get my parents out of Lithuania and to obtain good surgical training. As always with dreams, they create a challenge to make them a reality: without the challenge, however, the dreams gradually disappear.

After ten days crossing the Atlantic, we arrived in New York Harbor. I had brought twenty dollars with me on the trip and the temptation on the ship had been so great that I had spent eighteen dollars of it on miscellaneous things. I arrived in New York with a two- dollar bill that I still carry in my wallet today.

A band was there to greet us. As soon as I completed the landing procedures, I saw my cousins, Eleanor and Julius Kase, as well as Paul Geleris waiting for me at the pier.

PART III

Life in the United States

8 Internship and Residency: Adjusting to Normal Life

Eleanor and Julius Kase picked me up at the pier and we drove directly to their house. A room had been prepared for me in their apartment. From the moment I entered their house I felt at home. The love and compassion they showed me was overwhelming. Eleanor's mother, Emma Schecht, was a first cousin of my father. The first topic of conversation was the pictures taken before the war that Eleanor collected for me from different relatives, who, over the years, had received them from my parents.

The discussion shifted to the period of the war as well as to my life. I felt like I was with my own family with whom I was trying to get acquainted. They were a wonderful family and I felt privileged to be with them. Nina and Peter, their children, who were three and six, were polite and well-behaved.

Paul Geleris joined us at dinner that first night. I learned from Paul his plans for pursuing his medical education. He was working as a resident in pathology at the Metropolitan Hospital in New York and was planning to transfer in the coming year to Flower Fifth Avenue Medical School to continue his pathology training. He confirmed again that my internship had been approved at St Elizabeth Hospital in Elizabeth, New Jersey. I was to start at my convenience as soon as possible.

After spending a week or ten days getting to know my cousins, I had to fulfill my obligation and start my rotating internship at St Elizabeth Hospital. Paul Geleris came to pick me up and drove me there. I was already familiar with the layout of the hospital. I had become acquainted with the nuns and administration staff on my previous visit to the United

States, when I had worked there for two weeks as a junior intern.

The obligation of the intern was to admit patients to the hospital – private as well as ward patients – and to write a history and physical, including the onset of the disease symptoms, clinical findings and tentative diagnosis. St Elizabeth Hospital had a small but efficient medical library for interns. I found medical books there that I needed. The other interns never hesitated to lend me a hand and give guidance with any question I had or advice I needed. I was able to translate my medical thinking into English.

St Elizabeth Hospital was a beautiful introduction for me to American medicine. I appreciated most that while doing the history and physicals I was never pressured. I developed confidence in myself in being able to practice medicine. I rotated in different departments that gave me practical exposure to different branches of medicine. St Elizabeth Hospital had the only polio unit in the city and I, like every intern, had to rotate through the polio unit. Because my father had been one of the leading epidemiologists and contagious disease physicians in Lithuania, my exposure to contagious diseases never caused me fear, except during the few weeks when I worked in the polio unit in St Elizabeth Hospital. The Lithuania in which I grew up was a primitive country, but it did not have the plague of polio disease to the extent that I saw in the polio unit at St Elizabeth Hospital. It was hard psychologically to understand the polio epidemic that raged in the United States and to see the helpless children who were trapped in iron lungs.

My next assignment was to the surgery department. This was my first introduction to surgery in a private hospital. There, I confirmed that this was to be my vocational choice of specialization.

I had to limit my social activities due to two factors: lack of time as well as lack of money. I received thirty-five dollars monthly as a payment for my work at St Elizabeth Hospital. This had to provide everything for myself except lodging and food.

On a rotating basis, as interns, we had to cover the emergency room, where the variety of cases that I had to treat was overwhelming. The city policy was that every ambulance had to be accompanied by an intern. I rotated services on ambulances and went to various emergencies and was the first physician to arrive. Every day there was excitement and every day I had to face new challenges.

It was soon time for me to find a surgical residency. I remembered before leaving Italy that Professor Mario Dogliotti, Chief of Surgery, at the University of Turin (who was the sponsor for my doctorate presentation, 'Preservation of Skin Grafts in Different Temperatures'), had close connections with the Mayo Clinic in Minneapolis, Minnesota. He had always advised me that if I decided to have my training at the Mayo Clinic, he would like to help me to obtain the residency. I never forgot this offer and wrote to the Mayo Clinic, from which I obtained an application. Professor Dogliotti sent me a recommendation. After a few months, I received a letter from the Mayo Clinic advising that my application had been rejected. I wrote to Professor Dogliotti who replied that he felt my rejection could not have been based on my medical qualifications. He was puzzled.

I started a new search for my residency. I felt that my best opportunity would be in a Jewish hospital. I believed that my credentials were good enough to apply to Mt Sinai Hospital in New York; I knew they would not discriminate against me as a Jew – since it was a Jewish hospital. I obtained the application to Mt Sinai and filled it out very carefully including all my letters of recommendation. I felt that this time I would be successful.

I sent my application for a surgical residency to Dr John Garlock, chief of the surgical department, who was in charge of the residency program in Mt Sinai Hospital. About six weeks later I got a letter of rejection. Again, I was deeply disappointed. About two years later I found out the reason for this rejection. I had no family in New York. I was a refugee.

Cesare Reyneri and his brother Paolo, as well as William Gdud, had started their internship at St Elizabeth Hospital. My life at St Elizabeth Hospital was busy, with daily challenges. I decided to apply to city hospitals in New York City. I continued my search for a surgical residency. After studying the list of the city hospitals and consulting with several of my acquaintances, I decided that Lincoln Hospital in the Bronx would be my best choice for training. It was a busy city hospital for surgical training. I called the administrative office of the hospital and learned that there was still one opening for a junior assistant resident in a four-year program.

Dr Frederick Amendola was in charge of the surgical department and residency program at Lincoln Hospital. He was professor of surgery at Columbia University and also chief of surgery at Roosevelt Hospital in New York.

During my internship at St Elizabeth Hospital I became acquainted with Iyzik and Shoshanna Remba from Israel. Mr Remba was a New York correspondent for the *Jerusalem Post.* His assignment came to an end and the Rembas were planning to return to Israel. Before their return, I was invited to a farewell party at their house. I was hesitant to go; having sustained two rejections I was not in the mood for a party. As a courtesy to the Rembas, however, whom I had come to know fairly well, I decided to go.

During the party I met an internist who specialized in rheumatic diseases, and spent some time talking with him. He was very interested in my life and also in my plight in obtaining a surgical residency. I spent considerable time with him and when the time came to leave the party he asked if I would be available to come to his office on Park Avenue the following week. He gave me the days he would be able to see me. He told me he would have a surprise for me and asked me not to overlook this opportunity of visiting him in his office. I made special arrangements at St Elizabeth Hospital to be free and went to New York to visit him. I was surprised that on the door to the entrance of the office I saw his name and that of

Dr Frederick Amendola. Before entering the office, I realized the great opportunity that had been created by sheer coincidence. He told me that he shared an office with Dr Amendola and that he had made arrangements for me to have an interview with him and escorted me to his office.

As I sat in the chair facing Dr Amendola I felt the warmth and respect that Dr Amendola reflected talking to me. I was pleasantly surprised that Dr Amendola was fluent in Italian. By pure coincidence, he was well acquainted with Professor Mario Dogliotti, whom he had met at surgical meetings in Italy. He asked me if I had sent an application to Lincoln Hospital. I told him I had done this just a few days earlier. He also asked me to be sure to include Professor Dogliotti's recommendation. When I left the office I felt as if I was walking on a cloud. Dr Amendola, whom I got to know in the years to come, was a giant in the surgical world. In addition to being a giant, he was a gentleman beyond description and a very considerate person.

I returned to St Elizabeth Hospital to continue my work. In my heart I hoped that perhaps this time my prayers for a surgical residency would be answered.

Two weeks later, I received an official letter from Dr Smith, the administrator at Lincoln Hospital, who informed me that I had been accepted as a junior assistant resident in surgery at Lincoln Hospital for the full four-year program. He also pointed out that Lincoln Hospital had a pyramidal system. He explained in the letter that if I did not achieve the chief resident position, I would have to repeat my surgical residency in a different hospital. He added that most of his residents who did not reach the chief resident position usually shifted to surgical sub-specialties. In spite of the system under which I was admitted, I felt confidence and continued walking on air.

One day in the late afternoon, St Elizabeth Hospital dispatched an ambulance with me as the attending intern. We were taken directly to Newark Airport, where a commercial airplane had crashed during take-off. Ambulances from all the hospitals in the area were on their way to the airport. On arrival, we received a young woman and transported her to St Elizabeth Hospital. When her injuries were evaluated and treated she was put in a private room. Her face looked familiar, but I could not place it in my memory. The next day during rounds I noticed a tremendous number of flowers that continuously arrived in her room.

I learned that she was Mildred Smith, an American actress. I then recalled having seen her in the film, *No Way Out*. She played the wife of a black doctor, Sidney Poitier, whose screen debut it was. Richard Widmark was also in the film. During the following days she was visited by these actors and many other actors and personalities, including Louis Armstrong. Fortunately, her injuries were minor and within ten days she was discharged to go home. In gratitude to me for taking her from the airport and taking care of her, she and her boyfriend, who was the editor of *Ebony* magazine, invited me to join them and their friends for dinner in her house. During the dinner table conversation, I learned about the plight of black people in the United States. This was in 1952.

Halfway during my internship, during breakfast one day, one of the nuns came in and mentioned that two new interns from Germany would be joining us. Bill Gdud and I decided that we would extend all the courtesies to them but not get involved with them socially. Dr Wolfgang Zylka and Dr Kurt Quitman were both from the University of Cologne. They were delightful people and in no time we developed a close comradeship with them. We gradually tried to learn about each other. The most surprising thing was that Dr Zylka and Dr Quitman had both graduated from the University of Cologne, where my father had attended medical school and graduated more than thirty years earlier. I learned, for the first time, that the bombing raids in the Second World War destroyed much of Cologne, and that it was in the process of being rebuilt. The only structure that survived the bombing in the center of the city was the cathedral of Cologne. I learned from my friend Martin Gilbert that one of the six Royal Air Force bombing raids on Cologne – it was in fact the first 1,000-bomber raid of the war – had given encouragement to the Jews of the Warsaw Ghetto. Cologne had also been a strongly anti-Nazi city when Hitler came to power: its Mayor then, Conrad Adenauer, later German Chancellor, signed the post-war reparations agreement with the State of Israel in 1952.

Together with Dr Zylka and Dr Quitman, we often ventured to New York City, where we all enjoyed the museums, the theater, and other amenities that the city offered us. By the end of our internship a friendship had developed.

Years later, when I was in private practice, I learned some surprising news. I received a letter from Dr Zylka telling me that Dr Quitman had died from a blood disease. The interesting piece of information that Dr Zylka passed on was that Dr Quitman's father had been the chief radiologist at the university during the war and he had saved a Jewish family of four who lived in his house for the duration of the war and were able to survive with forged Aryan papers. Even though I knew Kurt Quitman relatively well during the time we spent together, he never mentioned this act of heroism that his parents performed by taking a risk to shelter a Jewish family.

Sometimes it is just such an experience that is needed as a reminder not to judge people before we get to know them.

June 1952 was an important date for me. It was the month I arrived at Lincoln Hospital and reported directly to the office of the administrator to meet Dr Smith. He also told me that single-room occupancy had been reserved for me and that he would have one of his secretaries walk me to my room. It was a very small room in the residents' quarters with a bed, a sink and a small table that I could use as my desk. The window had a 'magnificent' view – the wall of the next building. I did not have to worry about any distractions when I looked out my window..

Dr Smith's secretary called up one of the senior assistant surgical residents, Dr Allen Bedford, and asked him to give me a tour of the hospital.

We began to walk through the hospital where he showed me the layout as well as the facilities, including the laboratory and the X-ray. Allen took the time to explain to me the structure of the surgical training at Lincoln Hospital: 1st year - Junior Assistant Resident (4 residents); 2nd year – Senior Assistant Resident (3 residents); 3rd year – Senior Resident (2 residents); 4th year – Chief Resident (1 resident).

Allen explained to me my responsibilities as a first year junior assistant resident. Basically, I would function as a surgical intern. He also explained to me the function and responsibility of Units A and B. The responsibility of both units was to admit, work up and take care of all the patients admitted, including coverage of the emergency room. Unit A admitted patients on uneven days and B on even days.

Allen was assigned to Unit A and told me that he would be one of my superiors. After the 'royal tour', we stopped in the doctors' dining room and had some coffee. Allen had graduated from an American medical school. He was married and had two children. In the years to come, as I worked with Allen, I learned how dedicated he was to his patients. He often did not leave the hospital even on the days he was officially off duty. His dedication to his patients was unlimited. If a patient needed blood and there was no blood available in the blood banks of the hospital, he himself would donate a unit of blood and then look for volunteers if more blood was needed.

Each Wednesday we had the Grand Rounds, when we were joined by the whole surgical staff and attending physicians, including Dr Frederick Amendola, Chief of the Surgery Department.

After my second week working at the hospital, I was asked to do a presentation during Grand Rounds. I prepared myself diligently the day before.

I started my presentation by explaining that approximately three days earlier I admitted a young child to the hospital with the following symptoms and tentative diagnosis. During the rounds, I called the child a 'kid'. After the rounds, Dr

Amendola put his hands on my shoulders and told me that he knew it might be a misunderstanding, but he wanted me to know that they did not admit any kids to this hospital. He told me that he was sure I had not realized that kid means baby goat in English.

The emergency room was always filled with drama, so much so that a police officer was regularly stationed in the emergency room, just in case. In many cases, he had to intervene for one reason or another to protect the doctors from aggressive patients and/or their families.

Near the hospital was a large building that housed a nursing school. Its residents were women who were training to become nurses. I was told that this was one of the largest Black nursing schools in the United States.

The residents at Lincoln Hospital impressed me very much by their devotion to the care of the patients. The residents from the various departments were always willing to give me a hand and would spend time explaining things about which I asked. The staff was composed mainly of American graduates, most of them returning from the Korean War, as well as foreigners of different nationalities.

My salary was still twenty-five dollars a month. There was a tremendous amount of work that I had to carry out in admissions to the hospital, as well as other functions that were assigned to me. Just as my salary was limited, so were my social activities – markedly limited by time. I scrubbed every day in the operating room. I felt that I was privileged to watch both the simple and the complicated operations. After surgery, I would go to my textbooks and review what I had seen during the procedure.

It was at this time that I met Dr Bernard Kellerman, originally from the Swiss city of Basel, who had come to Lincoln Hospital for his internship. A friendship developed between us. One day he invited me to join him on a double date with two Swiss girls who were working at Swiss Air. I was very pleasantly surprised to meet my date and even more surprised that they had invited us to their small apartment where they had prepared dinner for us. Certainly neither Bernard nor I could afford to take them out for a meal of this caliber.

Bernard and I, as well as the people I met through him, all had a common interest: to learn the way of life in the United States and to visit museums and art galleries as well as the shows that were available in such a rich and cultured city as New York. Unfortunately, our time was very limited. Physically, Lincoln Hospital was not the best-looking hospital, but I must say that the care of the patients was good due to the dedication and devotion of the resident staff. Lincoln Hospital was located in the Bronx, a borough in New York City. It was not in the best neighborhood. When Bernard and I went to the city we always took our doctors' white jackets with us as they protected us on our walk to the subway station which was about a mile from the hospital. At the station, we put our coats into a briefcase and upon returning from the city put them back on, to assure a safe return to the hospital. In all the years I worked at Lincoln Hospital, I was never mugged or attacked, and I was not afraid to walk along the streets there. I do not know of any other doctor who followed this same procedure who was ever afraid of walking on the streets.

Pearl Good introduced me to Mira Jedwabnik, her childhood friend from Vilnius who was living in New York City. Just one day before the war broke out, Mira and her parents sailed on the last passenger ship leaving Europe. I was often invited to their house. Mira was an accomplished artist and was surrounded by interesting people. This was an intellectually stimulating reprieve from the hospital surroundings.

After six months, Dr Allen Bedford started to assign patients to me. I had the opportunity to carry out assigned procedures under the attending physician's supervision.

Lincoln Hospital had a morgue. One preserved cadaver was available for the surgical residents. On certain evenings, I would go down to the morgue and supplement my knowledge of anatomy by dissecting the cadaver. Lincoln Hospital became my life and I rarely left the hospital. The food was adequate and my room was private. I had time to read in my room and prepare myself for each day's surgical cases. Allen and I developed a close friendship. When we had time and opportunity, we would go to the dining room for a cup of coffee and spend hours discussing different cases. It was not easy for me to keep up with Allen, but by keeping up with him I must have left a positive impression on him. Every month that passed he would assign more surgeries to me. I was grateful for the experience I was receiving.

The year passed quickly and the time came for the selection of the Senior Assistant Resident. It was Allen's recommendation that helped me preserve my position in the pyramidal system and I was appointed by the board to continue my residency as a second year Senior Assistant Resident. I felt sorry for the Junior Assistant Resident who did not make it.

I continued my surgical residency with Dr Allen Bedford who was promoted to position of Senior Resident. As Senior Assistant Resident, my responsibilities increased with the daily challenges. I spent more time in the operating room and was assigned an increased number of surgeries to perform under the supervision of our attending physician. Eventually I was promoted to first assistant in surgeries.

During the weekly rounds certain cases were presented and discussed. Dr Amendola was invited to perform special surgeries, but in my status as a Senior Assistant Resident, I was not privileged to participate or assist in those surgeries with him. During rounds on the day of surgery, he often stopped and would chat with me a few minutes. I felt that he was interested in the progress of my surgical training.

Dr Jack Friedman had the responsibility for surgical training on service A. I spent a lot of time with him discussing the difficult patients that we had admitted. I liked Dr Friedman. He was not superficial and was a very stimulating teacher in the art of surgery.

The year passed incredibly fast. It was May again and after

the meeting of the board I was advised that I had been chosen to continue as a third year senior resident in surgery. There were only two chosen to continue in the pyramidal system. Our official titles were: First Assistants of the Chief Resident. The following year would be a critical year because only one of us would be chosen to be chief resident of the surgery department.

When I was in the first months of my third year residency as senior resident, an event happened in the operating room that changed the pyramidal system in the surgical residency. During a surgical procedure, Allen got into a verbal argument with the anesthesiologist who was caring for the patient. Unfortunately, Allen was unable to control his temper and proceeded to take off his gloves. He interrupted the procedure, went to the head of the table, and hit the anesthesiologist The anesthesiologist fell to the floor and moaned, 'I'm dying, I'm dying. Please notify my family that my last words to them were, I love them very much.' I was paged post haste to the operating room. I found the anesthesiologist lying on the floor mumbling. Allen looked at me and told me to take over the anesthesia (which we were all trained to do). Allen rescrubbed, put on gloves and continued the surgery. There was a heavy silence in the operating room. At some point the anesthesiologist was carried out of the operating room on a stretcher. The patient who underwent the surgery did very well and the post-operative course was uneventful. The anesthesiologist survived!

Following this incident, an emergency meeting of the board of the hospital was called. Allen was dismissed from his residency and I was appointed as Acting Chief Resident. For myself, I was extremely happy with the board's decision, but at the same time I was sad for Allen. I had developed a close and deep friendship with him and felt sorry for his fate.

Looking back on my conversations with Allen in the years we had worked together, I very often had told him that the most important thing a human being could do was to control his emotions. That is what differentiates humans from animals. It was the lack of control of his emotions that had caused such a disaster to Allen's career as a surgeon.

Now I was the Acting Chief Resident with all the decisions, burdens and challenges put upon my shoulders. I was happy with this responsibility and immediately started to reorganize the service under the help and guidance of Dr Friedman, but at the same time with some modifications palatable and enjoyable to the younger staff.

Dr Friedman, who was one of my strongest supporters, congratulated me on the appointment and offered his help and guidance in anything I should need. I took his advice in the year to come and throughout the year I consulted him on many of the challenges that arose in regard to patients as well as with relationships with my junior staff. It was my choice to assign the surgeries to myself as well as to my junior staff. I chose to perform all the surgeries I could physically do. Every time I did a surgery in the presence of the attending staff I was very well prepared on the clinical aspect of disease, surgical anatomy as well as the topographic anatomy. I did not neglect my junior staff and distributed more surgeries to them than they expected. This brought a tremendous loyalty from my junior staff. At the same time I put the responsibility on them to follow my example and to be clinically and anatomically prepared for each surgery that they performed. It would be their responsibility several times daily, in addition to their regular duties, to follow up each surgery that they had performed and develop a close relationship with the patient and the family. I felt this was extremely important for the recovery of the patient.

Dr Amendola congratulated me and expressed his confidence in my abilities to carry out the responsibility assigned to me.

In the late evenings, I continued my routine and went to the morgue where a cadaver was assigned to the surgical residents. Having given my surgical residents a larger number of surgeries and putting new responsibilities on them, I was never alone in the morgue and it was always satisfying to have a discussion on anatomical topography.

Lincoln Hospital was an active city hospital and the

21. Jack as a resident, Lincoln Hospital, Bronx, 1954.

number of surgeries performed daily was incredibly high. I was in charge of selecting patients for presentation in Grand Rounds as well as assigning the surgeon to present each individual case.

In addition to spending more time with Dr Friedman, I also had the opportunity to spend some time in conferences on special cases with Dr Amendola. My greatest reward was to be the first assistant to him during surgical procedures that he performed when he operated at Lincoln Hospital. He was an intellectual surgeon and all his lectures and my time spent with him were a treasured experience for me. In addition, he was a superb technician. The main thing I learned from him was respect for the tissue. I still remember that in addition to his rubber gloves he had cotton gloves with which he used to cover his rubber gloves. He always operated with two sets of gloves to decrease the trauma to the organs that he exposed during the operation.

I was also very privileged to operate and work with Dr Friedman, who was my teacher and guide during the time I ran the department as the acting chief resident. He was an incredibly dedicated and demanding teacher and I benefited from his discussions.

On 14 July 1954 another event occurred which left an imprint on my life. I was in the elevator when a young man entered. I asked him if I could help him. He introduced himself as Arnold Einhorn and stated that he had just come from Paris and would be starting his internship at Lincoln Hospital. We chatted for a few minutes and I learned that he was already a trained pediatrician in Paris, but was interested in settling in the United States. That would require him to repeat his internship as well as pediatric training. It was Bastille Day and I invited him to join me in the doctors' lounge to celebrate Bastille Day with a cup of coffee. He smiled and said, 'In Paris, we don't celebrate Bastille Day with coffee.' Nevertheless we had coffee and spent a little time talking. With this cup of coffee began a lifelong friendship.

Subsequently, Arnold started his internship and was assigned to my surgical service. I felt happy and privileged. He also was a survivor of the Holocaust, an inmate of the Vichy French concentration camp at Agde, a former combatant in the Jewish French underground and a veteran of the British Eighth Army after escaping, by crossing the Pyrenees Mountains from France to Spain from Nazi-occupied France.

Arnold was extremely academic-minded and was a great help to me in the challenges I faced as acting chief resident on the surgical service. When we had time, we had long and stimulating conversations. He is brilliant: a connoisseur of art, music and literature, and I learned more from him than I could offer him.

Arnold always talked about the girl whom he left in France – Yvonne. He was planning to marry her. One day, Arnold told me that he was going to the pier. The ship carrying his girlfriend Yvonne would be arriving that day. I was very happy to meet her. She was charming and beautiful. A short time after Yvonne arrived in the United States, they decided to get married. I was honored to be his best man and witness at his wedding, and honored that he was mine at my own wedding one year later

After his internship, Arnold served a pediatric residency and chief residency at the Jacobi Hospital of the Albert Einstein College of Medicine. Immediately upon completion of his Chief Residency there, he was appointed by the Albert Einstein College to be Director of the Department of Pediatrics of their South Bronx affiliate, Lincoln Hospital and Medical Center. Rapidly ascending the academic trail, he became Professor of Pediatrics at the Albert Einstein College of Medicine. After serving twenty years on the Einstein full-time faculty he moved to Washington, DC to assume the positions of Chairman of Pediatric Medicine, Physician-in-Chief and Training Program Director at the Children's National Medical Center, with the rank of Professor of Pediatrics and Associate Dean of the George Washington School of Medicine and Health Sciences. Eighteen years later and ready to retire, George Washington University bestowed upon him the title of Professor Emeritus of Pediatrics, but he was enticed to join also the faculty of Georgetown University where he now serves in addition as Professor of Pediatrics.

My third year of residency passed very quickly. The month of May arrived and the board met. I was hoping to be appointed as the official Chief Resident as I was required to have four years of surgical training. My year as acting chief resident was appreciated by the hospital and by the attending staff. At that meeting, in May 1955, I was appointed Chief Surgical Resident at Lincoln Hospital. I felt very grateful. I realized that I had reached the top of the pyramidal system, and that I was the first foreign graduate to achieve this position. My friend, Cesare Reyneri, pursued a residency in internal medicine. His brother, Paolo Reyneri, pursued his Ear, Nose and Throat (ENT) residency. The graduates of Casa dello Studente all pursued different specialties and were successful in their fields. Paul Geleris completed his pathology residency and joined the public health services. Bill Gdud pursued his residency in general practice.

The last year of required training to complete my surgical residency was 1955/56. As Chief Resident, I assigned the most challenging surgeries to myself and continued working with Dr Amendola and Dr Friedman.

There was a very large Puerto Rican population in the Bronx. Schistosomiasis is an intestinal parasitic disease endemic in Puerto Rico. It is transmitted to humans while swimming and bathing in fresh water (lakes) infested by water snails carrying the parasites. The parasite penetrates the skin. Only a certain percentage of the population, however, is affected with clinical schistosomiasis that manifests itself by causing liver cirrhosis. As a consequence the pressure in the portal veins is markedly increased; it leads to esophageal varices (enlargement of esophageal veins which can cause fatal bleeding).

Dr Amendola was internationally known for having classified gastrointestinal bleeding in reference to age, recurrence and indication for surgical intervention. He was interested in the surgical treatment of esophageal varices and I had assisted him in several surgical procedures in the treatment of severe esophageal varices. He asked me to present a lecture on schistosomiasis which I did on the following grand rounds.

1955 was an important year. On 9 January 1955 I had became a citizen of the United States of America. What a good feeling! Another goal was achieved.

In December 1955 one of my staff physicians, Dr Peralta, was married. I was invited to the wedding. Richard Schwimmer, an oral surgery resident, was also invited and he brought his date, Joyce Sklar. We were seated at the same table during the reception. During the few hours I spent sitting next to Joyce, I realized what a fantastic person she was. Her beauty was secondary to her wonderful personality.

The next day I complimented Richard on the choice of his

date. He mentioned to me that they were not seeing each other very much. I told him that when and if he stopped seeing her I might be interested in getting to know her a little better.

About six weeks later, while having dinner in the hospital, Richard told me that he had stopped dating Joyce. I told him I would trade my 'little black book of phone numbers' (he was always impressed with the airline stewardess I had been dating) for her number. He agreed. I called Joyce and made a date.

As chief resident, my salary had been raised from twenty-five dollars to one hundred dollars a month. Joyce and I went out on our first date in March. My free time was limited and we had to the make the most of it. Joyce lived in Brooklyn and I lived in the Bronx. Manhattan was the most convenient place for us to meet. I found an Italian and a French restaurant, which both had a flat fee and a fixed menu. The cost of the meal was three dollars. This became our regular meeting place.

During our meals we learned about each other. Joyce had graduated from Brooklyn College and was an elementary school teacher in the New York City Public School System. She was teaching second grade in an underprivileged neighborhood and discovered that, at night during the winter months, many of the children would hide in the stairwells at school to keep warm because there was no heat in their homes. Joyce described to me how she would bring them food and clothing. She would also visit their apartments to meet their families and see the living conditions. The children did not receive nutritious food at home. Their main 'diet' was sugar candies available at the candy store for pennies. The burden these children carried made it difficult for them to concentrate in school. Teaching in these communities is a big challenge. I was fascinated by Joyce's compassion and energy.

Every time we met and enjoyed our evenings together, we learned more about one another. I learned that Joyce had a clear understanding of the things that are important in life and the things that are not important. This paralleled my own

22. Joyce Sklar when Jack met her.

philosophy. I found Joyce's beauty indescribable and I fell in love with her. She gradually became a true friend who was not afraid to express her own ideas and thoughts even if they were different from my own thinking. I never met a more exciting woman than Joyce,

I was still deeply involved with my work responsibilities as Chief Resident. I had to spend a lot of time at the hospital, so our dates were not too frequent. I had a great advantage, however, in dating Joyce; I did not need to give advance notice for our dates. That made it much easier for me. She understood that my time schedule was inconsistent. I compensated for our infrequent dates by talking to her on the phone almost every evening.

I was still extremely excited with my position as Chief Resident and all the benefits I had in learning the art of surgery. My new dilemma was what to do the year after I finished my residency. At that time I would be fully eligible to take the required examination and to be certified for the American Board of Surgery.

I remembered the walks I had taken in the forest with my father and Dr Zacharin when I was a teenager. Dr Zacharin was the leading surgeon in Lithuania. I expressed my interest in becoming a surgeon and Dr Zacharin encouraged me. My father said: 'Surgeons are very good technicians, but they are not intellectual physicians as compared to internists.' I never forgot his words.

An opportunity presented itself at the University of Pennsylvania in Philadelphia. Dr Isidore Ravdin offered a postgraduate course for young surgeons who had already completed their surgical training. After having studied about the program, I felt that it might be a great opportunity for me to take and to become an 'intellectual' surgeon and change my father's opinion about surgeons. I discussed it with Joyce, who was very supportive. After I had presented all the pros and cons to Joyce, she encouraged me to continue my education for another year. Another big supporter in my decision was Arnold, who had his heart in academic surgery.

I contacted Dr Amendola and made an appointment to see him. I felt that he would have more time to spend if we met in his office. I went to see him and to my pleasant surprise, he was extremely supportive of my idea. He mentioned to me that Dr Ravdin was a good friend of his and that he would be more than happy to write a letter of recommendation to Dr Ravdin and introduce me to him. I felt it was important for me to get Dr Amendola's blessing to pursue my career along this line.

I also mentioned my ideas to Dr Friedman, who invited me to his house for dinner. At the dinner table I could not have received more support for my thoughts and ideas. The circle of support from my teachers, Joyce and Arnold was so overwhelming that I immediately wrote a letter to the University of Pennsylvania asking them for an application.

The real problem was that the course required $1,000 to cover my tuition fee. I had learned that every library had a scholarship book. Many thousands of scholarships were listed for people of different races and religions in various academic fields. I went to the library and spent several weekends studying the book. After having gone through numerous pages, I found the addresses of thirty foundations to which I could apply. Joyce typed the thirty application letters for me.

In the meantime, I received a letter from the University of Pennsylvania saying that the board had met and approved my admission for the postgraduate course. I was delighted and hoped that one of these letters would bring some positive good news. A few weeks later, I received replies to all thirty letters. One foundation decided to lend me the money to be repaid two years after being in private practice.

My funds were approved and my admission to the university, for the postgraduate course in surgery, was confirmed.

My entire surgical residency at Lincoln Hospital, one of the busiest hospitals in New York, was rewarding, especially in the last two years when I was in charge of the surgical department as an acting chief resident and later as chief resident. My rewards consisted in being able to choose for myself the number and type of surgeries I performed.

Every week at Grand Rounds, I tried to select the most challenging cases, especially the ones that were diagnostically mystery cases. I learned the logic that the different attending physicians used to try and solve the diagnosis of the patient.

My residency was coming to an end. It was already May and I decided to do a daring thing to surprise Joyce. My friends Ignash and Alina Pressman were both ex-students from Casa dello Studente. Ignash was an engineer and worked at Otis Elevators. Alina was training in anesthesiology at one of the county hospitals in Brooklyn. One Saturday afternoon they invited me and Joyce to join them on a visit to the New York Botanical Gardens. It was a beautiful spring day. In the evening we went to the Pressman apartment. After dinner, I proposed to Joyce. She was absolutely surprised. I told her that I did not expect an answer on the spot. I said that I would appreciate it if she would sleep over at the Pressmans because I had to return to the hospital that night. The next day, after rounds at Lincoln Hospital, I would come and take her home to Brooklyn. I knew she was not expecting to stay overnight, so I had bought her a toothbrush as a present.

The next day, after seeing my patients at the hospital, I returned to the Pressman apartment. Joyce accepted my proposal. On the subway train to Brooklyn, I asked her not to tell her parents. I wanted to have the privilege of asking her parents for her hand in marriage.

During the next few days at Lincoln Hospital I confided in Bob Propper, an oral surgery resident, about my proposal to Joyce and how I wanted to go to Brooklyn to tell her parents, Abraham and Kate Sklar. Bob and I were good friends and had skied together and double dated many times. He had a car and volunteered to drive me to Brooklyn and wait for me downstairs while I spoke to Joyce's parents. I was grateful for his generosity. It was another week before I had the time to take up his offer. Bob drove me to Brooklyn. He parked, while I ran upstairs to talk to Joyce's parents. I was very brief in describing my love for Joyce and followed with, 'I would like to marry her if it is all right with you?' At this point I told them

23. The wedding of Jack and Joyce Brauns, 24 June 1956.

24. Joyce's parents, Abraham and Kate Sklar, 1956.

that there was a friend of mine waiting downstairs and I had to leave.

I left Joyce's house a few minutes later and Bob drove me back to the hospital. When I returned to the hospital, I called Joyce. I found out that her parents were still sitting in the same chairs they were sitting in when I had left them. They were perplexed, had lost their sense of time, and suggested at first that Joyce and I finish school and then think about marriage. It was hard for them to realize that their last child would be leaving for a life of her own. When they awoke from their stupor they gave us their blessing. They were happy. Joyce and I decided that we would get married at the end of June.

My work at the hospital continued. I was so happy and the time passed extremely fast Then suddenly, without realizing it, we were already in the middle of June. Our wedding date was set for 24 June 1956.

After I completed my residency at Lincoln Hospital, I went to Dr Amendola's office to thank him for all his surgical education and wisdom during the years of my surgical residency. He asked me if I still remembered the time that I made the presentation where I talked about a kid being admitted. He had a good memory and it was a pleasant surprise that he had not forgotten such a small detail – one that I had been trying to forget.

Also following the completion of my residency, Joyce and I made a special call to see and thank Dr Friedman for his guidance and support in my surgical training. .

Our wedding day started a new chapter in my life. I would not be alone anymore and I would have a beautiful and intelligent companion. The only sad thing about my wedding was that my parents were so far away in Lithuania and unable to share this celebration. The only way I could share my wedding with them was by sending them some photographs. I also was very sad that my younger brother, who had lost his life during the war in Stutthof Concentration Camp, was absent. At the wedding, I saw most of my friends from Casa dello Studente, as well as some old and new relatives. During the wedding, I looked at Joyce and felt very grateful to be blessed with a wife who would be my companion and friend. We stayed a few days in a hotel in Manhattan Beach, Brooklyn, where Joyce was teaching. She was obliged to finish the school year where she was teaching, and had to play piano at the graduation.

The postgraduate course at the University of Pennsylvania

would begin on 15 September 1956. We decided not to rent an apartment until school time in September. We therefore went on an extended honeymoon. We planned to explore the eastern seaboard from New York to Florida in our new 1956 Ford Mainliner; it was my first car – the cheapest car there was. Because of our restricted budget, we would sleep in small hotels on the way or rent small flats to enjoy the locations we were planning to visit. Joyce was very understanding and did not mind traveling on a tight budget. My cousins, Eleanor and Julius Kase, had moved to Florida by then and we planned to visit them.

It took us about a month to get to Miami, having first enjoyed Washington, Virginia and the beautiful beaches in the Carolinas. This month was an important one for both of us. During this time we had the opportunity to get away from our busy daily lives and learn about each other, our thoughts and ideas, and we made plans for our future life. When I got to know Joyce more, I appreciated her even more.

We arrived in Miami Beach and met my cousins, Eleanor and Julius Kase. This gave both of us an opportunity to appreciate the wonderful family I had in Julius and Eleanor. After a few days in Miami, we decided to explore the Keys. We drove leisurely through the Keys, finally reaching Key West where we stopped at a small airport. There was a big sign posted: 'Flight to Cuba: $25.' That was affordable and sounded adventurous and exciting. We found a parking space for our car and took the flight to Cuba and within a short time we landed there. We checked into a small hotel and spent a week in Havana. It was a completely new culture to us. An Italian movie company was filming a picture called *Copacabana* in the famous nightclub of the same name in Havana. The director, crew and camera people stayed in the same hotel we were in. I was able to communicate with them in Italian. They invited us to join them as extras. We were delighted and that was our first exposure to a movie set.

Like everything that comes and goes, after a week we had to say goodbye to Cuba and flew back to the United States.

Joyce had applied for a teaching position in King of Prussia, Pennsylvania, about half an hour away from the University of Pennsylvania in Philadelphia. She had an interview with the Superintendent of the Marian County School District, and was hired to teach second grade in the Candlebrook Elementary School in King of Prussia. The next challenge was to find a place to live. It was a very small town and at that time there were no apartment dwellings. We looked in the ads, drove around, and the only place we could find was on the second floor of a funeral home. It was dark and gloomy there.

After searching for a few more days, we met an elderly Italian couple living in a one-family, two-story house in King of Prussia. They were very willing to rent the second floor, consisting of four empty rooms and a bathroom. It was a large house within walking distance of the school, and only twenty minutes by car to the University of Pennsylvania. We were close to Valley Forge and also to Lafayette Hills where our good friends, Dora and Stanley Wulc, from Casa dello Studente, lived and with whom we spent a lot of time. This friendship flourished.

There were some disadvantages. Being on the second floor of a one-family house, there was no door to the upper part of the house, and thus no privacy. I spoke to the landlady and asked if I could build a wall along the staircase and install a door to the second floor. She was very accommodating. I went to a local lumber yard where I found the owner. After giving him the measurements, I asked him if he could pre-cut the wood required to construct a small wall with a door. A week later he used his own truck to bring the pre-cut pieces and necessary supplies to the house and carry them upstairs. Within a few days, the door was installed and we had our privacy.

The landlady purchased a used stove, painted silver on the inside, from the Salvation Army and we bought a refrigerator. The emotion of having access to my own refrigerator, filled with food of my choice, is indescribable. It was almost a dozen years since I lived in an apartment with a kitchen I could call my own. We bought four folding chairs and a small used table. We used an old bookcase to store the food and dishes.

For our bedroom, we bought a mattress and bedsprings. We made a cabinet for our clothes from sheets of pre-cut plywood and made shelves on one side and then hung sliding hardware to hang shirts, and so on, on the other side. We covered the wood with wood-grained contact paper so it had a better appearance. We got heavy cardboard boxes from the supermarket and put a heavy stone in each, covering it with matching contact paper. These became our night stands. We also bought two folding Japanese paper lanterns. With the help of wire hangers and a socket we made instant lights for each side of the bed.

For my study we bought a large, aluminum folding table for the desk and I used Joyce's chair from college and used the desk lamp from my days in Lincoln Hospital.

The fourth room was used as a living room where we entertained friends. We got a sturdy cardboard box from the supermarket and painted it black. This became the base for our coffee table. We got a four by four foot piece of plywood and stained it to use for the top. From a distance, the table appeared to have a black onyx base. We piled up bricks and placed shelves on them for our books. We hung shelves on the wall to display a few decorative wedding gifts. We bought a lounge chair; a butterfly-type metal frame covered with black canvas, and covered the outside radiator with a special covered board and used it for display. Joyce made curtains for the final touch.

After that was completed, we basically had a four-room furnished apartment that was our first apartment together, something we were proud of. Our goal was to stay there for only one year and then proceed to settle in California.

The academic year at the University of Pennsylvania exposed me to the art of surgery from a completely different perspective – the academic one. Exposure to the faculty as well as to the guest speakers was stimulating and enlightening.

It was an exciting year. At Lincoln Hospital, I had learned the practical aspects of surgery and the daily challenge of the care of the patients. At the University of Pennsylvania I was exposed to the academic approach to medicine, writing and publishing articles. The year passed very quickly and the time came for us to move again, this time to California.

I applied for a license to practice medicine in California. I was accepted for the examination and flew to California for my oral exam. Joyce's cousins, Marcia and Larry Israel, were very hospitable and let us use their car. After the exam we flew back to Pennsylvania to pack our belongings and prepare to drive to California.

Before leaving Pennsylvania we decided to sell all our 'furniture' and put an ad in the paper. Surprisingly enough there were several people who were interested in buying all the furniture in our apartment, including the refrigerator. Once everything was picked up, our apartment was again empty. The landlord asked us not to dismantle the door and the wall leading to the second floor. With everything packed, including our skis, we were on our way to California.

It was an experience to drive across the United States from east to west. We had the opportunity to stop at our leisure and explore the beautiful places that we encountered. I highly recommend that everyone take the time to cross the United States by car. It gave us the opportunity to understand what a magnificent country the United States is. It took us ten days to drive and we arrived in California a few days before the written State Board exam.

William Z. Gdud settled in La Puente, California, set up a general practice and changed his name to Good. Paul Geleris settled in Glendora, California and set up his pathology laboratories only about ten miles away. We decided to join them in California.

The next question was which location we should choose. I was determined not to compromise and to seek a practice limited to surgery. The warm reception from Bill and Pearl Good and Paul and Marilyn Geleris was heartwarming. At that time, the Goods had three children: a boy, Lenny, and baby twins, Michael and Hannah. Paul and Marilyn had two young sons, Andrew and Joseph. Even being so busy with the children and the new medical practices, they always found time to spend with us and help to guide us in the right direction. I greatly appreciated the friendship we had developed in the Casa Dello Studente. The Good and Geleris families became aunts and uncles to my children.

California is a beautiful state with mountains, desert and the sea. It reminded me a lot of the climate and nature that I had only seen previously in Italy. One of the most panoramic places that I saw during my trip across country was when we stopped for some time in Lake Tahoe, in northern California.

Joyce and I set out to see where in California I should start my practice. There was no question that some places were more attractive nature-wise and some other places were less attractive. Some surgeons, who were practicing in the more desirable areas, advised me that it is a little better a few miles away, not to stop here, but to continue to look in another area. I learned that, despite the fact that there was a need for surgeons in every place, in a very desirable location there was a tightly-controlled group who tried to keep newcomers away.

After researching all my options, and after Joyce and I sat down to evaluate them, we decided the best place to settle was in La Puente, where I would have the support of Bill Good and people with whom he worked. I discussed these thoughts with him and told him of my decision.

I received a notice from the California Medical State Board of Examiners that I had passed my exam, and my license to practice medicine and surgery was issued. There was a suite available in the same medical building where Bill Good had his office. I rented it. Joyce and I were busy setting up the office with all the equipment and furniture required.

Slowly I built up a surgical referral practice. Bill Good sent me his surgical cases and introduced me to the physicians in the community. Gradually my practice grew. I was happy to be in California.

Here again, the three of us from Casa dello Studente – Bill Good, Paul Geleris and I – found ourselves living close to each other, practicing in nearby towns in California.

25. Paul Geleris, Zev Gdud and Jack, founders of the Casa dello Studente, Turin, 1946. A friendship of 60 years started there.

26. William Z. Gdud, Paul Geleris and Jack, practicing medicine in La Puente and Glendora, California.

As a human being, you can achieve almost everything that you want to achieve. You should always remember, however, that with good friends around, the same achievement is much easier and is endured with less pain. I was privileged to have two such good friends, Bill and Paul, and their families, who went out of their way to make my transition to settling in California a real pleasure.

Joyce, upon our arrival in California, had applied for a teaching position in the local elementary school. Since the school year had already started and we had only one car, it seemed practical for her to work in my office. She became the receptionist and office manager. This way we had a lot of time together and she was able to understand my life as a practicing surgeon.

After having applied to be certified by the American Board of Surgery, I was advised of the dates of the examination and I began preparing myself for it.

At one of the meetings in the local hospital, I met Dr H. Donel Elshire (Don) who was a young surgeon who had started his practice at approximately the same time. During our conversation I found out that he was also studying for the boards. We decided that it might not be a bad idea to start studying together. The American Board of Surgery examination had a very high 'mortality' rate. Some of the surgeons used to fail once or twice before they were able to pass and be certified. It was a great challenge.

Don Elshire was an intelligent, young surgeon who had trained at the county hospital in Los Angeles and was dedicated to the art of surgery. By studying with him I got to know him and I liked him. I was happy that the feeling was mutual. We both had a passion for surgery and devotion to our families. At some time we decided to join our practices and form a partnership. We kept two offices, my office in La Puente and his office in Glendora. His interest was in vascular surgery and my interest outside of general surgery was pediatric surgery. We both pursued our interests by attending different conferences and postgraduate courses to further our education. As soon as the partnership was formed and our schedules worked out, we both realized how fortunate we were, as the partnership created more free time for ourselves to be able to spend time with our families. We also had another thing in common: we both liked to travel. Don, his wife and two children were avid skiers, as were Joyce and I.

The American Board of Surgery examination was scheduled in San Francisco. The day before the examination Joyce and I flew to San Francisco. Don did not feel that he was completely ready and postponed the board examination until the next examination date. I felt that my additional training, the fifth year of surgery at the University of Pennsylvania, gave me tremendous confidence. I believed I was very well-prepared. However, I was still scared of the examination. We, the candidates, learned the names of the examiners and it brought terror to our minds.

Dr De Bakey was assigned as my examiner. He was a renowned surgeon based in Dallas, Texas. Needless to say, the name of Dr De Bakey brought a tremendous fear to my mind. I entered the room and sat in the chair in front of him. He asked me how I felt and if I was ready for the examination. After my affirmative answer, he presented a case to me and asked how I would handle that case. During my year stay in Pennsylvania, we had special sessions handled in the same way. We, the students, had to figure out step by step the diagnostic examination as well as the treatment approach. When I realized the type of examination this would be I immediately felt very comfortable and relaxed. I think I even was able to smile and give my answers to Dr De Bakey. He listened closely, but it was difficult to detect his reaction to my presentation.

I had come to a point in the examination where I owed my answer to the education that I received at the University of Pennsylvania. I recalled an identical case that had been presented during a lecture there and I was therefore prepared for the answers. Step by step diagnostic studies were required in establishing the patient's sustained trauma. I responded to the question asked by Dr De Bakey, saying that I would accompany the patient to the X-ray department. He looked at me and asked why. My goal was to demonstrate the presence of a small pneumothorax. It is essential that an X-ray be taken in expiration instead of inspiration. He looked at me with a big smile on his face and said, 'Good thinking.' A few minutes later, I found that my half an hour was over and I felt that this one pearl of wisdom I learned at the University of Pennsylvania was worth the whole year I had spent. This half hour with Dr De Bakey inspired tremendous confidence, so that my fear dissipated when I faced the other examiners.

After the examination, Joyce was waiting for me and we decided to go to the 'Top of the Mark' lounge in the Mark Hopkins Hotel to celebrate. We went, but my mouth was so dry that I could not even take a sip of water. It took me the rest of the day to recover from the 'psychological examination trauma'. Two months later I received a congratulatory letter from the American Board of Surgery confirming that I had passed the exams and was officially certified by the American Board of Surgery.

Don and I built up a solid surgical practice. We were both devoted to surgery and had tremendous respect and consideration for our patients and our practice grew very fast. We became known in our community and received a lot of respect.

Don took his board examinations six months later and passed. We were both board-certified surgeons. Two years later we became eligible to apply to the American College of Surgeons. To be a member of the American College of Surgeons is a prestigious honor. Any board-certified surgeon can apply for membership, with certain requirements of ethics and surgical performance. We received the applications and diligently filled them out and mailed them back. Six weeks later, to my surprise, I received a letter saying that my application had been denied and no further correspondence was required. Needless to say I was deeply upset and decided to find out why my application had been rejected.

The first step was to consult Dr Amendola. I called and made an appointment at his office in New York and flew there. He was very cordial. He listened to my story and was puzzled that I had been denied admission to the American College of Surgeons. He asked me to return in two days. In the meantime, he promised that he would call his good friend, Dr Stephenson, who was the secretary of the American College of Surgeons. I stayed in New York and revisited Dr Amendola a few days later. He learned, in the process of investigation, that a letter received from one of the surgeons, an officer of the American College of Surgeons practicing in the same community, had made a derogatory statement about me saying that my practice had grown very fast and therefore 'I must be involved in unethical behavior.'

Dr Amendola said to me, 'Dr Brauns, I have known you for so many years and I do not believe that unethical behavior was the reason for the growth of your practice.' We talked at length and he asked me about a few surgeons. He felt there might have been a personal grudge or competitive anger, for the surgeon to try to keep me out of the American College of Surgeons in order to enhance his own surgical standing in the community. He promised not to let this go by.

I asked him if he would also call Dr Ravdin, the Chairman of the Board of the America College of Surgeons, who knew me fairly well in the year that I spent at the University of Pennsylvania.

Approximately two months later, I received a letter from Dr Stephenson telling me that the board had had a meeting and it was decided to conduct an investigation of the charges.

A few weeks later, an investigator from the American College of Surgeons appeared at my office, as well as at the hospital, to check all my records in reference to surgical reports, transactions, those who assisted me in surgery, and the financial records.

The efforts of Dr Amendola and Dr Ravdin to help me out finally paid off. Approximately two months later, I received a congratulatory letter stating that my records had been checked and it was the decision of the American College of Surgeons to admit me as a Fellow of the American College of Surgeons.

Interestingly enough, Dr Elshire faced the same fate as I had, but because of the results of the America College of Surgeons investigation of me, he was also cleared because we were partners. We decided to find the surgeon in our community who had made these derogatory remarks. It took some time and we learned that the person was one of our colleagues, who pretended to be our friend. He was extremely nice to us when we talked to him; he resented both of us, however, for coming to this community and building up such a large and successful practice. Over a cup of coffee, we decided to continue our relationship with him, because we were the winners and he was the loser.

That year I went to Atlantic City to the meeting of the American College of Surgeons, where I was initiated as a Fellow of the American College of Surgeons.

The moral of the story is that you must not allow yourself to be derailed by somebody who makes false accusations. Dr Amendola and Dr Ravdin helped to pursue justice and clear my name as well as that of Dr Elshire.

Our practice was growing and we had less and less time to spend with our families. We met a young surgeon, Dr Mark Anapoell, who worked in the community. He approached us and asked if we could use some help. He stated that he would be leaving the group he was working with and had heard about our reputation. A close relationship had developed between Don Elshire and me as far as trust was concerned and it was a big decision to invite a third person to join us. Because of our devotion to our families, our quest for more free time and our passion for surgery, we decided to include Mark in our group. He was a very well-trained surgeon who had attended Flower Fifth Avenue Medical School in New York. We reached an agreement and formed an equal partnership. Mark maintained his own office in West Covina.

Our surgical group was doing a large number of vascular

surgeries, mainly done by Don. I was doing a lot of general and pediatric surgeries and most of the pediatricians were sending their patients to us. Mark was doing general and vascular surgeries. We were a well-coordinated, happy team.

One day in 1960 I picked up a newspaper and found a short article mentioning that Nikita Khrushchev and his wife were planning a visit to the United States. I thought this might be my opportunity to get a petition or letter to Mrs Khrushchev asking her to obtain the permits for my parents, Dr Moses and Basia (Betty) Brauns, to leave the Soviet Republic of Lithuania and join me. Many times in the past my efforts had failed.

I remembered that Dr Robert Fry, an anesthesiologist with whom I worked, told me that he personally knew ex-Congressman Patrick Hillings, who had gone to school with Vice-President Richard Nixon in California, and who might be able to help me.

I made arrangements to meet Dr Fry to share my ideas with him. I told him the story of the separation from my parents since the war, and that my parents were still in Lithuania, part of the Soviet Union. Now that Mr Khrushchev was visiting California, perhaps Vice-President Nixon could help me in giving my petition, on behalf of my parents, to Mrs Khrushchev. One of my concerns, however, was the confrontation that Nixon had with Khrushchev at a fair in Moscow. Maybe this might hinder my plans, but Dr Fry agreed it was a good idea for me to meet his friend ex-Congressman Pat Hillings and make the arrangements.

The following week I met ex-Congressman Hillings and discussed with him the historical events that had led to our separation, and that my biggest request, an impossible dream, was to get my parents out of Lithuania. He was a very warm and compassionate person. He listened carefully and then told me that he would contact Nixon and see if something could be done.

Nixon, who was in the midst of his election campaign, was the speaker at a Catholic fund-raising event in the Beverly

Hilton Hotel in Los Angeles. Joyce and I attended the event. Ex-Congressman Hillings made arrangements with the Secret Service for me to meet with Nixon during the evening. I went to this event with my heart palpitating and waited. After the people starting leaving, a member of the Secret Service approached me and said that he would escort Joyce and me to the end of the reception line to meet Vice-President and Mrs Nixon. We were very excited.

When we met Vice-President and Mrs Nixon they extended their hands in greeting and Nixon listened attentively while I presented my story. I told him that getting my parents out of the Soviet Union to reunite with them was my biggest and most impossible dream. I had brought a letter written in Russian, composed by myself and Bill and Pearl Good. Pearl has a very beautiful handwriting and perfect knowledge of Russian and she helped me to compose this letter. The letter compared Mrs Khrushchev to my mother, stating that Mrs Khrushchev had had two sons. One of her sons had been killed during the Second World War. My mother also had two sons; one had been killed by the Nazis, and I was the only remaining son.

Nixon, after listening to my whole story, still holding my hand, said to me, 'Mr Khrushchev is no friend of mine, but I will do everything I can to help you. I cannot promise that anything will happen, but as you said, it never hurts to try.' In the meantime Mrs Nixon was holding Joyce's hand and also listened intently to my story. We thanked Vice-President and Mrs Nixon and we left.

I was so emotionally drained from this meeting that I could not fall asleep that night, thinking that perhaps there was a chance after fifteen years to see my parents.

A few days later I received a telegram from the White House, signed by Nixon, telling me that he had made the arrangements to deliver my letter to Mrs Khrushchev. I was thrilled by the telegram and my hopes increased. My dreams of seeing my parents were intensified.

Mr and Mrs Khrushchev had their problems in California.

For security reasons they were not allowed to go to Disneyland and that upset Khrushchev. It was thought best not to give him the letter in Los Angeles, but to choose a different city.

Approximately ten days later I received a notification from the Soviet Embassy in Washington, signed by Ambassador Menshikov, that Mrs Khrushchev had received my letter in Texas and that Dr Moses and Basia Brauns would be granted permission to leave the Soviet Union. I sat down in a chair where I stayed for a long time as if I had been struck by friendly lightning. My dreams to get my parents out of the Soviet Union had become a reality. Joyce and I hugged each other and cried with excitement.

Joyce was expecting our first child and at the same time my impossible dream to reunite with my parents was coming to pass. Two of the most important events were happening simultaneously.

A couple of weeks later I received a letter from my parents, through Israel, advising me that they had been contacted by the Soviet Foreign Ministry and had been advised that within ten days they would be receiving a visa to leave the Soviet Union. The news must have brought tremendous excitement to my parents; this was a dream that they had had for years, since our separation. The letter I received from my parents was overwhelming and suddenly I felt that my impossible dream might become a reality. I still kept my fingers crossed because nothing happens until it really happens.

I had regularly corresponded with my parents through Israel because it was politically safer for my parents to receive mail from their son in Israel than in the United States. At the courtesy of Rabbi Gdud (father of Bill Good) I sent all the mail to his house in Hadera in Israel, which was forwarded to my parents and then vice versa.

I wrote a letter to my friend Avraham Tory, who was practicing law in Tel Aviv, and asked him to prepare the papers for my parents to join me in Israel. Avraham Tory had been the Secretary of the *Altestenrat* (Jewish Council) in the

Kovno Ghetto and was a close friend of my father. He felt privileged to be able to help my father come out of the Soviet Union. After a few days all the papers were filed and mailed to my parents. In two months, my parents received an exit visa to go to Israel.

Finally I received a telegram from Avraham Tory advising me that within a week he would pick my parents up at the airport in Tel Aviv and that they would be staying with him until all the papers were arranged for them to proceed to the United States. Ironically, his wife, Pnina Tory, who had been visiting their daughter in Berkeley, California, was at our house when we received this telegram. I was so happy, but my happiness would not be complete until I really knew they had landed safely in Israel. Last-minute plans for one reason or another can always change. A week later, my parents arrived in Israel and I spoke to them for a long time on the phone. I was so excited. It had been fifteen years since I had seen my father and sixteen years since I had seen my mother.

My parents received their visas to proceed to the United States. They sent a telegram advising us of their departure from Israel to Los Angeles. Arrangements were made for them to fly with Trans World Airlines (TWA). On the planned departure date, TWA went on strike and they provided my parents with two tickets to San Francisco on Lufthansa, and then a connection on an American carrier to Los Angeles. It was 28 December 1960.

There was no time to fly to San Francisco to meet them. I made a phone call to my friends, Cesare and Barbara Reyneri, who lived in Mountain View, California, close to San Francisco. They graciously agreed to greet my parents at the airport and spend a few hours with them, and then guide them to the next airline. They stayed with them until the flight was ready to board for Los Angeles. I will always be grateful to Cesare and Barbara for doing this, and for sharing the excitement of greeting my parents in the United States.

We asked Pearl and William Good to come to our house

and babysit for Suzette Claire – our daughter who had been born on 4 October 1960, just two and a half months earlier – so that we could go to Los Angeles Airport to pick up my parents.

In my parents' lives as well as in my life, our emotions were often curbed. Our lives made us curb our emotions. When the plane landed we were able to walk onto the tarmac and watch them come down the stairs. I first saw my mother coming down the steps followed by my father. I realized that my dreams had become a reality. I would not only be able to see my parents, but I would be able to touch them with my hands. We hugged for a minute and then we walked to the car to drive home. We were so numb with emotion no tears were shed.

Their faces were happy and beaming as was mine and I was so pleased to see the love and affection that Joyce showed them as well as what my parents showed Joyce. They had only known Joyce from pictures that I continued to send them along with pictures of our precious baby Suzette, their first grandchild, whom they were very anxious to meet.

On the way home, with all the excitement of the reunion, my father was still focused on his past life in the Soviet Union and insisted that we go to the nearest police station and report their arrival. I do not think he was convinced when I told him this was not obligatory in the United States.

We arrived home, greeted by the Goods. Pearl set the table meticulously and tea and cakes were ready. It was a joyous reunion.

The next morning they asked how often they could shower, once a week or twice a week? When they saw the Sunday edition of the *New York Times* they wondered why we received so many papers. The size of it was not conceivable in their minds.

Six months before their arrival, in June 1960, we had purchased a house in Covina. We prepared a bedroom and bathroom for them. My parents gradually settled in and we all enjoyed being together and sharing our experiences, trying to catch up on the conversations we had missed for the past fifteen to sixteen years.

They were overjoyed to meet their granddaughter, Suzette, but were astounded that we allowed our German shepherd dog, Thunder, whom we adopted as a puppy when we purchased our house, to stay in our house with the new baby. In the Soviet Union dogs carried various diseases and my father was concerned for health reasons. My mother's reaction was different. When she saw Thunder lick Suzette it awoke her memories and she stated that unquestionably a German shepherd, who licked her face, played a role in saving her life. My mother had told me the story about this through many letters I received from her after the war. That was the reason we chose a German shepherd dog. Now she told us this story again, in person.

When Stutthof Concentration Camp was being evacuated in 1945, the inmates were subject to long marches, and those who could not keep up with the marches were executed on the spot along the road by SS officers who followed the column. At one point during the march my mother was run over by a German military car and sustained a compound, comminuted fracture of her right ankle. She was immobilized by the injury and lay helpless in the snow.

Two events saved my mother's life. An SS man with a German shepherd dog appeared. Instead of attacking my mother as the dog had been trained to do, he sniffed and licked her face. The SS guard was surprised. Coincidentally at this moment a group of German refugees in carriages drawn by horses arrived at the scene. They were escaping the war zone. The SS guard had intended to shoot my mother since she could not walk, but he could not carry out this order due to the presence of the German refugees, and he left her lying in the snow. Her hair was prematurely gray and her body was emaciated, therefore the SS guard assumed she would die shortly anyway.

The refugees, seeing her lying in the snow, picked her up, hid her in their cart and transported her to the city hospital of

Stargard. Apparently the refugees belonged to a secret underground organization that rescued people from the atrocities of the Nazis.

An unpleasant scene between the hospital personnel, the doctor on duty and the refugees occurred. The hospital staff told the refugees that no Jews were allowed to be treated in a city hospital so they took my mother to a farmhouse where the people hid her in the attic and provided for her care. The same doctor who was not able to attend to her in the hospital made periodic visits to the farmhouse to treat her for several months. He belonged to the same secret organization as the refugees.

Several months later my mother was liberated by the Red Army and transferred to a military hospital. After she was discharged she returned to Vilnius. Miraculously my mother's injury gradually healed and eventually she was able to walk with a slight limp. The dog's compassion saved my mother's life by licking her. It distracted the SS man and in those minutes when the refugees passed by he was not able to shoot her.

My mother always remembered the good deeds of the all the people, including some Germans, who risked their lives to rescued her, and the German shepherd who saved her life. She always talked about it.

I was extremely happy that my daughter would have the opportunity to get to know my parents. In the days to come, it was very exciting for Joyce and me to take my parents to different places and watch their reactions. These were not fancy or elaborate places, but places like the supermarket. My mother could not believe that such a large variety of food and consumer goods was available for all the people and not just the privileged as it was in the Soviet Union. Members of the Communist Party could go to certain stores and buy particular items that were not available in different stores. It was also very sobering for me because it reinforced my feelings of how lucky and privileged I was to be living in the United States.

Many immigrants from Lithuania read about the arrival of

27. Jack's parents, newly arrived in the US, with Jack, Joyce and the newborn Suzette, May 1961.

my parents and those who knew my father and mother before the war started to call. In the evenings we had gatherings of different friends who came to visit Basia and Moses (friends called them Betty and Mosy) and they all reminisced about the pre-war times. Irena Veisaite's father had immigrated to the United States before the war and coincidentally lived about an hour away from our house. He became a frequent visitor. Also, I was reunited with Si Frumkin, who came one evening with his mother and stepfather to greet and welcome my parents. Si and I maintain a close friendship to this day. Norman and Irene Lyons, and Kobek Beilinson with his wife Annette, and my father's cousin, Miriam Wanks, all friends from Lithuania before the war, came to the house, and continued to be frequent visitors for more than twenty years, until my parents passed away. I was happy that my parents had their own circle of friends and would not be lonely. They also established a network of friends in our community. Among those I worked with was Dr Reginald Denke, from Germany.

When his parents visited him, as they did several times a year, my parents extended hospitality to them, in spite of my parents' past experiences in Germany. My father always said, 'You cannot blame a whole race for the dreadful deeds of some.'

Within a few months Uncle Heinz, who was my main loyal supporter and had provided me with funds for my existence and made it possible for me to continue medical school in Italy for so many years, came to California with his wife Sonia. They stayed in our home for a month. The two brothers, Mosy and Heinz, were finally reunited after so many years. Heinz had immigrated to South Africa after the First World War and set up a textile business.

Shortly afterward my mother's sister Leny, and her husband Eugene Tal, who were living in Argentina, visited us. They immigrated there before the war and both practiced medicine. Now finally my parents met with all their few remaining relatives.

After a few months we built a separate apartment with bedroom, bathroom, living room / study and kitchen attached to our house for my parents so we both had privacy. We traditionally ate together every Friday night for an Oneg Shabbat (Sabbath meal) and Sunday for brunch. Otherwise we cooked separately and ate at different hours. Our lifestyles were very different and we all wanted to respect one another.

My father learned to speak English by diligently following an audio language program. He quickly became fluent, and in subsequent years wrote his memoirs in English. He spent his time corresponding with friends all over the world. At the same time he was also an avid stamp collector. He was very structured time-wise and was able to find time for everything. He enjoyed television and would never miss the law court presentation which was so different in its presentation of the democratic way of life from the land he came from. He checked the television guide daily. One day he asked me how 'Beatles' could be on Ed Sullivan's show. Of course he did not realize Beatles were not insects, but the name of a musical group.

28. Jack's parents visiting Uncle Heinz, Aunt Sonia and cousins Aubrey and Ella, South Africa, 1963.

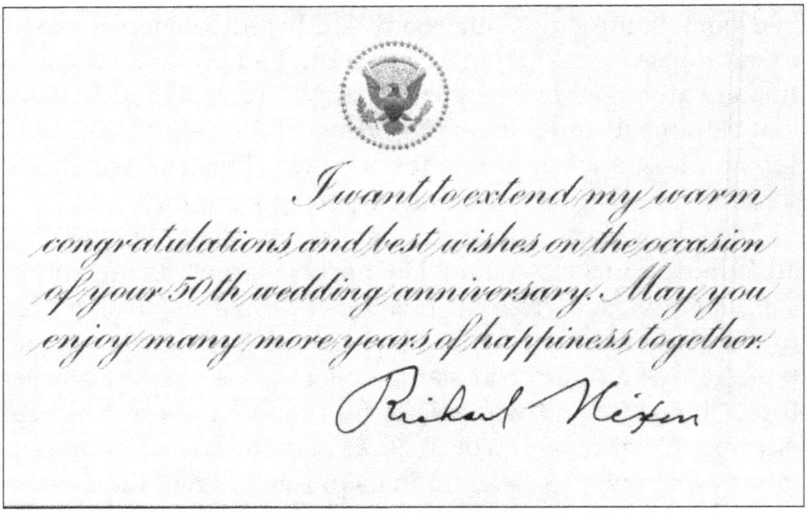

I want to extend my warm congratulations and best wishes on the occasion of your 50th wedding anniversary. May you enjoy many more years of happiness together.

Richard Nixon

29. Letter of congratulation from President Nixon, 1972.

My father also enjoyed working in the garden. We planted an orchard for him. I cannot describe the pleasure he experienced not only caring for the orchard, but also harvesting the fruit that the orchard produced. He described to me his thoughts during Stalin's era in Lithuania: If he could be granted one wish in those days, it was that he would be able to eat an apple or an orange every day.

My mother joined the Brandeis book club which was active in our community. The club made her welcome and benefited from all her knowledge of German, Russian and French literature. My parents adjusted to life in California very quickly.

For me the most exciting thing about having my parents in our house was the conversations that I had with both of them. They were conversations that I had missed over the last fifteen years. Medicine was my father's passion and I was always interested in his thinking. My parents were always positive. They never argued. They adapted to the American culture and we all lived together on the very best terms for twenty years.

They became like second parents to our children and they gave us the opportunity to travel because my mother and father felt comfortable staying at home and taking care of the children. They felt secure in knowing many of our friends and knowing that they could depend on them for help if they needed it.

Joyce and I were able then to travel and join a medical group visiting China. It was one of the first trips arranged after Nixon established a relationship with China.

The Chinese government extended an invitation to a group of orthopedic surgeons from the United States, to learn about medicine in China. We were shown a thyroidectomy done under acupuncture in Shanghai. We also visited the patients who underwent reattachment of limbs, which the Chinese pioneered, in the same hospital.

On another occasion we joined an American radiology group traveling to Kenya, which was combined with a safari. It was an eye-opening experience to visit the hospitals and witness the difference between Nairobi and the countryside hospitals. The safari took us to places which fascinated us with their beauty in nature and a totally different culture. We made a promise to take our family there one day to share the impressive sights.

In Thailand we attended a conference of the International College of Surgeons hosted by the King of Thailand. I learned that medicine all over the world is basically the same, but with cultural differences in each country.

One day after my parents had been here for a while, my father asked me what surgeries I had done that day. I told him, described them, and told him what I did and why I did it. About three days later, my father asked me how patients X, Y and Z were doing. I told him that they were fine. He asked me if I had called the patients' families. I told him that I had not, but that the patients' families knew my phone number and if they would like to know anything they could just call me.

My father was visibly upset and said, 'Remember that the patient, whether a child, a parent, an uncle or grandparent, is a most important family member of that family. They might be very humble people and might not want to disturb you. It is your obligation to call them and keep them informed of the patient's progress. This is the basic responsibility that you have.' I promised my father that I would be making calls from then on to the family of every patient who was in the hospital, to keep them informed of their progress, and to follow their progress at home after they had been discharged from the hospital.

When I returned to the office, my nurse prepared for me a list of the three to five patients who were in the hospital, along with their phone numbers. Before I began office hours every day, I would call and inform each family of the progress of their hospitalized loved ones. In time, it became my routine. In the 1960s, it was not customary for a physician to call his patients. I never knew why my practice grew so fast, but one day I realized it was not only because I was an experienced surgeon, but also because I was one who communicated with the patient and called the family to keep them informed. It became a habit for me; I did not feel any wasted time in doing so.

Twelve years after my father died, I did a hernia repair on a patient. Immediately following the surgery, he went home. As a rule, I would call the patient at home the day after surgery to find out how he was doing. The patient's wife answered the phone and told me that he was doing very well and he was feeling well except for one problem: he was nauseated and throwing up.

I talked to the patient and he confirmed what his wife told me. He told me not to worry about him because he was drinking a lot of water to compensate for the loss of the fluid that he was eliminating. I advised his wife to go to the drugstore and get a medication for the nausea and I would call them back a few hours later. When I called back, his wife again told me how well her husband felt, and that the nausea and vomiting had stopped, but she noticed a twitching in his facial muscles. I talked to the patient and he told me the same thing. He advised me not to worry about him because he felt very well. I advised his wife to put him in a car or call an ambulance and I would meet her in the emergency room.

An hour later, I met them in the emergency room. He received some medication for the twitching. I decided to stay at the hospital until I saw that he was completely out of danger. A few minutes later the emergency room called and told me that he had had a convulsion. I returned to the emergency room. The patient was not convulsing at the time I saw him. I called a neurologist immediately to evaluate the patient. The blood work that I had drawn on his admission returned, and I learned that his potassium was at an extremely low level, explaining the events of his post-operative course. The neurologist arrived and found no other reason for the convulsion and confirmed that the culprit was the patient's low potassium level. He was admitted to intensive care overnight. In the morning, he was completely normal after he had received the proper dose of potassium to supplement his potassium levels. Subsequently he was discharged home.

The moral of this story is that if I had not called him and found out the symptoms he had, most likely he would have continued vomiting, continuously depleting his potassium to a point of no return. My father, from his grave, had saved a life. I was still indoctrinated by him to call my post-operative patients, and he was responsible for having saved this patient's life. If I had not called, because the patient felt he was doing so well, he most likely would have died and the cause of death probably would have been classified as connected to heart failure. I do not know how many patients I helped by calling them, but I know about this particular call that saved the patient's life.

I continued practicing surgery with Dr Elshire and Dr Anapoell in our community. We earned a good reputation, but the main thing was that we had the privilege of spending time with our families, due to the surgical coverage that we offered each other through our partnership.

In 1962 we were blessed with the birth of our second daughter, Janine, and in 1965 the birth of our third daughter, Alicia. I felt blessed to be surrounded by five women: Joyce, Suzette, Janine, Alicia and my mother. My father and I were the beneficiaries of the love generated by the women in our household. So too was Thunder, our German shepherd and his son, Blitz, born a few years later.

While practicing general surgery, which included a lot of industrial emergency surgery, I felt there was a tremendous need for Industrial Medical Clinics. I formulated the concept and created, with my partners' support and encouragement, the first Tri-City Industrial Medical Clinic in the City of Industry, California, and subsequently the second one in Gardena, California. The clinics served a large number of industrial facilities and were very successful.

Because of our involvement with industrial clinics I had the opportunity to bid for an Industrial Medical Facility at the Los Angeles Airport when it was expanding. I had many innovative ideas for emergency care at the airport, including the introduction of mini-ambulances built from golf carts which could easily travel in the underground passageways. Unfortunately the final decision was between two choices, our facility and a very large and powerful hospital with 'deep pockets' They were chosen.

After the war I rekindled my interest in photography. First I got a still camera and during my students years I took many pictures. In later years I bought a movie camera. This was a very important hobby for me and it also kindled the interest of my children in photography. Separately, I taught each of my children, who learned very fast, how to take pictures and how to develop them. All of them became very interested in photography. I built a black and white darkroom at home which I enjoyed very much and at the same time stimulated the interest of the entire family. Over the years Suzette became proficient in underwater photography stills, Janine in portraits and landscapes, and Alicia in stills and in filming and editing videos and movies. Their pictures enhance our home.

Joyce and I knew that schools would provide the required education for our children, but we felt that it was our responsibility to provide the extra education that would stimulate their interest in different directions and expose them to the philosophy and appreciation of life itself.

Most of the children born to Holocaust survivors are deprived of their grandparents, uncles, aunts, and cousins. We were extremely fortunate because Joyce's family members were living in the United States during the war and my children had the privilege of having grandparents, Abraham and Kate (Kitty) Sklar, and their family. Unfortunately, Joyce's father, Abraham, died when Suzette was three years old. Joyce's mother, Kitty, then moved to Los Angeles from New York.

The actual awareness of the Holocaust started early for my children. The friends who visited my parents were mostly Holocaust survivors and the stories they heard were the beginning of their Holocaust education. It continued through their lifetime with all the events they encountered in school and in museums. They participated and attended the opening of the Kovno Ghetto Exhibit in the Holocaust Memorial Museum in Washington on 20 November 1997, where all the stories were documented. It was like looking through a window into the past life of the Brauns family.

I learned early in the raising of my daughters that one-to-one contact as well as contact all together is essential to a strong, healthy relationship. Everyone recalls the many times when just one daughter and I spent quality time together – whether going for an ice cream or making a small trip together – when each of us could communicate and open up to the other. It was a great opportunity to learn about and encourage their varied interests. When the opportunity presented itself, Joyce and I separately made trips with each child.

Alicia went to the American School in Switzerland for the last two years of high school. It was located in Lugano. My friend Beno, his wife, Busia, and their daughter, Irit, lived in Lugano, so while in Switzerland, Alicia was not alone. Joyce and I also visited her separately several times during the two years.

The school made a field trip to visit the site of Dachau Concentration Camp, just outside Munich, which is now a museum. This visit made a huge impact on her and she sent me a poem expressing her feelings:

> November 16, 1981.
> Dear Dad,
> I visited the place
> Where what they used for lace
> Was so much barbed wire,
> It made my heart turn on fire.
>
> You lived there for a year
> I have to shed a tear.
> It must have been so awful,
> They were so unlawful.
>
> I respect you so much
> You have a special touch

Everyone could see
How much you mean to me.

It makes me so mad
What they did to you dad
But what can I do?
Except love you.

With every lasting love, Alicia.

Alicia felt it was important that her sisters and her mother must also see Dachau, so when Suzette and Janine visited her during Christmas break she made a special trip with them. She also took Joyce at another time.

During the spring break of 1982 the American School in Switzerland arranged a school trip to Moscow and Leningrad. Alicia felt that she would also like to visit Lithuania, to make the experience more meaningful, and our family decision was that Joyce should join her at the same time the school was going. I made special arrangements so mother and daughter could go on their own to trace family roots in Lithuania and travel to Tallinn, Viljandi, Moscow and Leningrad.

They received red-carpet hospitality from Irena, my adopted sister, who accompanied them to many places and introduced them to many of my friends, including Dodik and his family and other people who remembered my father, describing in great detail how caring he was to his patients. They learned about the life of the survivors who came back from the Soviet Union after the war. Alicia learned about the importance of education through the many young people she was exposed to.

On her return, Joyce told me: 'You suffered immensely during four years of the war, but you survived. In April 1945 you were liberated and joined a free society and started building your own life. Unfortunately some of your friends, who were evacuated to the Soviet Union and then returned to Lithuania when the war ended, were not as lucky. When we visited them thirty-five years after the end of the war, we found they are still living in fear and apprehension, struggling to survive day by day.'

When the children were very young, in the early 1970s, we utilized traveling and spending time together to supplement our daughters' education. It was important to start an appreciation of the world, beginning with the United States.

On our first road trip we exposed them to the wonders and beauty of nature in the national parks in the western United States. We also explored the west coast by car to San Francisco and another time flew to San Francisco and took a cruise to Vancouver, and to several ports in Alaska.

When we stopped in Vancouver our friends Barney and Nettie Prosterman met us at the pier. Barney was an orthopedic surgeon who was one of my senior residents at Lincoln Hospital. We had corresponded over the years and it was good to meet his family in Vancouver and renew our friendship.

Our next adventure took us to England, a different culture but one where everyone could be comfortable with the language and meet some of the friends with whom I was brought up in Lithuania. Our family visited my friends, Lord and Lady Kagan – Joseph and Mara – and their three children who lived in Yorkshire. Joseph and Mara were born in Lithuania and knew my family there. Before the war Joseph had been sent to England to study textile engineering and was brought back by his family in 1941, just for a visit, about a week before the war started. Unfortunately, he was caught in the turmoil that involved the Jews in Lithuania. A Lithuanian family risked their lives to save the Kagan family and they were hidden during the German occupation, and were saved. At the time, he was already married to Mara.

We slept in their guest house in Yorkshire – a medieval castle. I told them ghost stories and never forgot my children's faces when I pretended to be a ghost coming out from behind the curtain.

We were lucky to have Mara as our personal hostess and guide. She took us to the English countryside as well as London and introduced us to the history, heritage and current life.

Israel played an important role in my life. From childhood I learned about Zionism and my commitment as a Jew to Israel. Since I went to a Hebrew high school in Kaunas, my Hebrew was fluent. I wanted to expose my family to Israel.

Many of my close friends from childhood lived in Israel. We felt that it was essential that my children meet these friends they had heard so many stories about, to establish a close relationship, and to meet the younger generations. We made several trips and focused on different places each time.

The most dramatic adventures were organized by Zev Birger. During one visit he arranged a jeep trip through the Sinai Desert and we all camped at the foot of Mt Sinai.

Another time we took a four-day trip by jeep to the Negev. We climbed Masada, walked through Ein Gedi, swam in the Dead Sea, and on the way to Eilat visited King Solomon's mines. In Eilat we went scuba-diving and experienced the wonders and beauty of the undersea life of the Red Sea. At that time we were also able to stay in Taba which was later handed back to Egypt.

It was fascinating and impressive for my children to observe for the first time in their lives the intermingling of the Biblical Past Life with the present Modern Life. Walking the streets of Jerusalem and Tel Aviv, the shore of the Sea of Galilee, and towns of northern Israel was an unforgettable experience.

The benefit of these travels was to create memories that could never be taken away. All the trips were motivated by education.

I always remember my own life with my parents. I will never forget the details of the trips my parents took me on in the summertime. My father was always so busy and summertime trips gave him the opportunity to be away from the city where we lived and to be full-time with the family. Joyce and I tried to offer our own children the same type of family togetherness. Today, I have the most incredible relationship with members of my family and I feel these trips, being together away from the pressure of the daily grind, were the reason for it.

One day we received a call from Dora Wulc. She and her

husband were both former students of Casa dello Studente, and were living in Philadelphia. She had discovered that during the summer all the facilities at French universities were closed except for the linguistics department – in order to give foreigners an opportunity to study French and be exposed to French culture. We had a telephone conference and decided that all of us, including Dora Wulc and her children and the Brauns children with their friends, would go to Angers in the Loire Valley for one month to study French. It was a well-organized course and was taught in French. Class credits were transferred to the children's schools in the United States. There were about 500 students from different countries around the world. During the weekends the university organized trips and picnics to the Loire Valley.

As a reward for studying French we went to Club Med in Pompidou, near Limoges, and the specialized English Riding Club where all the lessons in the skill of riding English-style were in French. Dismounting upside down was one of the more difficult routines. I quit at that point.

Although Joyce and I did not have the same interest in riding horses, we learned early in our daughters' childhood that they were going to make many choices based on their individual interests. Our property in Covina allowed us to have horses, and there were many horse trails close by. Because of their enthusiasm for learning to ride, as well as for taking care of the horses, we bought our first horse, Sugar, and were able to board her in our neighbor's stable. Their stables and corral were directly behind our property and we were permitted to build a gate in the fence for easy access.

Alicia wanted her own horse and earned the money by doing jobs around the house. She was short of $100 to buy Jubal and her sister Suzette gave her this extra money.

My daughters' love for these horses was incredible. I always told them that I hoped they would love and care for their husbands as much as they loved and cared for their horses because, if they did, they would have happy marriages.

The next summer we chose Grenoble. Dora Wulc and her

daughter Karen, the same age as Suzette, joined us. The dormitories were occupied so we all slept in a nunnery. The most pleasant surprise for me, when I came to visit them, was that I received a special dispensation to sleep in the library during my stay.

We discovered that Club Med was a wonderful vacation place for a family interested in sports and togetherness, and we arranged to go to Club Med in Tahiti. It was there that Suzette and Joyce took a resort course in scuba-diving. The rest of us had the opportunity, through snorkeling, to be exposed to the wonders of underwater life there and to experience life in a tropical paradise. There we met people from all over the world and made many friends like Georges and Nathalie Carles from France. They visited us in Los Angeles and invited us to stay with them in their hotel in Serre Chevelier. We also met Judy and Paul Beckett from Los Angeles with whom we maintain a close friendship. They are like family. We have made many ski trips together and celebrate family functions.

The prerogative in the family was that any trip abroad had to be of educational value. Suzette and Janine wanted to continue to study French and get academic credits at the same time. The University of Georgetown in Washington had a summer program in Dijon and transferred credits to American universities. While they were there they played on the soccer team.

Joyce, Alicia and I joined them after their session was over and we made a family trip together by train to visit Nathalie and Georges Carles in Serre Chevelier in the French Alps. Their hospitality was overwhelming. They took us to their summer log cabin in the Alps and it was a fantastic union with nature. No electricity. We had to draw water from the well for cooking, but had running water in the shower. On daytime trips we hiked to high mountains where we were able to pick Edelweiss. The scenery was breathtaking.

From Serre Chevalier we took the train and stopped in Cannes to visit my Kaunas and Casa dello Studente friend

Beno Elstein and his wife Busia who were staying at Cap Ferrat. They embraced us with great hospitality. Here we experienced the beach and luxurious modern accommodation. It was a privilege to experience such different modes of living, from the mountains to the beach.

While Alicia attended Menlo College in Atherton, near Stanford University, she took the opportunity to go with a group from the school to Avignon in France as an exchange student. Each student was assigned to live with a local family.

Of the numerous educational trips, one of the highlights was a photographic safari adventure in Kenya. Joyce and I made our promise to return a reality. I always loved animals and felt it is not enough just to love animals. You have to try to understand the animals to really appreciate them. Our children were then in their late teens or early 20s. The whole family rode in a Land Rover, exploring the National Parks in Kenya and with an expert local guide had the opportunity to observe the interactive behavior of the wild animals in their habitat. The animals were so used to the Land Rovers we could drive up to within ten feet of a family of lions and they would just ignore us and go on with their daily routine. It was great fun and fascinating to watch them play, eat, sleep, hunt, and so on. We observed the difference between animal and human behavior. Few animals kill for the sake of killing; they kill to survive. It was an unforgettable experience. We were all challenged in our photographic skills and were able to bring back many images to reinforce our memory.

I am often surprised and amazed at how little appreciation some American-born people have for the privilege of living in the United States. By traveling around the world, my goal was to help my children appreciate the privilege of being able to live in the United States.

I am lucky to have met and married Joyce, who shared with me the same philosophy. The children also benefited from us living together with my parents, whose influence reinforced the appreciation of life and a positive attitude when facing challenges.

After the war I had lived in Turin, one hour from Sestriere, one of the foremost skiing locations in the Italian Alps. After Joyce and I were married, she perfected her skiing. It was our goal to teach our children to ski, not only as a recreational sport, but also as a way for our family to spend time together. We trained and skied with them.

My partner and friend, Don Elshire, his wife Roberta and their two children, Don and Robin, were also excellent skiers. Jointly we purchased a condominium in Mammoth Mountain, California. This was a good investment because it provided each of our families with a place to stay where we skied year after year.

Since education combined with travel was a prerequisite all three took advantage of this and went to Whistler Mountain in the Canadian Rockies, to Toni Sailor Summer Ski Camp. Suzette took the freestyle program and Janine and Alicia the racing program.

On one of our family ski vacations we went to Club Med in Copper Mountain, Colorado. A weekly slalom ski race was held for the guests. It is hard to describe the pleasure I had seeing my daughters, the youngest participants, win: Suzette, first place–Gold; Janine, second place–Silver; and Alicia, third place–Bronze. In other words, the Brauns' younger generation conquered the slopes, and although it was not an important race, it was still a great satisfaction for me to see them win.

On another ski vacation, Natalie and Georges Carles invited us back to their hotel in Serre Chevalier to celebrate the New Year, and to ski the Alps. We had stayed in their hotel during the summer, and being invited in the winter was a treat. Georges had converted an old barn into a hotel and they called it La Vieille Ferme. He is an excellent chef. His little hotel was famous for his superb cuisine.

During our stay, Natalie and Georges organized the skiing trips. None of us will forget the experience of crossing the Alps on skis, from France to Italy. We skied to Sestriere, Italy, had lunch and after lunch, skied back to Serre Chevelier,

France. The weather was excellent and it enhanced our incredible adventure. It was certainly a unique and unforgettable way to celebrate the New Year. The hospitality of our French hosts was extraordinary.

Suzette was focused at a young age. She liked to excel in whatever she did, in sports or at work. She graduated from the University of California, Davis, in managerial economics with an emphasis on marketing. Her first job was selling Dale Carnegie courses. She worked for Hewlett Packard and Bank of America and then several years later moved to Los Angeles. She helped to create the National Ambulatory Hernia Institute (NAHI) where she became the marketing director. Through Suzette's untiring efforts and creativity, she established and serviced fifteen centers of Excellence for Hernia Repair in California and formed the sister corporation in Florida which grew to five offices. She designed and prepared all the marketing materials, and implemented special events and conferences. She established a customer base and long-term relationships. This work led her to become the CEO of NAHI. Suzette's enthusiasm, positive attitude and genuine interest and compassion for people are great assets in her work.

Suzette met Jay Rivera and they married in Fiji on 28 December 1998. Our family met them and witnessed their union, giving our blessings. We are so happy to have Jay as part of our family. I enjoy spending time with him and appreciate his intelligence, kindness and devotion to our family and his own. Jay and Suzette had a baby boy, Joshua Ben Rivera, born on 21 October 2000. I can say this little baby has become the joy of our lives.

Suzette is interested in sports such as scuba-diving, and snow-skiing, and over the years participated in many marathons. She is very competitive. She was on the ski team at the University of California, Davis, and also represented and raced in corporate ski races for Hewlett Packard and the Bank of America.

Most recently Suzette has formed her own medical marketing company.

Janine has a tremendous sense of humor and a positive approach, which led her to explore different avenues of life, utilizing all the things she had been exposed to growing up. She went to the University of California, Davis, for two years.

Her quest for travel and French culture catapulted her to Paris where she enrolled at the Sorbonne. Zev Birger had lived in Paris for several years working in the film industry. He gave me the phone number of Dr Jacques and Vicki Ciepielewski, so Janine could call someone in case of emergency. She was invited to their home for Oneg Shabbat and they became friends. During her stay she had the opportunity to work in Jacques' dental office. On her return to the United States she continued her education at California State, Long Beach, where she graduated with a major in industrial arts.

Janine made a great contribution to my work by translating the earliest documentation of hernias from French medical books, enabling me to make a film on the history of hernias. She also created the corporate logo for the National Ambulatory Hernia Institute. She took time off to go to Colorado to teach skiing to people with disabilities, including the blind. Her diversified interests lead her to different fields. She is a creative artist and combines unusual art with photography. She made a collection of photographs from her travels, highlighting her two treks in Nepal.

Janine began work in computer graphics and is currently working as a script supervisor in the film industry.

Alicia is a bright and sensitive woman. She has always been interested in nature and photography, and while studying in Switzerland she photographed landscapes. She attended Menlo College in Atherton, California (Menlo Park) for two years and then transferred to Chapman College in Orange, California where she graduated with a major in mass media communication with an emphasis on film and television.

Because of her interest in filming, Alicia wanted to do a full-length feature about her father's experiences during the war. After reading *Surviving the Holocaust: The Kovno Ghetto Diary* by Avraham Tory, and meeting Avraham and his wife Pnina in Israel, she was inspired to write a movie script based on this book.

Avraham Tory granted Alicia the legal rights to write the script and make the movie. Alicia dedicated several years to researching the material and interviewed many survivors in Israel. Joyce and I accompanied her to record their stories.

Alicia co-wrote the screenplay with David Elton, and they devised a six hour mini-series. They called it *The Last Leaves of Winter*. The script received a positive response for the writing and the story but financially it was not affordable, not commercial enough, to generate the kind of money it needed.

Alicia helped to make the presentation for the Kovno Ghetto Exhibit to the Board of the United States Holocaust Memorial Museum in Washington, DC. She also made an outstanding contribution to our family memories by filming several professional videos of our trips, to Israel and skiing in Mammoth Mountain, editing them with a soundtrack.

At the present time she works in the movie industry as a camera assistant and is branching off with her own creative projects.

She has filmed hummingbirds from the point of hatching to flying, which she witnessed in her backyard, and then put the footage together into a story to create a video.

I never pushed our daughters into medicine and I am happy that they found their own interests and devotion in the fields in which they were interested. It was wonderful for Joyce and me to see how our daughters developed their own lives and bloomed like flowers. They contributed so much to my life.

The entire family, including Joyce, actively participated in helping me with all my projects, big and small, doing all kinds of tasks for which I am very grateful.

It was in the mid-1970s when we met Jim Tagami for the first time. He was highly recommended as a landscape designer, who specialized in Japanese gardens. He came to inspect the proposed area that had to be restored after we built an addition to our house.

After spending several hours in our house, reviewing different aspects of the garden, including the elevation drop that we wanted to landscape, he returned a week later with several sketches for our inspection. He advised us that in order for us to understand what he wanted to do, we had to take a trip together to Mt Baldy, about twenty miles from our home, in the San Bernardino Mountains. We drove there and walked around the creeks and streams. Jim showed us the natural flow of the waterfall, the creeks and the boulders surrounding the streams and the perfect balance that had been created by nature. The sights and sounds were also connected. Jim helped to open our eyes to become more aware of our surroundings. He was confident that he could create our garden and mold nature in our yard. He felt that a Japanese garden would bring the serenity of nature into our crowded lives. The emphasis was that the Japanese garden is alive and enhances the quality of human life. Joyce and I were in search of peace and tranquility which the Japanese garden would provide for us.

On my first trip to Japan, I visited many Japanese gardens and really began to understand the significance they played in the lives of the Japanese people. I was fascinated, and after I returned from Japan, I enriched my library with several books about Japanese gardens which I studied and read to enhance my knowledge. The most fascinating thing about Japanese gardens is that living people are represented by specific trees dedicated to them, and also immortalized with special rocks placed within the garden.

After we had several meetings with Jim, with his outlines of the proposed garden, I found out that when he built gardens he was never able to follow his proposed plans exactly because everything he did had to flow with the land and be natural. His philosophy is that nature cannot be planned. To create an outstanding garden it is essential to let nature play its own role. His philosophy is to create the garden so that it can adjust itself to nature.

It took Jim approximately ten years to construct the garden. First he hauled in the big rocks and then designed a water system that would have three ponds and a waterfall from one pond to the other. The rocks and boulders were individually selected by him.

Choosing the proper trees was extremely important. He knew Frank Yamashita-San, a master in raising and pruning Japanese pine trees. He invited him to see his project. Several trees were selected by Yamashita-San and Jim for the completion of the garden. Yamashita was impressed with the garden and was surprised that such a young man as Jim could have the ability and sensitivity to create it. He brought us appropriate trees for the garden. He chose black (male) and red (female) pines for the base of the gardens. The black tree representing me and the red tree representing Joyce were planted at the bottom of the third pond. These two trees were the supporters and base of the garden holding the pond together as we were the supporters of our family and held our family together. Three pine trees were brought in, representing each of our daughters. A double pine tree from the same trunk was chosen to represent my parents who had lived together for the past fifty years. The original two palms represented Joyce's parents. Jim selected special boulders and rocks which represented each of the members of the family for eternity to be placed near the individual trees. Yamashita-San and his wife pruned these trees for more than twenty years; after his wife died, he retired a short time later, but he continued to prune our trees for several years. Frank Yamashita-San died in the year 2000, having lived more than ninety years. I had learned a lot from him and feel his presence was a big influence on giving a special meaning to the garden. At present, Kitajima brothers, who are pupils of Frank Yamashita-San, care for and prune our pine trees.

Approximately ten years after Jim Tagami's first visit to our house, the water was turned on and the garden became alive. There were several large boulders which helped to create the waterfall. Many pebbles are in the ponds, much like one would find in natural streams. Because of the elevation of the property, the waterfall descends with great force, creating a magical and exquisite sound which also vibrates through the garden and the house. Jim placed some lanterns within the proper setting of rocks in the garden, beginning their path at the base just before the meditative path. They create a pleasant mood and light the garden. After the water came the fish. We bought baby koi, who in time grew to be over twelve inches in size with intricate patterns and bright, bold colors. They became the moving flowers of the garden.

One of the fascinating parts of the garden is the walk constructed from railroad tires that goes through the garden. The path curves: I learned from Jim that in Japanese gardens this is very important. As you go up and down each step, you stop and inspect the garden. Surprisingly, with each step the view of the garden changes as the path twists and turns. The garden also changes with the time of day. With the movement of the sun, the shadows change the appearance of all the life in the garden. As the seasons change, the new colors appear. Since the inception of the garden I had an opportunity to visit Japan several times and see many Japanese gardens. The more I walked among them, the more I appreciated the existence of our small Japanese garden at home. I am grateful to Jim for having exposed and brought the Japanese culture and the nature of the garden into our lives through this garden.

Jim has a daughter, Sencee, who was about seven years old when we started building the garden. Jim brought her daily and she became a part of our family. Sencee was a delight and she inherited many of the creative genes of her father to appreciate nature, art and design. At the present time, she is a senior at the Art Center College of Design in Pasadena, one of the most prestigious art schools in the United States. I am very grateful not just for the garden but also for the close relationship all of us have developed over the years with Sencee.

Jim also understood my interest in creating a vegetable garden, and set aside a small part of our property for a vegetable garden, where he installed a drip system for watering. I planted every variety of vegetable and fruit including spinach, tomatoes, cucumbers, onions, radishes, garlic, different types of eggplants, and artichokes.

Janine became very involved with the garden and helped Joyce and I in preparing the soil and planting.

For the Jewish holiday meals, horseradish is an important condiment. It was Janine's idea to grow the radish root in our garden and for us to harvest it, grind it and prepare it from scratch. It became our ritual.

One of the amazing things that I believe is part of my concentration camp past concerns potatoes. I decided to plant potatoes in my garden. I set aside a considerable amount of space in the garden and planted them. Why I did it is hard to

30. Jack, Joyce and teenage daughters in the Japanese Garden, 1979.

explain. Potatoes played an important part in my survival in Dachau. I always enjoyed eating potatoes after the war, not just during the war where they were a mainstay of life. The reason I planted so many potatoes in the garden was because it was a symbol of security. The potato yield was tremendous. After a few years, I decided to expand my potato gardening to even more varieties. Alicia took me to a nursery and there we discovered many more different types of potatoes. We bought and planted purple and blue potatoes, white potatoes, Idaho potatoes, little yellow potatoes and big yellow potatoes. In other words, whatever variety of potato was available on the market, I grew. Every different kind of potato on the market appeared on our table. It is interesting that if you close your eyes you do not know the color of potato you are eating: to most of us they all seem to taste the same.

Jim also changed the watering in our orchard to a drip system, adapted especially for an orchard which gave us the opportunity to grow grapes. I felt that we almost were self-sufficient through the vegetable and fruit gardens. I was proud to be able to contribute vegetables from my garden to our dinner table. My daughters come regularly to harvest the fruit. There is no question that the vegetables taste superior to the ones bought in the store. This interest in the garden stimulated all my children's interest in gardening and in the appreciation of working with nature, working with the land. In their own homes they spend a lot of time in their own gardens.

There is no way to describe the hunger I experienced during the war. It was one of the cruelest things imposed by the Nazi regime. We ate what we could when we could and we were always searching to satisfy our hunger.

When the war ended, the people who were liberated from the concentration camps had lost the ability to eat and digest food. Many of the people who were liberated died, unfortunately, as a result of the generosity of the liberators who gave them too much food. Fortunately, when I was liberated in

Dachau, a quarantine of forty days of progressive increase in food intake to control food given to the liberated survivors was imposed by the American forces, who had learned from past experience the danger of giving too much food too soon.

I was liberated with my father, who educated me on the inability of the digestive system suddenly to absorb a large quantity of food that the inmates had been deprived of for several years. The most difficult task for me was not to eat the delicious chocolate that I would get periodically, in spite of its being prohibited, from different members of the American forces. On my trip from Dachau to Budapest, I benefited from the generosity of the Russian kitchens on the railroad. Fortunately, most of the food offered by the Russian kitchens was in small quantities, only to fill the size of the small metal container that I had with me.

When I came to Italy and enrolled in medical school, I was always hungry. The amount of money that I received as a stipend was only ten dollars a month and very often I had to share my income with some books. The delicatessen store at that time was full of food to buy. Not having any money, however, I used to pass by the delicatessen and try to inhale the smell of the food.

When I settled and began to raise my family, a dilemma arose in my mind – how to teach the children to appreciate food and at the same time not to abuse the quantity of the food. The discipline that I tried to teach the children I myself learned how to follow. The children were not obligated to finish everything on the plate. I tried to give them the ability to balance their nutritional intake. Today, as I write this book, at my age, I have a new dilemma. The dilemma that I had in my early years was to eat as much as I could. My dilemma now is to try to eat as little as possible. I learned to appreciate good food as Joyce is a superb cook and very conscious of the nutritional benefits of food.

When I married Joyce, being so obsessed with food at the time, my wedding present to her was an Italian cookbook. My wedding present paid off. Through the years, Joyce's preparation of food and the understanding of my problems are greatly appreciated. Even today when I go to a restaurant, I try to order small portions because if the restaurant places a big plate of food in front of me, I cannot psychologically leave anything on the plate, and in a way I am obligated to finish everything (at least in my own mind).

Our practice grew and the number of patients grew. Don Elshire, Mark Anapoell and I did not want to give up the free time that we were spending with our families. One of the physicians in our community introduced us to a surgeon from Philadelphia, Dr David Rilling, a Fellow of the American College of Surgeons, who was then living on the east coast. He had been a leading surgeon in the Vietnam War and as well as general surgery was also certified in chest surgery. We could not have wished for a more qualified and a nicer person to join us. David, with his wife Karina, settled in California, and he joined our surgical practice. He was an intellectual as well as being a superb surgeon. I learned many fascinating aspects of surgery from him. He was interested in the practical aspect of surgery as well as the academic aspect. Our families enjoyed each other's company and we spent a lot of time together.

David spent some time at the Shouldice Clinic in Toronto, Canada. It was the center for, and pioneer in, inguinal hernia repairs under local anesthesia. It was David who introduced to us the local anesthesia approach to inguinal hernia repairs and introduced us also to the Shouldice technique.

A 34-year-old male was referred to us for consultation. He was a good worker, but had an alcoholic history with severe liver damage. There was no way that an inguinal hernia repair under general anesthesia could have been carried out on him. The insurance carrier stated he would have to be classified with a permanent disability. Dave took over the case and the inguinal hernia was repaired under local anesthesia. The patient went home a day later and within a few weeks was discharged to return to normal and customary work without any temporary or permanent disability. The insurance company was very appreciative and many insurance companies started to refer inguinal hernias cases for repair.

Illness in his family caused Dave and Karina to leave California and return to Philadelphia. Our group was back to three surgeons.

Discussions over policy problems caused a rift in our partnership. I decided to leave the group that I had formed and went back to practicing solo. I maintained two offices, one in La Puente and one in Brea, and still tried to spend a great deal of time with the family.

There was a surgical group in practice in Orange County, namely Dr Robert Moran, Dr Clarence Petrie, Dr Jeffrey Johnsrud and Dr Ben Novak. They were always available to cover my practice and I really liked them for their personalities as well as being excellent surgeons with an incredible concern for the patients.

After some time, appreciating the quality of work that they did and the friendship that they showed to me, I associated with them and I became a member of the group.

Dr Robert Moran was extremely interested in hernia repair and introduced a new type of hernia repair called the Moran Repair that the group was practicing with successful results. From the average of 12 per cent around the United States, the recurrence rate in Dr Moran's hands dropped to 0.4 per cent.

One day while having dinner I brought up the idea to Dr Moran of forming a special surgical entity, separate from our surgical practice, that would be dedicated to the repair of hernias. That is how the National Ambulatory Hernia Institute was formed, and how the first office of NAHI was established.

Dr Moran supported the idea. Working with my new partners, I discovered how fortunate I was to have associated with them and to work together on such an interesting project.

Every surgeon practicing in the United States knew how to do hernias. The average surgeon, however, would usually perform two or three herniorraphies a month. I hoped that with the National Ambulatory Hernia Institute we would offer surgeons who were involved a minimum of ten to fifteen hernia repairs a month. That would increase the skill of each surgeon, and at the same time we would be able to improve our technique, with a decreased recurrence rate.

I must say that a lot of credit for my idea of the surgery center came to me though my association with David Rilling, who talked to me a lot about the Shouldice Hospital in Toronto, as well as following in the footsteps of Dr Shouldice and establishing a center dedicated completely to hernia repair.

I also felt that all my training at the University of Pennsylvania helped me to establish the National Ambulatory Hernia Institute. The success of NAHI would depend on our organizing it and the training we would offer to our surgeons.

Dr Moran's hernia repair technique was not difficult, but it was a little more sophisticated than the technique that was currently used in hernia repair. Dr Moran's technique used the Shouldice repair and inserted a piece of mesh under the transversalis fascia to strengthen the repair. I felt that this was a brilliant idea, to utilize the best available technique (designed by the Shouldice clinic) and improve it by reinforcing it with polypropylene mesh.

I went to the drawing board and designed a plastic model of the inguinal area on a scale of 1:1 that was anatomically correct. It allowed the repair to be carried out on the model with the insertion of mesh. The surgeon could practice and get acquainted with the anatomy and the technique of the repair.

We lectured at the American College of Surgeons meetings. I made films of our technique, together with the new model I designed to be used by surgeons as a learning tool. During the New Orleans meeting, Professor Volker Schumpelick, professor and chief of the Surgical Department at the University of Aachen, and one of the most renowned hernia specialists in Europe, visited our booth. He was impressed with the model and said that within the next few months he would be giving a course in hernia repair for the European surgeons. Approximately 200 leading surgeons from all over Europe had already registered for the course. He asked if Dr Moran and I would come to lecture on our repair and perform some surgeries using Dr Moran's technique. I felt a great blessing that my model had been successful in catapulting me into the international academic educational environment.

Since my liberation in Dachau, I had never gone back to Germany. This opportunity presented me with a moral dilemma about whether or not to go back to visit Germany even for educational purposes. The next month or so, this dilemma occupied all my thoughts. Finally, I remembered my father telling me, 'Don't forget what happened, the cruelty and viciousness of the treatment to which we were subjected during the Second World War by the Germans. However, you cannot punish the children of those perpetrators who carried out this cruel act.' Dr Schumpelick left me with an excellent impression. I felt that he fell into the category in my father's thoughts. He was only about ten years old when the war ended.

I wrote him a letter and accepted his invitation. A few months later I landed in Cologne, the city where my father had gone to medical school and obtained his MD. Often when speaking with my father, he told me about the generosity and love that he felt from the German people whom he had been exposed to, his teachers as well as his fellow students. He never felt any anti-Semitic sentiment during his years of studying in Germany, from 1918 to 1922.

Dr Moran and I were met at the airport by two young surgeons who had been asked by Professor Schumpelick to bring us to Aachen, about an hour's drive from Cologne airport. The warm treatment and hospitality that Dr Moran and I received in Germany is unforgettable. I had brought my model with me and gave my lecture in German. I also gave each of the participants the opportunity to do the surgical repair on the model. Needless to say, by giving the lecture in German, I surprised Professor Schumpelick. Through the years, a friendship and mutual respect developed between us.

A year later there was a big meeting in Switzerland and everyone known to be involved in the repair of hernias was invited to lecture. Dr Moran and I both went to the meeting and presented some lectures. Our lectures were reprinted in the medical textbooks published in English. This time the lecture was given in English. There were about sixty participants, and we spent the entire time together for one week. I was stimulated by the new acquaintances and the discussions we had. During this time we had the opportunity to meet many leading surgeons. We learned different approaches to hernia repair, and we learned their thoughts and philosophies. I met Dr Dalila Greco, the leading woman surgeon from Milan, who specialized in hernias. Subsequently she invited me to Milan to give a lecture in Italian, which I was very proud to do.

This meeting in Switzerland catapulted Dr Moran and me, and mainly the National Ambulatory Hernia Institute, into the international arena. Our articles were printed in Japanese and Italian medical journals and literature, as well as international medical literature. It was a tremendous challenge and brought us a great deal of satisfaction.

The National Ambulatory Hernia Institute grew from one office in Fullerton to fourteen offices in California. Then I flew to Florida where I met Dr Bill Welch, who successfully established five NAHI offices in Florida. It is interesting that in meeting Dr Welch I understood his tremendous qualities and abilities, not only as a surgeon but also as an organizer. I am happy that at the present time we have about nineteen offices with about thirty surgeons working for NAHI in California and Florida.

Since the creation of the National Ambulatory Hernia Institute, I have been able to publish many papers. I also designed several more models for different hernia repairs and I produced twelve educational films, narrated by Dr Clarence Petrie that contributed to the education of hernia repair.

NAHI, with the help of Dr Moran, made an impact in the field of hernia repair.

I met Jeff Goldschen many years ago before I started to organize the National Ambulatory Hernia Institute. So when I was in need of some educational films to educate other doctors, as well as to present some papers that accompanied a medical film, I called Jeff. He is an intelligent and talented man. We were able to work together and produce the most incredible educational films. It was his idea to mount the camera in the operating room lights to avoid blocking the view with hands and shadows. I am grateful for that. Our films were used and presented at the American College of Surgeons meetings, where we received commendations for the quality. Together with Jeff Goldschen we created the first inguinal hernia CD-ROM with the participation of sixteen national and international authorities.

In addition, the National Ambulatory Hernia Institute was in need of a website, in the early stages of website formation. It was through Jeff's efforts that he constructed an excellent educational website with educational material and films available upon the patient's request We also presented it in five languages, and structured it in a way that many patients from all over the world had the possibility of coming to us to have the surgery done in a number of different locations in California and Florida. This brought NAHI to incredible heights and I owe this growth from the films, CD-Rom and the website to the efforts and intelligent planning of Jeff Goldschen. Our association has resulted in a long-lasting and close friendship.

I described earlier how Jim Tagami and I became good friends during the creation of the Japanese Garden He was born in Los Angeles; his family was interned during the Second World War, as most of the Japanese-Americans were. After the war, he went to Japan with his father. It gave him the opportunity to learn the Japanese culture as well as finish high school in Japan. He spent a lot of time with his grandfather, who had a great influence in his life. When he returned to the

United States he was interested in landscape design but also wanted to do business in Japan. He was instrumental in arranging the National Aeronautics and Space Administration (NASA) exhibition in Tokyo.

As a result of working with the NASA exhibit, he established a lot of important connections. Because of his background he is able to understand the Japanese people and the cultural differences in Japan.

He made and established a very close relationship with Dr Hirokata Iwai, President of Iwai Medical Clinic and Highly Advanced Medical Technology (HAMTEC).

Jim became interested in the ways of Japanese medicine. He eventually tried to establish a 'Pacific Rim Program for the Medical Care for Japanese Citizens Temporarily Working in the United States' with the help and guidance of Dr Hirokata Iwai in Japan and Dr Warren Fox and myself in the United States.

At that time Dr Warren Fox was a member of the Board of Directors of Brea Community Hospital, Brea, California. We wanted to set up this program with the hospital and local Japanese doctors' offices. Jim, Warren and I tried hard to make this a reality.

Jim also became interested in the Proton Beam Therapy System (PBTS) at Loma Linda University Medical Center in Loma Linda, California, and met Dr James Slater, the Chairman of the Department of Radiation Medicine. He introduced Dr Slater to Dr Iwai in the hope that one day we could set up a Proton Therapy Center in Japan.

We had many meetings in Japan and in Loma Linda. We were invited to the yearly HAMTEC meeting in Tokyo and Dr Warren Fox presented the paper, 'Establishing the Pacific Rim Program for Medical Care of Japanese Citizens Working Temporarily in the United States'. Dr James Slater gave a lecture, 'An Update of Proton Therapy'. At this meeting I also had the opportunity to represent the National Ambulatory Hernia Institute and gave a paper on 'The Moran Repair for Inguinal Hernias'. These articles were published in the HAMTEC Journal 1992/93.

The HAMTEC meeting is important in the Japanese medical structure and is usually attended by staff from the Ministry of Health as well as the Minister himself.

My acquaintance with Dr Iwai led to a long friendship. Dr Iwai is active in the Japanese medical community and is extremely intellectual. He expressed interest in Israel at a time when there was only a limited commercial relationship between Japan and Israel. Dr Iwai decided to change this. With his connections, and with the blessings of the Japanese Ministry of Commerce, he organized a delegation of the Japanese conglomerates for a trip to Israel to start a new relationship with Israel.

I asked Zev Birger, who was then working in Mayor Teddy Kollek's office in Jerusalem, to arrange the meeting with all the Israeli ministers and several Israel industries during the seven-day stay in Jerusalem. The delegation was received with great respect. The results of the meeting can be seen today in the relations that Israel's industries and Japan have established.

Dr Iwai was appreciative of the arrangements made by Zev Birger. Zev arranged Dr and Mrs Iwai's tours through Israel to be interesting and physically as easy as possible for them. Dr Iwai reciprocated by having the book, *A Holocaust Memoir – A Daughter's Gift of Love*, written by Trudi Birger, Zev Birger's wife, translated into Japanese and published in Japan. Dr Iwai was interested in the Holocaust and always listened attentively when I related stories about my life and about the years during the Holocaust He visited Yad Vashem, the memorial in Jerusalem for the six million Jews who perished during the Second World War. He and his wife were visibly moved.

Another time, Dr Warren and Robbie Fox, Jim Tagami, Joyce and I were invited to attend the celebration of Dr Iwai's 75th birthday at the Grand Otani Hotel in Tokyo at which 800 people were present. I felt privileged as an American to be asked to give a speech to honor this powerful and exceptional man.

Through the years our relationship and friendship continued. Dr and Mrs Iwai visited the United States several times and we visited Japan several times. I began to get to know Dr Iwai and discover the kind of outstanding human being he is. His interests are diversified and we were able to discuss many subjects together – medicine, history, art and philosophy. We are grateful to him for having immersed us in the Japanese culture, for his hospitality and for the many experiences we had in Japan because of him and his family.

On 8 February 1995, the Japanese community in Los Angeles decided to commemorate the work of Sempo Sugihara, the Japanese Consul in Kaunas in 1941.

Kiyoshi Kawai was appointed as the chairman of this commemoration. He appointed me as co-chairman. I gladly accepted. I was one of the few people who had the opportunity to have met Sempo Sugihara before the Second World War, in our apartment in Kaunas, Lithuania. He was the first Japanese person I had ever met and it stimulated my curiosity in the Japanese culture as well as in Japan itself.

I made my presentation at the 'Tribute to a Contemporary Moral Hero – Sempo Sugihara'. I felt that the Japanese community of Los Angeles appreciated it very much.

For years, I was determined to recapture the time that I lost during the war: four years of my life. For many years I tried to work out how to do this. I could not find an agency that had a recovery system for my lost years.

Finally after many years of thinking and evaluating, I decided to do the following: the retirement age is customarily 65. I decided to recapture four years and reduce my retirement age so that I would retire at the age of 61. In the four years recaptured in this fashion, I was able to do a lot of things that I always wanted to do and never had the time to do, plus many things I could not have done while I was still in practice. I was still blessed with good health and a good memory. Exactly four years before my official retirement age, I notified my partners about my decision. Interestingly enough, everyone was very surprised, as I was still in good health and had a successful practice built up with great partners. Why did I retire? The phone calls that I received asked if I was sick or was there another reason that I retired. My answer was: 'It is a principle.' I wonder if many of my friends understood this approach to my lost years.

I discussed my decision with Dr Moran and I explained to him that I would have so much more time to dedicate to establishing and securing the success and growth of the National Ambulatory Hernia Institute.

The National Ambulatory Hernia Institute also propelled me in my academic involvement. My free time was divided between the National Ambulatory Hernia Institute and the time I spent working on my Holocaust memoirs.

After my liberation from Dachau I was excited and happy to have survived. Very often I asked myself how I had the strength to endure the challenges that I faced during my difficult years in the ghetto as well as the concentration camps. Many of the survivors had the same question: where was God? How could this have happened? Six million Jews were killed and of them, there were one and a half million children who were brutally killed by the Nazis and by the collaborators. During the years, I tried to find answers to these questions. I read several books and I also met with different people who I thought might be able to answer the questions. I tried to meet people, some in the United States and some in Israel, who I felt could enlighten me on the subject. However, I never received a satisfactory answer. My search for an explanation continued for many years.

Approximately forty years since our liberation, Bill and Pearl Good and Gabriel (Gabik) Sedlis, and Joyce and I finally had a chance to spend time together in Mammoth Mountain, California. We were all close friends from the Casa dello Studente where we had skied together in the Italian Alps. This time, skiing in Mammoth, we felt that in spite of our age, we were still excellent skiers who enjoyed flying through the mountains.

In the evening, Joyce prepared an excellent Italian dinner

for us. Gabik had brought his harmonica and Bill his balalaika, and we were happy that Alicia was also with us. We sang many songs from our student years. After we got tired, we switched to jokes. There were some new jokes and some old jokes. However, one joke stuck in my mind.

The joke was about two fishermen who lived in Biblical times near the Sea of Galilee and fished. One of the fishermen was extremely religious. He observed the Sabbath, he went to the synagogue every Friday night, he threw back all the little fish he caught, and he gave part of his catch of the day to the poor people. The other fisherman was a secular Jew who did not go to the synagogue and did not observe the Sabbath as a religious Jew would be doing. They lived next door to one another and were fisherman by trade. One day there was a great storm and the religious fisherman's boat smashed against a rock and sank. The fisherman grabbed part of his boat and was holding onto it. He did not know how to swim. At this point the secular fisherman risked his own life to try to save his colleague's life. He came very close to the man and the religious fisherman told him, 'Go away, and don't touch me. You are not kosher. I don't want to be touched by you', and he drowned. On his way to meet God, he was very angry. He accused God of having neglected him, for not having saved him, in spite of him being so devoted to God and his commandments.

Suddenly he heard a voice that said, 'I would just like to ask why you did not accept the help of the secular Jew whom I sent to save you?'

From Mammoth to our home in Covina, about a six-hour drive, everyone was fast asleep and I was alone with my thoughts. This joke came back to me and my thoughts started to intermingle with my past life. In rethinking my own life, there are definite times when I was saved without knowing who it was that had saved me.

IN LITHUANIA, WHEN I WAS PUT UP AGAINST THE WALL TO BE SHOT

I was lined up to be shot by Lithuanian fascists, just as a German motorcycle scout leading the German army into the city became lost in the labyrinth of the old city, and stopped in front of the house to check the map. The sound of the motorcycle and the Lithuanian fascists' fear of the arrival of the German army saved me. The Lithuanians fled.

ON NERIS BRIDGE

Before the closure of the Kovno Ghetto gates and moving the Jewish population behind them, the Jewish Council organized a group of volunteers to visit every house in the ghetto and measure it to assess and lay out an orderly resettlement of the people in the ghetto. I volunteered to help.

On the way to the ghetto, the murderous Lithuanian fascists blocked both sides of the bridge and tried to arrest all the Jews including the volunteers. It was a desperate situation where I found myself in the wrong place at the wrong time. The people they arrested never returned. An unknown Lithuanian farmer on his way to market with his cheese saved my life by telling me to get into his cart. He drove safely past the checkpoint and saved my life. I took him to my mother at home so that she could pay for the cheeses he gave me. By the time my mother came down, he was gone. I can still see his face before my eyes.

ON THE BRIDGE CROSSING FROM THE LARGE GHETTO TO THE SMALL GHETTO

The Contagious Diseases Hospital where my father and I were headed was set on fire on 4 October 1941. An elderly man stopped my father and talked to him and those ten minutes saved our lives. We arrived ten minutes late. The bridge was already closed. A Lithuanian guard on the bridge prevented my father and me from crossing the bridge; it was already closed and we were unable to reach the hospital. I knew then and I know now that if I had crossed the bridge I would not be here to tell the story of my life. So many other episodes in my life that occurred were inexplicable – why I did certain things or why I had to do certain things.

WHEN WE ARRIVED IN KAUFERING

In 1937, my father saved the life of Mrs Helmanowitsch who had typhus abdominalis with internal bleeding. In 1944, when we arrived in Kaufering, a sub-branch of Dachau 2, her husband, SS Rottenführer Helmanowitsch, was in charge. He recognized my father and did not forget that my father saved his wife's life. He played an important role in saving my father's life and mine, as well as many other inmates in Kaufering.

OF STANDING IN THE *APPELL PLATZ* IN KAUFERING: WHEN I VOLUNTEERED TO WORK FOR ORGANIZATION TODT

I volunteered to be the master of my own destiny, not knowing what was in store for me, but knowing that generally it was dangerous to volunteer. When I was in Dachau, Hans Schmidt, from Organization Todt, had come to Kaufering to recruit carpenters. I volunteered, not knowing that it would save my life.

Every day of the four years was associated with tremendous danger. Certain things could not be helped, they happened. Many people died; they died because they were in the wrong place at the wrong time.

I was thinking about my life and I came to this simple conclusion. There is no question that there are certain things in my life that I could not help. I was saved because I was in the right place at the right time and I was not in the wrong place at the wrong time. It must have been a superior force that guided me and helped me through certain circumstances.

Life plays strange games. We face challenges, but it is the strength of the individual that plays an important part to face all the challenges of life. During my trip back from Mammoth Mountain, I convinced myself that you need to have faith in yourself and the knowledge that a superior force might be there to help you, and this is the strength of God. I stopped searching for the existence or non-existence of God, and I stopped searching for the answer to why God forgot about me during the war or allowed the massacre of one and a half million children to take place.

I sustained many sufferings and humiliations only because I was born as a Jew and lived as a Jew. I cherish Judaism; I will never renounce Judaism because I was persecuted. I enjoy its rich and beautiful philosophy as applied to the daily life.

In 1985, my daughters, Janine and Alicia, attended a Brandeis University summer session in Simi Valley, California, to take an intensified course in Judaism to supplement their Jewish education. One day I received a letter and brochure from them about a three-day retreat for married couples that Brandeis was offering in the fall of 1985. The selected speakers included Martin Gilbert, the official biographer of Winston Churchill and author of many Holocaust publications; Rabbi Telushkin, rising theologian and Jewish philosopher; and also Dennis Praeger, later a brilliant talk-show host on ethics. I discussed this with Joyce and we decided to participate in the lecture series.

Simi Valley is an hour-and-a-half drive from our home. We arrived at five in the evening in time for the first dinner for the participants and lecturers. It was a beautiful camp located in tranquil surroundings. At this first dinner, we were seated with Martin Gilbert. This was the first time I had met him, but I will never forget the discussion that we had during our dinner conversation. He asked me a blunt question, 'How much do you know about the Pogroms in Russia?' (Pogroms are defined in *Webster's Dictionary* as 'an organized persecution and massacre of a minority group, especially Jews in Czarist Russia'). I answered the question by telling him that I did not know too much, but I still remembered everything my

31. Joyce and Jack with Martin Gilbert, their first meeting, Simi Valley, 1985.

grandmother used to tell me – which really was not very much. He looked at me, smiled and said, 'You know, the reason why your knowledge is so vague is because at that time we did not have many historians who recorded the events of that time. Most of the people who were affected by the trauma of the pogroms and were lucky enough to survive were humble and intimidated people who did not volunteer to describe their pogrom experience. They may have been willing to describe their experience only to their very close relatives or members of their family.'

Martin also asked me how much I knew about the Turkish massacres of the Armenians. I was proud to tell him that I had read the book by Franz Werfel, *The Forty Days of Musa Dag*. I was a teenager at the time, and was impressed. I never realized that the same fate of the Armenian people would one day be awaiting me. He commented that it was the only best-selling book written about the Armenian Massacres, and it was written by a Jew.

After that dinner, I realized the significance of historians and the importance of recording the tragedy of the Holocaust. I still remember the lecture that Martin Gilbert gave at the Brandeis retreat. It was 'Churchill and the Jews'. He left a tremendous impression on me and it was the beginning of a new friendship.

Martin was born in London in 1936. He was educated at Oxford. Following his graduation, he became a research assistant to Randolph Churchill. After Randolph's death in 1968, he succeeded him as the official Churchill biographer. He is also the author of a definitive history of the Holocaust, twelve historical atlases, and comprehensive studies of the First and Second World Wars. He was made an Honorary Fellow of Merton College, Oxford, in 1994 and was knighted in 1995. I learned about the tireless and resourceful detective work Martin had to carry out to be able to write about the life of Churchill in his book, *In Search of Churchill.*

Meeting Martin Gilbert opened a new chapter in my life. Our friendship continued and he was often a guest speaker at the Claremont Institute in California. I always made an effort to go to these lectures.

In 1995, Sir Martin Gilbert wrote me a letter telling me that he was preparing a book, *The Day the War Ended: May 8, 1945*, and asked me how much I remembered of that day. I told him that I was still living in Dachau on that day – following my liberation. He asked me if I could send him a page or two about my recollections of that day. I agreed to do this and subsequently sent them to him. He published my letter in his book.

On my next visit to London, while having dinner at Martin's house, he presented me with that book as a gift. After having heard many of my stories, he encouraged me. He felt I should be writing down all these stories in an autobiographical context.

At that time, I was still practicing surgery and my time was very limited. I did, however, work with Martin and the producer Herb Krosney on the film, *The Buried Secrets of Kovno Ghetto*. This was shown at the opening of the Kovno Ghetto Exhibit at the United States Holocaust Memorial Museum in

Washington, on 20 November 1997. Since then I have spoken at many institutions and schools and showed the film, which is shown periodically on the A&E History Channel during the Holocaust memorial day, each April, and at other appropriate times. The film is still available by calling the History Channel, who will send a copy for a nominal charge.

Subsequently, I made another film with the help of the producer Jeff Goldschen. It was called *Medicine in Kovno Ghetto* and was based on the paper that my father, Dr Moses Brauns, wrote on the contagious diseases while he was in the ghetto. Our dear friend Irene Lyons, who knew my parents before the war, translated the paper for me. Martin offered to do the introduction to the film. He has played a very important part in my life.

I will always be grateful to my children, Janine and Alicia, who as participants at the Brandeis summer session had sent the retreat information to me and insisted we participate. Otherwise, I might have missed this great opportunity.

I flew to Washington and visited the United States Holocaust Memorial Museum with Joyce and Alicia, to make the presentation to the board for an exhibit on the Kovno Ghetto. Joel Elkes MD joined us. Avraham and Pnina Tory flew from Israel to meet us. We stayed in Washington for ten days and for several days met with the board of the museum. Schayka Weinberg was the director of the museum. After many meetings with the board, complete with explanations and presentation of the original diary, we convinced the board to establish a temporary exhibit (two years) on the history of Kovno Ghetto.

Why did they agree? The credit goes to Avraham Tory, who meticulously wrote the diaries and who, with the help of Pnina Sheinzon, hid them underground for safekeeping. They brought these original documents with them for inspection.

Avraham Tory had collected all the documents and every Gestapo order. He asked the artists who were incarcerated in the Kovno Ghetto to paint certain events. All this was put with the diaries, and saved. After the war, the Torys retrieved most of the boxes of the material they hid.

In addition, Kaduchin, a photographer living in Kovno, had taken more than 1,000 photographs of the events in the Kovno Ghetto, a remarkable documentation of this tragic time. We were able to find these photographs and present them to the museum.

The Kovno Ghetto was one of the best-documented ghettos. This made it possible for the United States Holocaust Memorial Museum to have a powerful visual documentation of the history of Kovno Ghetto.

The Kovno Ghetto Exhibit at the United States Holocaust Memorial Museum in Washington opened on 21 November 1997. It was both dramatic and breathtaking, but at the same time painful. It was a visual documentation of my past life.

The opening included a showing of the film, *The Buried Secrets of Kovno Ghetto* directed by Herb Krosney, in Lithuania, and narrated by Sir Martin Gilbert. Herb and his wife Mary Stewart (who participated in the filming) flew from Israel for this event. My film, *Medicine in Kovno Ghetto* was also shown. Jeff Goldschen, his wife Lori and their children came. Jeff also filmed the museum opening.

I began to lecture on the Holocaust at different universities and museums. One of my most successful presentations was in the year 2000 in Providence, Rhode Island, for both the Jewish community and the Episcopalian community. It was the idea of my niece, Geralyn Wolf, my wife's sister's daughter, who is the Episcopalian bishop of Rhode Island – one of the few female bishops in the United States – to organize a two-day conference, 'A Remembrance of the Holocaust'. She introduced me to Tara Lisciandro, the director of the Rhode Island Holocaust Memorial Museum, who helped us with the arrangements.

On the first day I showed *The Buried Secrets of Kovno Ghetto* to a large audience. This was followed by a discussion with the audience, and with my friend, Zev Birger, who had been in the Kovno Ghetto with me. The next day I presented

Medicine in Kovno Ghetto, with special invitations sent out to the physicians and faculty members of the university, and to the local physicians.

I had first met Geralyn (Gerry) when she was a little girl, at the time when Joyce and I got married. I have always enjoyed being with her. Her quick wit and smile make everyone she is with feel good. I admire her search for knowledge and her interest in so many fields. She converted from Judaism to Christianity. In 1996 she became the Episcopalian bishop of Rhode Island, but in spite of having changed her religious beliefs, she is still devoted to the heritage of Judaism.

Unfortunately, her sister Valerie died unexpectedly, and in respect for Valerie's wishes to be buried in the Jewish tradition, Gerry said Kaddish (the prayer for the dead) for her every day in the early morning in the local synagogue for a year. The members of the congregation recognized her as Bishop Wolf and wholeheartedly welcomed her for this good deed.

I enjoyed visiting Gerry's art studio to see the whimsical and imaginative 'Beeple People' she creates, exhibits and sells. I appreciate Gerry very much and admire her many talents, organizational skills, and communicative abilities, her tireless efforts to help people to try to make them understand and appreciate one another. I feel proud and lucky that she is part of my family.

In 1950, Casa dello Studente in Turin, Italy was closed; its graduates each went his own way. We were dispersed all over the world, including the United States. Everyone was involved with building up their own life.

The United States National Holocaust Memorial Museum was sponsoring an international reunion of the survivors of the Holocaust, 'Life Reborn: Jewish Displaced Persons 1945–1951', on 15 January 2000. I decided to use the opportunity and to have our first reunion, fifty years after the closure of the Casa dello Studente.

Nathaniel (Nuti) Firestone, an ex-student of Casa dello

32. Jack and his niece Geralyn Wolf, at the two-day conference 'A Remembrance of the Holocaust', Rhode Island, 2000.

Studente, and Joyce worked together with me to make all the arrangements. We invited all the former Casa dello Studente students and their family offspring. Unfortunately, some of the students from Casa dello Studente were missing from this reunion. Some had died and others were too unwell to attend.

Approximately thirty former students and their families came to the reunion. After having spent four years living together and becoming one family, we finally had our first reunion fifty years later. We shared the joys of our achievements and at the same time mourned and shared the pain of our wartime experiences. Some of us had kept in touch during the years, but some I met again for the first time since having been with them in Casa dello Studente. Some came with their children and a few brought their grandchildren to this reunion. We celebrated life.

I was the Master of Ceremonies. I really enjoyed this responsibility, especially introducing each of the speakers from Casa dello Studente and reminiscing about that time of life that we spent together. We also utilized this occasion to present and acknowledge a plaque of appreciation for one of our co-founders, Dr Paul Geleris. It was extremely interesting for all the children and grandchildren of the Casa dello Studente residents who were present. They listened to the testimonies of the achievements of their parents and their parents' friends and the challenges that they had to face to achieve their educational goals.

Of the fifty students who had lived in Casa dello Studente, all graduated from university in different fields, among them medicine, physics, chemistry, architecture, music and international law. It was exciting to hear from the former students what they had achieved in their lives.

We also learned, for the first time, of their experiences during the war. At the student house none of us spoke of the horrors of the war. Everyone was focused on being free and on obtaining an education.

The achievements among this small group of fifty people were incredible. I will mention a few ex-graduates and their accomplishments.

Stanley Wulc, engineer and physicist, founded Vector Manufacturing Company, specializing in space telemetry. He pioneered high-density packaging of electronic instruments. Many major national programs in missile development, airplane testing and satellite instrumentation carried his company's equipment. One of the programs involved testing astronauts under stress during space flights. One result of this especially developed technology was the creation of electronic monitors for post-operative patients, used in intensive care units in hospitals.

Paul Geleris, a board-certified pathologist, established eleven private outpatient medical laboratories and five in-hospital laboratories in the San Gabriel Valley, California. He introduced the 'Pap' test and the 'central laboratory' concept in California. He employed 185 technical and specialty staff in Glendora, California.

Benjamin (Beno) Elstein, doctor of chemistry, developed phosphate fertilizers in Israel. He was responsible for the revival of the King Solomon's copper mines near Eilat. Bernard Roizman, the Joseph Regenstein Distinguished Service Professor in Virology at the University of Chicago, discovered and isolated the herpes zoster virus. He had obtained his doctorate from John Hopkins in 1956. Joseph Gutherz majored in music and became a famous cantor and vocalist in performing arts. My room-mate Edmund Bass, a veterinarian, developed the concept of 'the sterile cow and horse' to produce serum for different medical and veterinarian applications. Nathaniel (Nuti) Firestone received a degree in Architecture and Engineering from Yale University. Gabriel Sedlis received a Master of Architecture degree from Harvard University. Dora Wulc graduated with Honors in Chemistry from Virginia Polytechnic Institute and University. She worked for Merck & Co. as Assistant Editor of the 6th edition of the *Merck Index*. Pearl (Perella) Good, doctor in chemistry, was a research associate and did membrane lipid research in the chemistry department in Pomona College, Claremont, California. William Good, a board-certified family doctor (voluntarily re-certified four times), is a meticulous diagnostician, and a humanitarian. He is totally devoted to his patients, is active in medical and hospital organizations. William is still practicing solo in La Puente, California.

I could go on and on about everybody's achievements. All fifty students became professionals and contributed their knowledge and skills to society.

The reunion was hampered by the thought that we might never see one another again. We discussed having another reunion in a few years and hope that it will become a reality.

There were five marriages among the students living in Casa Dello Studente and they are still married: Pearl (Perella) Esterowicz and William Z. Good; Lucia Borychowska and Benny Mandil (Lucia died in 2001, several months after the reunion); Dorina Kapize and Piero Morawetz; Med Hochberger and Nello Salomon; Dora Kaplan and Stanley Wulc.

All of the students were survivors of different concentration camps. All of them had endured incredible hardships. All of them were extremely grateful to the Italian people who helped them to overcome the difficult years and gave them the possibility of obtaining an education and begin a healthy life, integrated into a normal, sane society. It was good to know that in spite of all the difficulties, and in spite of Hitler's desire to eradicate the Jews, we did survive and produced beautiful children and grandchildren.

We also invited Cesare Reyneri and his wife Barbara. Cesare and his brother Paolo (who unfortunately died a few years ago) had played an important part in obtaining the lease for Casa dello Studente.

I mentioned the reunion of Casa dello Studente to Jeff Goldschen, who volunteered to come to Washington, to make a film, *The Reunion*, a dramatic presentation of the reunion. The emotion of the evening was transmitted to the film, which is a testimony to that reunion.

We then came up with the idea to make a film about the history of Casa dello Studente, its inception, life and achievements of its residents. At the present time, Jeff and I are working on the project and hope that one day it will come to fruition. We sent *The Reunion* to Martin Gilbert. He was very enthusiastic about it, comparing the story to his recently published book, *The Boys: The Story of 732 Young Concentration Camp Survivors*. He volunteered to narrate the film for us.

Sir Martin Gilbert, who is a strong advocate of education, especially for young people, said in his narration of the Kovno Ghetto film: 'We know what we lost during the war, but we will never know the potential of the one and a half million children who were killed, the potential of their children's children, and what they could have contributed to the world.'

On my way to New York, I was seated on the plane next to a man who was reading a German newspaper. We started a conversation. I learned that his name was Wolfgang Jacobi. He is a doctor of engineering from Munich, Germany. I also learned that he was only five years old when the war ended. He mentioned to me that his father was a very high-ranking official in the Wehrmacht, a professional soldier who enlisted in the German Army after the First World War.

I also learned that he has two daughters who are both attorneys. His youngest daughter, Jessica, was in Washington at that time, taking postgraduate legal courses at George Washington University. She was planning to visit the Holocaust Memorial Museum in approximately two weeks. I asked him if he would be kind enough to send me the impressions that his daughter Jessica related to him about her visit to the Holocaust Museum. We said goodbye at the end of our flight and we were both sorry that it had been such a short flight and that we did not have time to continue our conversation and discussion.

I was extremely impressed by Wolfgang Jacobi's intelligence and knowledge and I liked him as a human being. We corresponded after our first meeting. He sent me a few German books that had just been published. I reciprocated by sending some books that had been published in the United States on various topics.

The next day I presented my paper about medicine in the Kovno Ghetto, at the Yivo Institute in New York.

When we filmed *The Buried Secrets of Kovno Ghetto,* the History Channel had an annual budgetary restriction and could fund only a one-hour film, but we needed enough for two hours of film. To avoid waiting a whole year for the new budget, several people contributed some money to complete the funding for the film. Wolfgang Jacobi was one of the first who volunteered to send a contribution. His generous contribution made it possible for us to finish the film with an additional hour.

A month after having met Wolfgang Jacobi, I received a letter from his daughter, Jessica Jacobi – who was born in 1969 – with her impressions of her visit to the Holocaust Memorial Museum in Washington, DC. She has given me permission to reproduce it here. Three paragraphs will give a sense of a young German's concern and commitment to understanding the Holocaust.

> I get out of the elevator and I see what the American soldiers saw in 1945: a pit in the ground filled with burned corpses, each mouth still open with a cry. The photo covers the entire wall opposite the elevator that brings me to the beginning of the exhibition. American soldiers are standing around the pit, speechless even on the photo, their hands hanging down helplessly…
>
> This museum has succeeded to make the Holocaust comprehensible for me again. It does not deal with numbers, which are beyond imagination anyhow. It individualizes. At the entrance I receive the pass of a Jewish woman, a little book, which tells her life story. The museum is built up chronologically. I am wandering from the top downwards through three levels and for each period of time the pass tells me what happened to this woman…
>
> After three hours in the museum I am physically and psychologically exhausted. Much to my regret it is quite crowded in spite of the restricted number of entrance tickets and I constantly have the feeling that I'm standing in somebody's way – blond and tall. Of course there is no cafeteria in this museum. At the end of each level there is a room all in white where you can sit and rest – a necessary repose indeed. After three hours I have not by any means seen everything and yet I have experienced so much.

I was extremely impressed that a young person who grew up in Germany after the war had been exposed, not only to the story of the Holocaust, but also through education, to understanding the Holocaust.

My relationship with Wolfgang Jacobi has continued and flourished. Periodically, we exchange letters, faxes and phone conversations and discuss different topics of interest to us. He knew the importance to me of the book, *Gluck Haben-Ubungssache,* by Dr Ernest Rothe, published in Berlin in 1931, and he, with ingenuity and perseverance, searched many antique stores and succeeded in finding a copy which he mailed to me. It was exciting to me to read this book again, at the age of 78 after having read it for the first time at age 13.

9 *Medicine in the Ghetto*

From 4 to 6 November 1996, the Yivo Institute in New York City sponsored a symposium of lectures on medicine during the Holocaust. I had the privilege of presenting the lecture on medicine in the Kovno Ghetto, written by my father during the period of incarceration in the Ghetto, 1941–44. My father's original papers are in the archives of the Holocaust Memorial Museum in Washington, DC.

We were lucky that my father was a historian and wrote everything down on paper. He described the prevalent diseases in the ghetto and their morbidity.

The story of *Medicine in the Kovno Ghetto* depended upon the mosaic of life in the ghetto.

On 19 July 1941 the Department of the Lithuanian Municipality entrusted my father with the task of preparing a sanitary medical project for the future ghetto.

On 4 August 1941 a project was submitted to establish in the ghetto a general hospital and a contagious diseases hospital. The Lithuanian Municipality did not provide anything for the proposed project and ordered the Jews to supply all the necessary equipment for the establishment of the hospital. The hospital inventory and medical equipment were collected and assembled by the medical personnel, who received the supplies from the ghetto inmates. The ghetto medical department was also responsible for 153 children from a children's home and fifty elderly people from the old-age homes.

There was a little ghetto and a big ghetto with a bridge connecting them. In the little ghetto on Paneriu Street there was a brick building which housed a school. All the rooms and even the bathrooms were overcrowded with people.

A five-year-old child became ill with acute appendicitis and had to be operated on. The child could not be admitted to a hospital in the city. He had to be operated on inside the ghetto where there was no hospital. In the overcrowded school building, Dr Zacharin, the only surgeon in the ghetto, arranged the surgery. He found a room in the building which was occupied by a couple. The couple was removed from the room and the room was cleared of its contents. In this room, a table was placed for the patient and a little table for instruments and for material. Outside the room in the hallway, a table was placed for the sterilization of instruments. Under these circumstances, the surgery was performed. The boy's wound healed and he recovered.

Following the surgery, the people were evacuated from this building and in this building a general hospital for the ghetto was established with departments for surgery, internal medicine and gynecology.

When the gates of the ghetto were closed, a hospital was established for contagious diseases in the little ghetto. This was a two-story wooden house which had been used by the Lithuanians as an old-age home. The house was far from suitable for infectious diseases. There were no isolation facilities, no adequate water supply or sewage disposal, and no adequate heating. However, there was no alternative. Equipment was gathered from the inmates in the ghetto.

On 14 August, all the Jewish patients from various city hospitals, TB sanitariums, children's homes and medical institutions were brought into the ghetto. The patients with contagious diseases were separated and placed in the Hospital for Contagious Diseases. Amongst the patients were those who suffered from typhoid fever (typhus abdominalis), scarlet fever, diphtheria and stages of tuberculosis.

On 15 August 1941 the gates of the ghetto were closed and the nightmare began for an infectionist-epidemiologist. Here is my professional evaluation of that nightmare:

CAUSES FOR THE OUTBREAK OF EPIDEMICS

A. SANITARY CONDITIONS

1. No running water.
   Water supply only from the wells.
2. No bathing facilities in the dwellings. No public baths. The first public bath was opened in 1942.
3. No sewers
   After the closing of the ghetto, the emptying of excrement from the outhouses was halted.
4. With the population increasing to 29,000 in the ghetto, all the outhouses were filled in no time.

   The winter of 1941 was one of the coldest winters. No new holes for the outhouses could be dug. In addition, the outhouses were dismantled and the wood was used for heating, in order to survive the cold winter. Excrement was exposed as frozen icicles.

   The nightmare for the epidemiologist was what would happen in the spring, if the excrement melted and inundated the ghetto. But spring came and new holes were dug by the ghetto inhabitants. The old ones were covered with dirt. Unfortunately, some of the outhouses were too close to the wells.
5. With the increase of the population to 27,500, 1.5 meters by 1.5 meters was allocated for each person.
6. The heating conditions were a disaster. A very small amount of wood was distributed for heating and cooking on a weekly basis. Periodically, no wood would arrive for distribution to the ghetto inhabitants.

B. STARVATION

Hunger began on the first day of the ghetto's establishment. In Lithuania, there had always been enough food and, therefore, nobody stored food away for another day. After closure of the ghetto gates, people began to smuggle food into the ghetto through the barbed wire, or by carrying it when they returned from work outside the ghetto. Many people were shot to death while doing so, but there were always men, bold in spirit, who continued to bring in food. The main foods that were sent into the ghetto for the Jews were bread, meat, potatoes and sauerkraut. All these products were of an inferior quality. The bread was supplied by the Lithuanian commercial association, Parama. The bread sent to the Jews contained more moisture than usually permitted and it was moldy. A lot of the spoiled bread was not edible. Our hunger rations of bread were already reduced.

Another diminution of rations was created by the fact that there were approximately two thousand inmates about whom the Nazis did not know. They were hidden in the ghetto. Most of them were children, aged and ailing people. For them, there was no allowance of food. The people of the ghetto shared their food with them.

Meat was supplied by the Lithuanian commercial association, Maistas. Sometimes, the association sent a batch of horses' heads instead of meat to the ghetto. These heads were already spoiled when they were brought to the ghetto and were not fit for human consumption. In the ghetto, there was no natural ice, artificial ice, or refrigerators.

The supply of vegetables was provided by the Lithuanian commercial association, Sodiba. Jewish workers from the ghetto were sent to the association to pick up the vegetables. They noted many barrels of sauerkraut with inscriptions: 'Spoiled – Only for use in the ghetto'.

The winter of 1942 was very cold. At that time the potatoes were frozen and spoiled in big quantities. The commercial association sent rotten potatoes.

The food in the ghetto was low in calories and lacked vitamins.

C. PSYCHOLOGICAL WARFARE: DESTRUCTION OF THE MIND

Continuous action with the destruction of the Jews living in the ghetto continued periodically.

On 28 October 1941 the 'Great Action', 9,200 Jews were killed. In February 1942, the Riga 'Action', 1,000 Jews were taken from the Kaunas Ghetto and transported to Riga.

On 26 October 1943 was the Estonian 'Action'. More than 1,500 Jews were taken from the Kaunas Ghetto to Estonia.

The most terrible action was the 'Children's Action' which took place on 26 and 27 March 1944.

There were many events occuring continuously – almost daily – somebody shot here, somebody shot there.

Mortality in the ghetto between 15 August 1941 and 1 January 1942 was four times greater than previously in the Kaunas population. In our newly established ghetto cemetery, row upon row filled up with the graves of infants and old people. The infants died as a result of diarrhea and bad nutrition.

The high mortality among the elderly was particularly bad in the homes for the elderly where there was much suffering. The elderly died of hunger, of hemolytic and gastro-enteric conditions, of heart ailments and other causes.

All these experiences – the worries, the fears, and so on – could not pass without any effect on the ghetto inmates.

An indicative example of change in their metabolic function, probably conditioned by a change of glandular function, can be seen in the amenorrheas of thousands of the ghetto women and girls and in the significant weight loss in people of both sexes. Such psychologically conditioned amenorrhea had also been observed during the First World War.

Significant changes in the diet – black bread, vegetables, decrease or elimination of fats and meat from the diet – and nervous excitement, stimulated peristalsis of the intestines.

The meatless diet allowed for the disappearance of gallbladder disease or at least a decrease in the symptomatology. The loss of the fat layers of the abdominal wall caused the reappearance of old hernias, though incarcerations were rare.

The same can be observed in cardiac conditions. Colleagues of my father who treated many heart patients in Kaunas were surprised at how rarely the patients came to see the doctor in the ghetto. One could not say that cardiac conditions did not exist at all. The patients in whom myocardial changes were determined electrocardiographically also felt well in the ghetto and even were able to work on the airport. They felt well, if one may say so. They were afraid to be sick. They did not wish to be categorized as invalids.

Acute pulmonary diseases did not occur in Viljampolé any more than they did before the war in Kaunas. On the contrary, 5,000 to 6,000 people, most of whom had never been subjected to hard physical labor, walked long distances daily to do hard work outdoors in all weather conditions, yet there were comparatively few cases of bronchitis and/or pneumonia.

Concerning TB in the ghetto, they still could not say what the future would bring, since it was a chronic disease. Regarding metabolic disorders, a favorable influence on diabetes mellitus and gout was noted – not in every case, but in most. One almost never saw gout there. The diet in the ghetto was well suited for these conditions. For example, their carbohydrate diet consisted mainly of black bread, potatoes, vegetables and no sugar for diabetes, and a meatless diet for gout.

Regarding disease of the skin, due to the lack of bathing establishments and washrooms, bad and crowded living conditions, insufficient soap and wood for warm water, all parasitic skin conditions such as scabies, impetigo contagiosa, and furunculosis scabies should have taken a firm hold in Viljampole. According to my father, however, he did not believe that this happened or that the number of instances of skin diseases was greater in the ghetto than it was before in Kaunas.

On 19 September 1941, a pharmacy was established. The Germans assigned one pharmacy in Vilijampole for the ghetto. It had very few medications. It seemed as if someone had removed all the good medication before the pharmacy was transferred for use in the ghetto.

The Lithuanian State Health Department inspector, Dr Baltrusaitis, promised on each visit to requisition and send us much-needed supplies for the pharmacy and disinfectional purposes. Unfortunately, he never kept his promise.

Towards the end, however, in roundabout ways, we were able to get a number of different medicines and very good items too. Ultimately, it became obvious that it was possible to obtain more and better medicines in the ghetto than in the municipal pharmacy in Kaunas. Since the source of this medication was illegal and the trail was in the hands of a few, it led to speculation. The source of this medicine was German military hospitals and various German pharmaceutical and military warehouses. The medication had been brought illegally to Kaunas. The case eventually came to court and the defendant in this case, an SS officer, Winzler, was given the death sentence. A short notice appeared in the paper that he was penalized for selling to the Jews medications which had been stolen from a German medical warehouse.

On Saturday, 4 October 1941 the Hospital for Contagious Diseases was set on fire. All the patients, physicians, Dr Davidovich and staff, were trapped, and perished. Reports were spread by the Nazis that the hospital was destroyed because patients who suffered from leprosy were treated there. This was another outrageous fabrication because no leprosy patients were present in the ghetto.

On the same day, in the Small Ghetto, the building housing the general hospital, children's home and home for the aged, was cut off from the ghetto. The patient's from the general hospital, children from the children's home and old people from the old-age home were taken to the Ninth Fort, and murdered there.

In mid-December 1941 a new general hospital was established in another part of the ghetto. Once again, the ghetto inmates supplied all the necessary equipment. The general hospital had departments of surgery; internal medicine; ear, nose and throat; women's specialties; pediatrics; ophthalmology and venereal disease. No new hospital for contagious diseases was established. At the main ghetto gate, a special infirmary was established. In March, 1942, an isolated section was established for the mentally sick.

The German authorities strictly prohibited pregnancies in the ghetto, with a warning of the death penalty to both the mother and the newborn. Fifty abortions took place each month.

It was known at the time that the Nazis murdered all Soviet prisoners of war who had contact with typhus exanthematicus. In fact, many thousands of Soviet prisoners of war were annihilated because of typhus exanthematicus which they never had. After the burning of the Contagious Diseases Hospital, my father, Dr Moses Brauns, decided that the diagnosis of contagious disease was to be eliminated in the ghetto. In a secret agreement with Dr Elchanan Elkes, Chairman of the Jewish Council, he started treating affected patients secretly, without isolation. The children were removed from the room to stay with relatives or family friends, and the Jewish Council allocated extra soap, and wood for heating purposes, for the patients.

No contagious disease was ever reported to the Lithuanian Health Department.

CHART OF CONTAGIOUS DISEASES

Disease	No. of Cases	Course of Disease	Mortality	% of Mortality
Spotted fever Rickettsia Prowazeki	70	Mild	3 cases	4.3%
Typhus Abdominalis	80	Mild	None	
Infectious Hepatitis	1	Mild	None	
Scarlet Fever	3	Mild	None	
Diphtheria	30	Mild	None	

RICKETTSIA PROWAZEKI

Spotted fever, louse-borne typhus (exanthematicus fever). During the period from the beginning of the ghetto, 15 August 1941, to the liquidation of the ghetto, 13 July 1944, my father treated about seventy cases of spotted fever. It was striking that most of the cases were single and mostly they had a mild course. The patients with spotted fever came from two places – inside the ghetto and outside the ghetto.

Inside the ghetto was a workshop which had a department of used clothing. The clothing came from the battlefield and was cleaned and repaired. The clothes were dirty and despite the fact they underwent disinfection in Germany or at the sanitary baths in Kaunas, sometimes they contained living lice.

In the summer of 1941, a camp at Ziezmarai was liquidated. The remaining inmates, about eighty, were brought to the ghetto. Among them were about nine patients suffering from typhus exanthematicus. The administration of Ziezmarai did not know about the presence of this kind of patient. All recovered without any complications. One of the nurses of the ghetto who also was in contact with the patients became ill. Her course was also very mild and she recovered.

Another epidemic of spotted fever occurred in February 1942, which was outside the ghetto, the source being the *Entlausung Anstalt*: the sanitary baths used by the Germans.

The ghetto sent a team of workers to the German sanitary baths. The baths were for German Army personnel who were on their way to their homes in Germany. Wounded soldiers also had to pass the *Entlausung Anstalt* on their way to Germany. Many of the wounded soldiers were infested with lice.

A Jewish team was employed on the dirty side of the baths while a Lithuanian team was used on the clean side. The function of the Jewish workers was as follows. First, the Jewish workers had to carry the wounded German serviceman from the train to the baths. Second, Jewish barbers had to shave them (there were about six barbers). Third, the clothes were removed from the soldiers. Often the ovens were not functioning well and the clothes had living lice. The sanitary baths became a source of the disease transmitted by the living lice.

The word typhus exanthematicus was replaced with the diagnosis of grippe (influenza, pneumonia and brain grippe). Nobody spoke of typhus or spotted fever.

Fortunately, outside the ghetto, in the German sanitary baths, the Jewish workers existed only quantitatively and were not on a roll call. The workers were replaced by other men and the Germans did not notice the absence of sick Jewish workers. About seventy cases of typhus exanthematicus were treated with only three fatal cases. This is about 4.3 per cent and it is not a very high rate of mortality under the circumstances.

TYPHUS FEVER, TYPHUS ABDOMINALIS

(Para typhoid A and B) and salmonellosis. At the time of the great action of 28 October 1941 there were eight patients in the ghetto with typhoid fever. They were all dressed up and passed the selection line without it being recognized that they were sick. They all recovered.

In the ghetto, there were also cases of typhus abdominalis.

In autumn 1942 and spring 1943, in two different parts of the ghetto, we had two different epidemical outbreaks of contagious bowel diseases that involved about eighteen to twenty cases each time. The course of the disease was very mild. Some were complicated cases with intestinal hemorrhage but they recovered. The source of this outbreak was two water wells. We tested the water in the ghetto laboratory and found cultures of bacilli abdominalis typhus. The wells were closed temporarily with the explanation that we found the bodies of two dead cats in them. After disinfections of the wells, they were opened again and nobody mentioned these incidents. During the period of the ghetto, eighty cases of typhus abdominalis (para typhus A and B and Salmonellosis) were treated.

INFECTIOUS HEPATITIS
One case treated, recovered.

SCARLET FEVER
This was very rare and always had a totally different course to the cases that happened in Kaunas before the war. There were only three children with scarlet fever, with a very mild course.

DIPHTHERIA
During the existence of the ghetto, there were about thirty patients with the disease. The majority of patients did not receive anti-diphtheria serum treatment. Some received treatment on the fifth day, some on the seventh day after the beginning of the illness. The different courses of the cases of diphtheria were varied from mild to serious. There was not a single fatality from diphtheria.

It is easy to understand how much the lack of sanitary conditions, starvation, psychological stress, and the uneasiness which accompany every war, could have an influence on the development of epidemics. But contrary to the expectations of those in the ghetto, there were no serious epidemics and the Jews did not die from them.

10 A Matter of Trust

Clouds were gathering over Europe. Everyone was concerned about different aspects of life in case of war. My father was concerned with the education of my brother and me. He decided that the best way to secure the education of his children would be to take out an insurance policy that would cover our educational expenses. Two prominent insurance companies were very active in Europe: Allianz in Germany and Assicurazioni Generali in Italy.

Both had good reputations and earned considerable respect. My father opted to go with Assicurazioni Generali of Trieste. In order to achieve that he had to take out the policy with a local insurance company, Rigaer Union Versicherunges AG. In the contract with the insurance company, it stated that as soon as the policy was in effect it would be co-insured with Generali. To achieve that, my father had to obtain special permission from the Ministry of Finance of Lithuania to make all the monthly premium payments in United States dollars, so that the final payment at the maturity of the policy would also be returned in dollars.

On 3 October 1930, my father started the transaction negotiations with the insurance company and on 8 October 1930 they were completed. My father then received the original policy from Rigaer Union Versicherunges AG as well as from Generali. In the meantime, he also made the financial arrangements and received permission from the Lithuanian Ministry of Finance to be able to make the premium payments in dollars. Generali was one of the top insurance companies in Europe. A provision was written in the policy that in case of war, the policyholder was exempt from paying the premium.

As described earlier, after being liberated from Dachau, my father reminded me that in September 1945 the policy would have matured and $2,000 would be available for my education. $2,000 in 1945 was a lot of money and would have completely paid for my medical education.

In spite of the many difficulties I encountered after my liberation from Dachau, I made a special effort to get to Italy and enrolled in the medical school at the University of Turin.

The International Refugee Organization and the United Nations Refugee Organization provided a ten-dollar stipend as living expenses at that time. When I enrolled at the university, however, the additional costs of books, laboratory fees, and other expenses strained my budget so that I had to sacrifice money from my food budget.

At that time, I corresponded with my father in Lithuania and he advised me that the original policy that had been buried together with all our documents had been located. He gave me the number of the policy, which was 332. My father was one of the few who had been able to save the original policy,

In October 1945, I made a special trip to Rome, and visited the headquarters of Generali on Piazza Venezia. The manager of the office advised me that, as far as he knew, no policy was ever issued in the Baltic States, but he offered me a cup of coffee and promised to look into the matter. I gave him my address in Turin hoping some day to hear good news. I never heard from him again.

In 1960 my parents came from Lithuania and brought with them the original policy issued by Generali. In 1961, I made a copy of the policy and revisited the office of Assicurazioni Generali in Rome. There was another manager at that time. He too shook his head and told me that he was not aware that Generali had ever issued a policy in the Baltic States: Lithuania, Latvia or Estonia. He confirmed that he would look into it and would advise me. I left him my California address, but I never heard from him again.

In 1998, Rabbi Abraham Cooper, Dean of the Simon

Wiesenthal Center in Los Angeles, went to Trieste. While he was there he spoke with the executive of Generali on my behalf. He carried with him a copy of the original policy and showed it to them. Again, with the policy in their hands, they wanted more time to do research.

It was not until 22 July 1999, that Generali responded to Rabbi Cooper's inquiry. Generali offered to pay a mere $5,000 to resolve my 54-year-old claim. I could not understand how a policy could be worth $2,000 in 1945 and only $5,000 in 1999. I decided that I needed to hire an attorney. I was lucky to find attorneys William Shernoff, Lisa Stern and Evangeline Fisher Garris, whose expertise is in suing insurance companies when they fail to honor obligations to their insureds. A lawsuit was filed on 8 May 2000, in the State Court of California. Due to legal maneuvering by Generali's attorneys, the case was transferred to the Honorable Michael B. Mukasey of the Southern District of New York, where it is pending along with all the other cases against Generali from all over the country. It has now been more than two years since the lawsuit was filed and the court has yet to move the cases forward. This lack of progress in the courts has been a major concern for litigants and politicians alike. In fact, Governor Gray Davis of the State of California wrote to Judge Mukasey urging that the court proceeding move forward.

Since I filed my lawsuit against Generali, I have been active in bringing attention to this issue. I was interviewed by Robert Lenzner, National Editor of *Forbes Magazine,* for the preparation of an article on Holocaust-era insurance claims and I spoke before the United States Congress concerning my outstanding claim for benefits.

I received a letter from the Congress of the United States, House of Representatives, and Committee on Government Reform, on 31 October 2001, asking me to come to Washington to testify, express my views and to provide information regarding my experience pursuing a claim for compensation on a Holocaust-era insurance policy on 8 November 2001 at the Rayburn office building at 10:00 a.m.

The committee's focus was on the work of the International Commission on Holocaust-Era Insurance Claims (ICHEIC).

I spoke for ten minutes, getting an extension for three extra minutes. I concluded my Congressional testimony with a quote from my father: 'A woman can either be pregnant or not. There is nothing in between. And the same thing goes with honesty. Either you are honest or you are not honest. You cannot be honest in the morning and dishonest at night or vice versa.'

I brought with me the original policy certificate that had been issued in 1930 in Trieste, by the Generali. It was an emotional experience for me and I found a tremendous interest among the congressmen and congresswomen who served on the panel: Representatives Henry A. Waxman; Connie A. Morella; Ileana Ros-Lehtinen; Janice D. Schakowsky; and Christopher Shays. They tried to help me resolve this injustice to which I had been exposed.

It has been sixty-two years since I first went to Italy in 1945 to claim the funds from the matured policy, but nothing has been settled to date. An insurance company has a moral and legal responsibility of trust that they acquire at the time they sell the policy, and I do not expect deceased people to help claim their own policies.

In my case, it was different. It was an educational policy and nobody had to die. I was fortunate enough that I survived the Holocaust and had the original policy issued by Generali in Trieste in 1930 with all the seals, etc. in my possession. In retrospect, I am grateful to the Italian people for their kindness and compassion during the post-war years. They gave me a bridge from Dante's *Inferno* back to a normal life in a free society. With my understanding of the Italian philosophy of life, it is my hope that the broken trust will be restored and that Assicurazioni Generali will eventually settle this claim.

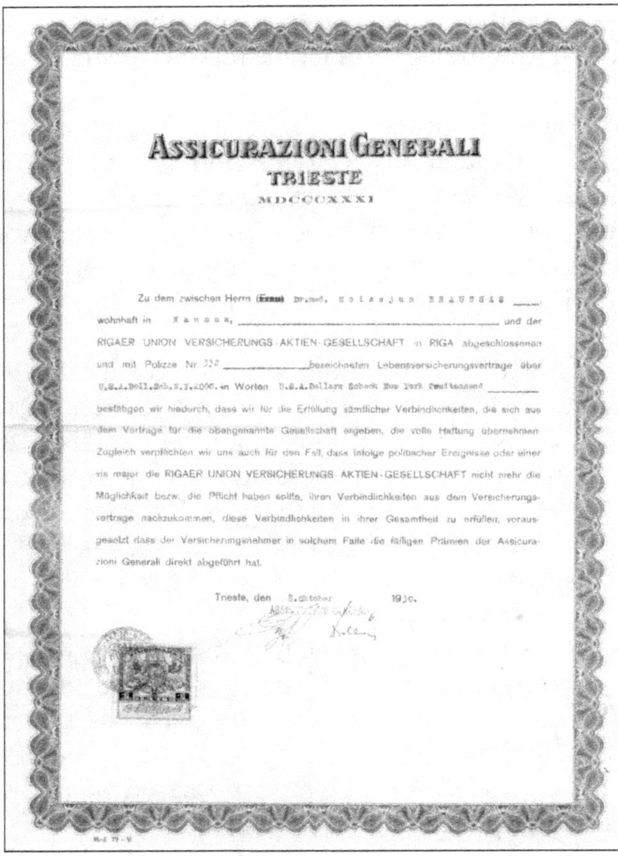

Assicurazioni Generali

Trieste

MDCCCXXXI

Zu dem zwischen Herrn (Frau) Dr. med. Moisejus BRAUNSAS wohnhaft in Kaunas, und der RIGAER UNION VERSICHERUNGS-AKTIEN-GESELLSCHAFT in RIGA abgeschlossenen und mit Polizze Nr. 332 bezeichneten Lebensversicherungsvertrage über U.S.A.Doll.Sch.N.Y.2000.- in Worten U.S.A.Dollars Scheck New York Zweitausend bestätigen wir hiedurch, dass wir für die Erfüllung sämtlicher Verbindlichkeiten, die sich aus dem Vertrage für die obengenannte Gesellschaft ergeben, die volle Haftung übernehmen. Zugleich verpflichten wir uns auch für den Fall, dass infolge politischer Ereignisse oder einer vis major die RIGAER UNION VERSICHERUNGS-AKTIEN-GESELLSCHAFT nicht mehr die Möglichkeit bezw. die Pflicht haben sollte, ihren Verbindlichkeiten aus dem Versicherungsvertrage nachzukommen, diese Verbindlichkeiten in ihrer Gesamtheit zu erfüllen, vorausgesetzt dass der Versicherungsnehmer in solchem Falle die fälligen Prämien der Assicurazioni Generali direkt abgeführt hat.

Trieste, den 8. Oktober 1930.

33. Assicurazioni Generali Trieste document, 1930.

11 *The People Who Stimulated My Brain Cells and Influenced the Course of My Life*

During my lifetime many people came into my life. Some stayed for a short time and some are still with me today, but all of them shaped my life in one way or another. They influenced me and affected my behavior, my thinking and my personality. In other words, all of them stimulated my brain cells and made me what I am. It is a big advantage to write an autobiography. It gave me time to think about who I am and the factors that made me what I am today.

My mother, **Basia Brauns**: she gave me life. She fed me. She took care of my every need; she always stimulated my mind and stressed the importance of speaking many languages. The knowledge of languages helped me to overcome many obstacles in life. In fact my linguistic abilities saved my life during the Holocaust.

My father, **Dr Moses Brauns**: there are not enough words to describe my father and the things that I learned from him from a humanitarian point of view. When I was young, I grew up with my father and my mother and my brother, a close family that had so much love to offer. I learned from my father the value of honesty and the value of responsibility. I learned from my father, that there is no compromise to the qualities of integrity, honesty, and responsibility. It takes certain risks to adhere to them, and my father did so without any hesitation. He lived his life with uncompromising integrity and incredible devotion to his family and to medicine.

Harry, my brother. I was only five years old, but I still remember when my mother came home from the hospital. My expectations for my brother were mainly to have a companion with whom I could play soccer. I remember my mother explaining the importance of devotion in building a beautiful relationship between my brother and myself. She always told me that it would be my responsibility to protect my brother. We grew up together. Before we played soccer, however, we played chess together. He was a phenomenal chess player and it was very difficult, in spite of our difference in age, for me to beat him at chess. I am very sad my brother is gone. He was killed in Stutthof Concentration Camp at the age of thirteen. It is difficult to reconcile myself to the fact that I had failed to protect him. I cannot stop thinking about what influence he would have had on my life. He was very interested in mathematics and in science. Regardless of what influence he would have had on me in my lifetime had he lived, the fact is that he is always on my mind.

Heinz Brown, my father's brother in South Africa, who did not abandon me. After the war he searched for my father and all our family and with persistence found me in Italy through a South African Army rabbi. Knowing that I was alone, he provided me with continuous support and made it possible for me to finish medical school. The regular letters of encouragement from him and his wife **Sonia**, were psychologically extremely important.

Irena Veisaite, my adopted sister, who lived with my parents after the war. They gave each other unconditional love and compassion from the horrible years of the war on the road to normalcy. For seventeen years, she filled the void of my absence, and also of the loss of my brother. When Irena and I were together in the ghetto, it was she who taught me Einstein's theory of relativity. I have read many times about this theory in the subsequent years of my life, but I never understood it as well as with Irena's explanation. It was also Irena who taught me the value and importance of friendship.

Mara Kagan, the matriarch of the Kagan family, a close

friend and also an extended member of our family. I appreciate her practical approach to philosophies of life.

Irene Lyons, who lived near my family in Kaunas before the war. She left the ghetto with false papers and lived with a Lithuanian family. When the family was evacuated to Germany she went with them as a foreign worker and got a job working for a German physician. She felt she was underpaid and had the courage to sue the German doctor and won the case. She married **Norman Lyons** and had two children. They came to the house frequently to visit my parents when they came to California. Our families became very close friends. She translated my father's lecture on medicine in the ghetto.

Nolik Ben Zion Schmidt, next to whom I sat in school when we were six to sixteen years old. He was my guide in art, dragging me to the exhibitions in the museums and stimulating my interest in art. Just before the liquidation of the ghetto he was in hiding, but was found and killed. His talent can be seen in the only painting of his that survived the Holocaust, depicting the resettlement of the Kovno Ghetto inmates from one section of the ghetto to another.

My high school teacher, **Mr Kessler**, who once became angry with me and said, 'You stink of laziness.' It took me some time and maturity to understand that I was lazy and I did not smell. I was changed by this statement, which left an impression on me for the rest of my life

Dr Ernst Rothe, whose book, *Gluck Haben-Ubungssache,* made a tremendous impact on me when I was thirteen years old. Dr Rothe was a contemporary of Sigmund Freud and Alfred Adler. The conclusion of this book, which became a guide for my life, is: 'You are the master of your own destiny.'

Zev Birger, a childhood friend from Kovno who spent the years of the Holocaust with me in the ghetto as well as in Dachau. We saved each other's lives in Dachau. His personality and vitality has always stimulated me.

Trudy Birger, who lived in the ghetto and knew my family. After the war she married Zev and they are living in Israel.

Over all these years she devoted her life to charity, establishing a dental clinic for children, both Israeli and Palestinian, in Jerusalem. She met an untimely death on 18 July 2002.

Consul General **Jaan Lattik** of Estonia, a close friend of my father, who spent a lot of time with our family on our visits to Estonia in the summertime as well as when he was Consul General of Estonia in Lithuania. Lattik was one of the first students at the University of Jerusalem, where he studied theology and where his Hebrew became fluent. On his return to Estonia he organized the first Hebrew High School in the Estonian capital, Tallin. Lattik was a Lutheran minister and became Estonian Minister of Education and subsequently the Consul General of Estonia in Lithuania.

Sempo Sugihara, the Consul General of Japan, stationed in Kaunas, who visited our home when I was a young boy. I felt he was an extraordinary person who evoked my curiosity and stimulated my interest in the Japanese culture. He was a person who, I later learned, had paid a very high price for having saved several thousand Jews on his own initiative. He told me always to strive to fulfill the goal that you believe in.

Rottenführer **Helmanowitsch**, who risked his life in repaying the debt of honor. He saved my father and me and many other people in the dark hours in Dachau-Kaufering.

Hans Schmidt and **Otto Jager** and **Max**, all foremen in the carpentry department of Organization Todt in Dachau-Kaufering, who went out of their way, risking their lives, to help me to survive.

Dr Nabriski, Dr Percikovitch and **Dr Oleisky**, all friends and medical associates of my father from the Jewish Hospital in Kaunas. We found ourselves all together in Dachau-Kaufering and gave each other the spiritual support needed to survive, acting as a family. If any of us got an extra piece of bread or any other food we always cut it in five pieces and shared it.

Dr Simon (Dolnitshky) Dolin, whom I met in Budapest after liberation. He was the first person who brought me the news that my mother had survived. He spent time and energy to convince me not to return to Lithuania, because it was unsafe, and because the future of Jews in Lithuania was very dim. He encouraged me to go to Italy to study. He was with his wife and son, five years old, who was born in the ghetto and then smuggled out in a sack of potatoes to a Lithuania acquaintance. A farmer hid him for more than four years, until the end of the war, and saved his life. Parents and baby were reunited. The baby grew up and became a physician. They all immigrated to the United States.

Avraham Tory, who as a young attorney in the Kovno Ghetto had the courage and perseverance to meticulously document the daily life there, including his collection of paintings, sketches and photographs. He left a historical legacy for generations to come. When he published the book – including all this data – in Hebrew, it inspired me to make an English edition and subsequently to create the Kovno Ghetto Exhibit in the Holocaust Memorial Museum, Washington, DC. Because of our association and his deeds I was also inspired to do the documentary about the Kovno Ghetto. He died on 24 February 2002.

Pnina Tory, wife of Avraham, who with bravery and courage helped him to save the documents during the ghetto years and carry the manuscript to Israel. She was supportive in every way and during their lifetime together they worked side by side on every project. Both Pnina and Avraham are very dear to me and all my family.

William Z. Good, my lifetime friend, who stood by me and guided me. Together we were able to overcome the challenges of our life for the past fifty-six years. I learned charity from him.

Pearl (Perella) Good, for years of a friendship which still continue, who helped me to compose the letter in Russian to Mrs Khrushchev, which resulted in my parents' release from the Soviet Union.

Paul Geleris, who with his great organizational ability brought about the Casa dello Studente, helping all of us to complete our studies in Italy.

Marilyn Geleris was supportive to me while I was a resident at Lincoln Hospital and I stayed at the Geleris home while I was preparing for my boards in California. Marilyn is active as a museum docent and also supported Paul in his philanthropic activities. Since Paul's passing on 31 May 2005, she has been actively supporting all his philanthropic endeavors, along with her two sons, Andrew and Joseph.

Stanley Wulc, my friend from Casa dello Studente, who is extremely stimulating in our endless discussions about philosophy of life, history, music, art, and photography. His expertise in these fields is always enriching and I am deeply impressed with his never-ending creative projects.

Dora Wulc, who encouraged me to write my memories. This was her idea since the days of the Casa dello Studente. Dora's intellect has always been a great stimulus to me. She is a close friend to me and all my family.

Gabriel (Gabik) Sedlis, friend from Casa dello Studente, who graduated from Harvard with a Master of Architecture degree. He was stimulating with his thoughts, ideas, and great wit. When we had a fire in our house he immediately flew from New York to help us to restore and redesign.

Benjamin (Beno) Elstein, who was a friend from Lithuania and also a fellow student in Casa dello Studente, and who became a lifelong friend. In spite of living in different countries we try to meet and exchange ideas.

Busia Elstein, a famous artist and designer who was always hospitable to me and my family. Sadly, she passed away on 22 December 1999. We lost a good friend.

Joseph Zarchin, my Boy Scout leader in Lithuania. He immigrated to Israel in 1939 on a student visa as a student of archaeology, and joined the British Army as part of the Palestine Brigade, and soon afterwards married Emmy. When he was stationed in Italy, he was able to find me and a close friendship was revitalized. Sadly he died on 4 April 2002 on his eighty-fifth birthday.

Emmy Zarchin, who offered me her hospitality from the day I visited her and her husband in Israel in 1948, as well as when I came with my whole family many years later. She and her children are like an extended family to us all. We adored Emmy and mourn her death on 3 December 1997. We miss her.

Hanni Krispin, my friend from Lithuania who lived in the Kovno Ghetto. We met after the war and cherish our friendship. She contributed to the documentary, *Buried Secrets of the Kovno Ghetto* with her testimony.

Dr Mayer Krispin, a general surgeon who practiced in Jaffa, who taught me to relax. When we visited Israel both he and Hanni took us everywhere and also introduced us to the gastronomical delights of Middle Eastern cuisine. The Arab owners of these restaurants were patients of Mayer and they held him in great esteem.

Avraham Ofek, brother of Mayer Krispin, who was a famous painter and teacher. He has permanent exhibits all over Israel. He told me that to understand and know a place you visit, you have to walk through it, smell it, and touch it. To understand Jerusalem he took us for a walk on the wall that encircles the old city, from the Damascus Gate to the Lions' Gate, to see the sunset. We could observe the old city on one side and the new modern city on the other, an unforgettable experience. Shortly afterward he died an untimely death from illness.

The **Reyneri Family, Cesare** and **Paolo** and their parents, and aunt and uncle **Teppati**, who lived in Turin and offered me so much love and compassion during the years I studied there. Cesare and Paolo moved to northern California and our friendship has been reinforced for close to sixty years. I will never forget how kind Cesare and his wife **Barbara** were to meet my parents at the airport in San Francisco to welcome them to the United States.

Professor Mario Alara, Dean of the University of Turin, who guided me during medical school through all my problems, and solved them.

Professor Mario Dogliotti, who presented my research paper, 'Preservation of Skin Grafts at Different Temperatures' to the University of Turin. This was necessary for me in order to obtain my medical degree upon graduation.

Dr Allen Bedford, a surgical resident in Lincoln Hospital, whose devotion to surgery rubbed off on me. His support and encouragement helped me to survive the 'Lincoln years' of my residency.

Dr Frederick Amendola, who was in charge of my training at the Lincoln Hospital in New York, and who inspired me.

Dr Jack Friedman, who spent a lot of time in the operating room with me, and who guided me in my surgical training in Lincoln Hospital, in New York.

Dr Isidore Ravdin, who together with Dr Frederick Amendola helped me and encouraged me to continue to fight against injustice.

Dr Arnold Einhorn, my lifelong friend, who stimulates my academic quest and my interest in the arts with his vast knowledge and encyclopedic mind. He has unlimited energy in the quest to teach pediatrics worldwide. His lectures are enhanced by the visual animation presentations he creates on his computer. He received the award of 'Teacher of the Year' for residents' training for many consecutive years.

Yvonne Einhorn, a devoted friend, who is a French chef extraordinaire and with creativity and ingenuity compiled an incredible cook book that we use and cherish.

Mira Jadwabnik Van Doren and her husband **John Van Doren**, whose creativity in the arts played an important part in my thinking.

Dr Robert Fry, ex-congressman **Patrick Hillings**, Vice-President **Richard Nixon**, and **Mrs Khrushchev**, who were the team who made it possible for my parents to get permission to leave the Lithuanian Soviet Socialist Republic.

Si Frumkin, who shared a similar fate with me in the Kovno Ghetto, as well as later in Dachau. Since we reconnected our friendship in 1960 he has stimulated my brain cells with his intelligence, tenacity and ingenuity. I feel that because of his relentless pursuit of getting the Jews out of the Soviet Union he tilted the scales and forced the Soviet government to let the Jews go. At the present time, he is an active journalist, relentlessly pursuing freedom for all people.

Bob Geminder, who survived the Holocaust in Poland by the ingenuity and courage of his mother, **Bertl Geminder**. She saved him and his brother who were less than ten years old. We met in California and our common background nourished our friendship.

Ben Wood, who was elected President of the Jewish Lithuanian Association in Los Angeles and was extremely helpful with reference to the exhibit of the Kovno Ghetto in the Holocaust Memorial Museum in Washington. He also helped with the documentary *Buried Secrets of Kovno Ghetto*. He, his wife **Hannah** and her sister **Esther** participated in the testimonies for the film. Sadly Ben died untimely on 23 May 1997.

Martin Gilbert. I am grateful for the opportunity to have met him twenty-five years ago. He has made a tremendous impact on my life. I learned the responsibility of an historian from him. He was my mentor in writing my autobiography. We became close friends. I was honored to be the best man at his wedding to **Esther Goldberg**, and Esther has become a very dear and important friend to me. Esther was instrumental in the publishing of my book and I am forever grateful.

Geralyn Wolf, who inspired me with her compassion and devotion to people.

My wife **Joyce**, my lifelong companion who supports and encourages me in all my endeavors. With her energy she is able to help me make everything I do a reality. She and I have worked together on many projects, sharing ideas, hopes and aspirations. I am deeply grateful to her for her determination that I should complete my autobiography.

My daughters, **Suzette**, **Janine** and **Alicia**, who always give me love and support and encourage me in all my projects. They constantly stimulate me and challenge me in my thinking. They were teenagers when their grandparents were sick and dying. They exhibited extraordinary kindness and compassion to them and unselfishly helped Joyce and me to give them companionship and love to make their last days easier.

Sencee Tagami, who has been devoted to me over the years. She became part of our family and enriched us all. I have watched her mature from a young child of seven years to today and witnessed her graduation with honors from the Art Center College of Design on 14 December 2002 in Pasadena, California.

Jay Rivera, my son-in-law, who is my good friend, fulfilling the role of the son I never had. He is devoted to his family with overwhelming love.

Joshua Rivera, my first grandchild, who was born on 21 October 2000. As soon as I enter the house and Joshua hears my voice, he calls, 'Papa, Papa', drops everything and runs with open arms to me. I wonder what is so special about my voice; I am sure it is mutual love. As soon as he reaches me, he gives me a radiant smile and takes hold of my finger with his little hand and takes me to his room to the shelf where his books are. He mumbles, 'Books, books, books', suggesting that I take a book. After I have pulled a book or two from the shelf, he goes to his chair and sits down, expecting me to read his books to him. I always oblige him and it is heart-warming to see the relationship that we have developed.

Herbert Krosney, director, who during the filming of *The Buried Secrets of Kovno Ghetto* was able to transfer the emotion of the tragedy to the television screen, even though he did not personally experience it. I keep in touch with him and his wife **Mary Stewart**, reinforcing a strong friendship.

Sara Bloomfield, director of the United States National Holocaust Memorial Museum in Washington, who helped Irena Veisaite and me bring seven historians from Lithuania to Washington and provided lodging and food for them. At the same time she arranged educational courses, exposing them to the tragedy of the Holocaust so that on their return to Lithuania they could teach the Holocaust at Lithuanian universities and high schools.

Martin Goldman, who was extremely ingenious and

constructive in solving the challenges that we faced in preparing the Casa dello Studente reunion simultaneously with the international reunion, 'Life Reborn: Jewish Displaced Persons 1945–1951', sponsored by the United States National Holocaust Memorial Museum, on 15 January 2000. He is the Director of Survivor Affairs at the museum and coordinated all the arrangements.

Christine Eisenberg, an expert in the field of Asian arts, who stimulated my interest to understand and appreciate them. She introduced me to **Graham Frazer**, whose expertise in Chinese art helped me to focus my interest. I collected Chinese Scrolls from the fifteenth and sixteenth centuries, that I recently donated to the Israel Museum in Jerusalem.

Dr David Thompson, who started his dental practice in the same medical building in La Puente, California with Bill Good and me. We maintained a close friendship over all these years. He taught me the philosophy of the Mormon Church.

Dr David Rilling, whose fresh new ideas helped to stimulate in me the concept of specialized centers for hernia repairs.

Dr Robert Moran, who was able to see my vision, and who stood by me in creating and promoting the National Ambulatory Hernia Institute.

Dr Clarence Petrie, who narrated the educational films for the National Ambulatory Hernia Institute. As an outstanding surgeon and artist he created illustrations of the surgical procedures that enhanced both our films and displays.

Dr Jeffrey Johnsrud, who had the responsibility of recruiting the most qualified surgeons to be part of the National Ambulatory Hernia Institute. He supported my ideas.

Dr Bernard Novak, who participated and represented the National Ambulatory Hernia Institute with his response to the inquiries on the website with his intelligence, knowledge and humor.

Professor Volker Schumpelick, Professor of Surgery at Aachen University; **Dr Dalila Greco**, surgeon, from Milan in Italy; and several other surgeons whom I had the privilege of meeting and getting to know. They stimulated my cerebral cells in reference to different approaches for hernia repair. This helped me to catapult the National Ambulatory Hernia Institute to an international status.

Jeff Goldschen, who helped me in all my endeavors to put my projects on film, on the internet, and to be exposed internationally. We developed a very close friendship.

Dr James Slater, who is Professor of Radiology, Director of the Proton Treatment Center at Loma Linda University Medical Center, the world's first hospital-based proton treatment facility. He introduced me to proton therapy, the most precise form of advanced radiation treatment. Through our friendship he became the source of my education in the field of science and physics.

Dr Hirokata Iwai, a man of integrity and principles and a giant in Japanese medicine. He is a humanitarian. His interests are far reaching.

Jim Tagami, who became one of my closest friends, and who never tires of educating me about the Japanese culture.

Dr Warren Fox. I appreciate his friendship, working together on our mutual projects, his diversified interests, his energy and devotion to everything he does, especially his family. Warren's wife, **Robbie**, has always shown interest in my past and I enjoy our discussions and appreciate her ideas.

Wolfgang Jacobi, who taught me that Nazism was not able to destroy German culture and philosophy. He constantly shares ideas with me and we have developed a very meaningful friendship.

Jessica Jacobi, who taught me about the power of education to help the young generation in Germany in understanding the Holocaust

Terry Thompson, CEO, Editor-in-Chief of Orange County *On Track* magazine, who was one of the first to expose my plight with Assicurazione Generale of Trieste, in reference to the educational insurance my father entrusted to them in 1930. She devoted the Summer 2000 issue to this story and illustrated the cover with a photomontage of me and my family before the war, giving it the title, 'A Matter of Trust'.

Robert Lenzner, National Editor of *Forbes Magazine*, my very good friend, who with his incredible knowledge, intelligence and integrity is constantly stimulating my brain cells. I feel he is directly or indirectly responsible for my invitation to Congress because of the article he wrote on 14 May 2001 in *Forbes Magazine* about 'Foot-Dragging on Holocaust Claims'.

Everyone is blessed with a lot of brain cells to be stimulated. I am sure that innumerable people who became a part of my life – regardless of whether they stayed for a short time or for a longer time – left an impression on my cerebral cells and shaped what I did because of the life I lived. I would like to thank all these people even if I have not mentioned them by name.

12 Letter to Joshua, My Grandson

I would like to end my memoirs with a letter I wrote to my grandson, Joshua, on 21 October 2002. He was then just two years old. One day I hope he will read this letter:

> Dear Joshua,
> You can not imagine the excitement in your mother and father's voices when they called to tell us that Dr Joseph Klerer had confirmed the pregnancy. You were on the way. I saw you for the first time even before you were born, when I watched the ultrasound. Even then, we found you to be very cute.
>
> On 21 October 2000, you left the warm ambience of the womb and saw for the first time the world as it is. Actually, you saw us surrounding you and admiring you. I doubt that you remember that event. We were very excited and very proud of your entrance into this world. Your mother's statement: 'I couldn't even bake a cake – and look what I baked!'
>
> I am writing this note on your second birthday. The love that your parents have given to you is indescribable.
>
> Joyce and I visit you at least two to three times a week to spend time together and to watch how you are developing. We have many photographs to remember our times together. I hope that I will still be around when you grow up to tell you all about life, and provide guidance through the wisdom that I acquired. I hope you carefully read my memoirs and the legacy that I left you about life.
>
> There is no way I can express with pen and ink and a few words my inner feelings about you, Joshua.

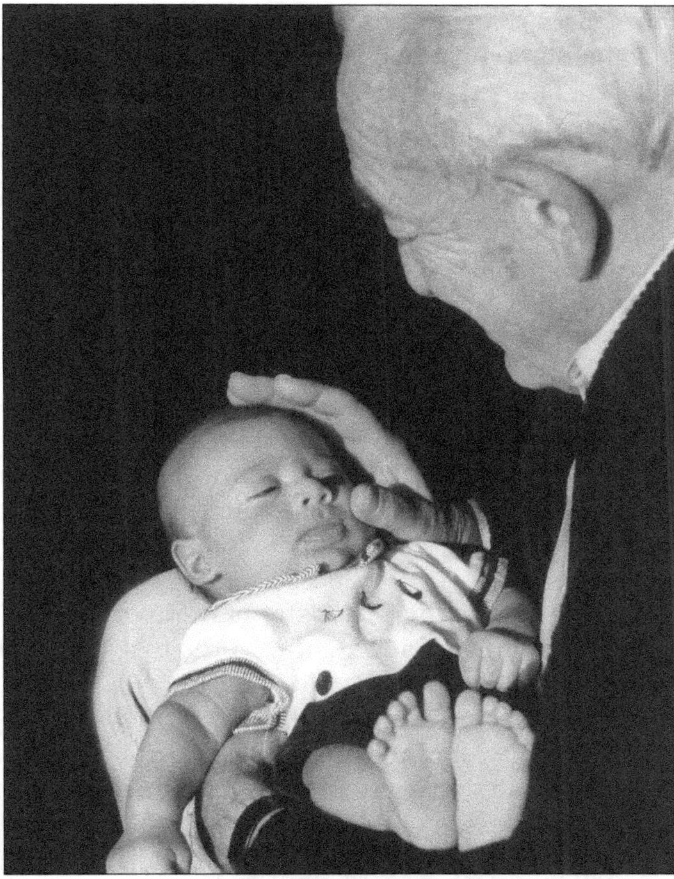

34. Joshua Ben Rivera, Jack's grandson, 2000.

My mother and father loved me very much and devoted their life to me. However, they never mentioned to me how difficult life can be and the challenges that I would have to face. They did not mention these things because of a lack of love, but because they wanted to protect me as best they could.

I am sure your parents will educate and teach you about the challenges of life that you might face in your own life. The world has changed a great deal since I was a little boy. However, the challenges of life in one way or another are unchanged. After you carefully read the book that I wrote for you about the legacy of our family, it is mainly to help you to overcome the challenges that you will face in your life.

From my own experience, in the lines and between the lines of the book, you will find that the main strength to overcome the challenges is related to education. It is essential that you make a special effort to benefit from all the educational avenues that will be available to you. Even when the studies are very hard and you ask yourself the question 'Why am I studying this subject?' or say,' I will never use this or that type of education in my life', remember my experience, that education that sounded so insignificant to me at the time I was studying became essential and eventually my lifesaver. Education will lead you to confidence in yourself. And with confidence in yourself, you will overcome any obstacle and challenge in life.

Even at a young age, it is extremely important that you understand and appreciate the words that I am writing to you.

While I was growing up, I realized the wisdom and guidance of my mother and father, and advise you to do the same. Listen to your parents' guidance for your life, as this is expressed with love.

Always remember: 'You are the master of your own destiny.' It is important for you to guide your own life by that philosophy. My mother used to say, 'If you want something done, do it yourself.' These are the main principles that have guided me in my life and I hope you will benefit from these words. Remember, your parents are your best friends. Use them as your guides for your exploration of life.

To be successful in life, you have to open your heart and be educated in a field that you are the most interested in. A very rewarding, satisfactory life will lead to a peaceful and exciting family life.

A little footnote to my message to you: the essence of

life can be compared to my mother's philosophy. Life is like a mosaic. When something good or beautiful happens you put in a bright color. When something bad or unpleasant happens you put it in a black color. As time passes, and you step back to look at your mosaic, you will see the bright colors become brighter and the black colors fade and become gray. Try to paint your life in many bright colors. That is what life is about. I have confidence in you. I wish you the best in your life.

All my love to you. God bless you.
Your grandfather,
'Papa' Jack

35. Brauns family portrait, Jack, Joyce, Suzette, Jay, Joshua, Janine and Alicia, 2003.

Life in the United States

www.ingramcontent.com/pod-product-compliance
Lightning Source LLC
LaVergne TN
LVHW010206110726
842469LV00013B/141